SKILLS FOR LAWYERS

SKILLS FOR LAWYERS

Kevin Browne LLB, Associate Professor

Annabel Elkington MA (Hons), Dip Law, Barrister

Gemma M Shield LLB (Hons), Solicitor

Stephanie Verlander LLB (Hons), MA, MCLIP

Published by

The University of Law,
2 Bunhill Row, London EC1Y 8HQ

© The University of Law 2025

All rights reserved. No part of this publication may be reproduced, stored in a retrieval system, or transmitted in any way or by any means, including photocopying or recording, without the written permission of the copyright holder, application for which should be addressed to the publisher.

Crown copyright material is licensed under the Open Government Licence v3.0.

EU material is © European Union, http://eur-lex.europa.eu/, 1998–2024.

British Library Cataloguing-in-Publication Data

A catalogue record for this book is available from the British Library.

ISBN: 978 1 80502 173 5

Typeset and Designed by Style Photosetting Ltd, Mayfield, East Sussex

Index by Moira Greenhalgh, Arnside, Cumbria

Preface

Knowledge of how a car engine works and the rules of the Highway Code is not enough to make anyone a good driver. Knowledge of the law and procedure is not enough to make you a good lawyer. Practice of law requires more than academic and technical understanding. To be a good lawyer you must develop the skills which will allow you to use your knowledge of law and procedure in an effective, ethical and efficient way.

The core skills are:

(a) writing and drafting;
(b) legal research;
(c) interviewing and advising clients;
(d) negotiation; and
(e) advocacy.

The chapters covering each of these skills provide essential introductory reading for those taking the Legal Practice Course and for anyone interested in pursuing a legal career. They can also be useful for trainees and qualified lawyers as a reference and in monitoring their own development and evaluating others.

Contents

PREFACE		v
CASE SCENARIOS		xi
	Road traffic accident / Personal injury case study	xi
	Potential transaction	xii

Part I	**WRITING AND DRAFTING**	**1**
Chapter 1	WRITING AND DRAFTING	3
	1.1 Introduction to writing and drafting	3
	1.2 Preparation and research	4
	1.3 Planning	4
	1.4 Drafting	10
	1.5 Checking	18
	1.6 Practical and ethical considerations	18
	1.7 Writing letters	23
	1.8 Writing reports and memoranda	24
	1.9 Spelling and grammar	26
	ANSWERS TO EXERCISES	29

Part II	**PRACTICAL LEGAL RESEARCH**	**33**
Chapter 2	INTRODUCTION TO PRACTICAL LEGAL RESEARCH	35
	2.1 Why should I read this section?	35
	2.2 The role of legal research in the office	35
	2.3 Problem-solving	36
	2.4 Principles of practical legal research	39
Chapter 3	ONLINE VERSUS PRINTED SOURCES	45
	3.1 Introduction	45
	3.2 Advantages of online sources	45
	3.3 Advantages of printed sources	46
	3.4 Accessing online sources	46
	3.5 Guidelines for searching online databases	46
	3.6 The free Internet: Google, AI and beyond	48
Chapter 4	GETTING STARTED	57
	4.1 Introduction	57
	4.2 Halsbury's Laws of England	57
	4.3 Practitioner databases	61
	4.4 Practitioner books	65
	4.5 Widening the net	66
Chapter 5	RESEARCHING CASE LAW	71
	5.2 Which source of cases has the most authority?	72
	5.3 How do I cite cases?	73
	5.4 Finding cases	74
	5.5 How do I update a case?	75
	5.6 How do I find cases on a subject?	79
Chapter 6	RESEARCHING LEGISLATION	83
	6.1 Introduction	83
	6.2 How do I cite legislation?	83
	6.3 Where can I find Acts?	85

	6.4	How do I establish whether an Act has come into force?	87
	6.5	Where can I find statutory instruments?	87
	6.6	Legislation on Lexis+ Legal Research	88
	6.7	Legislation on Westlaw	91
	6.8	How do I update legislation?	95
Chapter 7		RESEARCHING EUROPEAN UNION LAW	97
	7.1	Introduction	97
	7.2	General sources	98
	7.3	Primary legislation	99
	7.4	Secondary legislation	100
	7.5	Case law	103
Chapter 8		RESEARCHING FORMS AND PRECEDENTS	107
	8.1	Introduction	107
	8.2	Atkin's Court Forms	109
	8.3	Encyclopaedia of Forms and Precedents	110
Chapter 9		THE RESULT OF LEGAL RESEARCH	113
	9.1	Recording research	113
	9.2	Reporting research	114
	9.3	Cite it right	114
Part III		**ORAL COMMUNICATION SKILLS**	**117**
Chapter 10		INTRODUCTION TO ORAL COMMUNICATION SKILLS	119
	10.1	The importance of oral communication skills	119
	10.2	Listening	122
	10.3	Questioning	123
	10.4	Non-verbal communication	123
	10.5	Conclusion	123
Chapter 11		INTERVIEWING AND ADVISING	125
	11.1	Why is it important for a solicitor to be a good interviewer?	125
	11.2	Objectives of a solicitor/client interview	126
	11.3	Common failings	127
	11.4	Two ingredients for success – skills and structure	127
	11.5	The skills	128
	11.6	Client care and costs information	136
	11.7	An overview of the structure of the interview	137
	11.8	Structure and management of the initial interview	139
	11.9	The secret of success – practice	156
Chapter 12		NEGOTIATION AND ALTERNATIVE DISPUTE RESOLUTION	157
	12.1	Introduction	157
	12.2	The ethics of negotiation	158
	12.3	Negotiating styles	158
	12.4	Preparation for a negotiation	162
	12.5	The forum for the negotiation	169
	12.6	Other considerations before a meeting	170
	12.7	Overview of a negotiation	172
	12.8	The opening	172
	12.9	The middle phase: discussion and bargaining	173
	12.10	The end: closing a negotiation	175
	12.11	'Dirty tricks'	176
	12.12	Alternative dispute resolution	177
Chapter 13		ADVOCACY	183
	13.1	Introduction	183
	13.2	Skills	184

	13.3	The basics	186
	13.4	Opening the case	190
	13.5	Examination-in-chief	191
	13.6	Cross-examination	194
	13.7	Re-examination	196
	13.8	Closing the case	196
	13.9	Ethical issues	197
	13.10	Criminal cases: bail and mitigation	198
	13.11	Civil cases: interim applications	214
	13.12	Conclusion	238

BIBLIOGRAPHY 239

INDEX 241

Case Scenarios

ROAD TRAFFIC ACCIDENT / PERSONAL INJURY CASE STUDY

Summary

An accident occurred at the junction of Larkhall Road and Forest Road on Monday, 15 January 2018. A white van heading south on Forest Road was turning right into Larkhall Road. As the van was turning right it collided with a car heading north up Forest Road. The collision also involved a cyclist who was travelling alongside the car at the moment of impact.

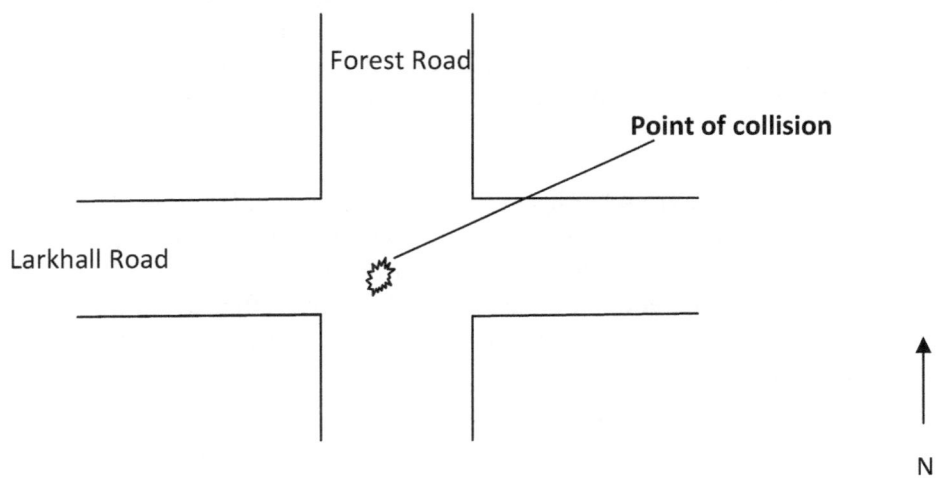

Vehicles and drivers involved

Van   White Ford company van owned by Armitage Deliveries and driven by Adam Worcik. Mr Worcik is a Polish national living in the UK and working as a driver for Armitage Deliveries. He sustained minor whiplash as a result of the accident.

Car   Silver Vauxhall Zafira owned and driven by Hina Patel, a senior midwife who works for her local NHS trust. Ms Patel suffered serious whiplash, a broken collar bone and a cut to her forehead which required seven stitches as a result of the accident. She has serious ongoing symptoms in relation to the whiplash injury, and the cut has left a permanent scar on her forehead (there is the possibility of further surgery to improve the appearance of this scar).

Cycle   Red Trek 200 ridden by Linford Chester, a freelance musician. Mr Chester suffered a broken left wrist and a cut to his arm which required 13 stitches.

Liability

Liability is disputed. Mr Worcik claims that Ms Patel was driving far too fast and that she was using her mobile phone when the accident happened. Ms Patel claims that Mr Worcik suddenly pulled into her path without indicating as she pulled out of the junction. Mr Chester, the cyclist, does not have a clear recollection of what happened.

Solicitors for the parties

Acting for Mr Worcik, the van driver	Acting for Ms Patel, the car driver	Acting for Mr Chester, the cyclist
Shea & De Sousa 67 Longbridge Road Stockwell London SW9 4RT 0207 479 4791	Alexa Hughes & Co 33 Millennium House Teddington KT4 6RB 0208 221 3445	Marshalls 114–116 Market Street Kingston KT1 4RT 0208 566 3228 inquiries@marshalls.co.uk

POTENTIAL TRANSACTION

Robert Grove Ltd is a large company specialising in restaurants/retail food outlets. Toast & Tea is a small chain of upmarket cafes owned by two brothers, Mark and Dominic Flowers, and a friend of theirs, Florence Lowe. The Toast & Tea owners are seeking to find a buyer for their company, and Robert Grove Ltd has expressed an interest in purchasing the chain.

Sellers

The owners of Toast & Tea have decided to sell, as their interests in the business are beginning to diverge. The chain has been very successful and currently owns 16 outlets in prime locations in central London. The cafes are old fashioned in design with a focus on service and quality which is reflected in the prices. Each cafe offers a children's room where under-8s enjoy supervised play. The cafes have won many awards for both food provided and provision for children/families.

The owners are keen for the transaction to progress quickly, as two of them have other ventures in which they would like to invest. They hope to achieve a purchase price of £22 million, but accept that in the current economic climate and given the current property market they may have to accept a figure closer to £18 million. Most of the value of the company is in ownership of cafe properties which have been purchased as freeholds/long leaseholds and in most cases have undergone valuable development work. The Flowers brothers were the major investors in the company and have a bigger stake, but Florence Lowe has acted as CEO and has been very hands-on in managing the chain.

Solicitors for the seller:
Mace McKenzie
Frobisher House, City Road, London EC2 5BR
0207 422 2134

Buyer

Robert Grove Ltd owns a range of pubs, restaurants and retail food outlets across the UK and Ireland. It has been looking to expand into the 'luxury' market. Toast & Tea's award-winning combination is attractive to it as a complement to its existing portfolio, and Robert Grove Ltd believes that given greater economies of scale it can make the business highly profitable.

Robert Grove Ltd would like to see Florence Lowe continue in her role or accept a position as an advisor for an agreed handover period. It is happy to proceed quickly but would ideally like any deal to include structured payments over a 12-month period. The current suggested purchase price of £22 million is based on valuation of Toast & Tea including its premises made at a time when commercial property prices were significantly higher.

Solicitors for the buyer:
Salinger & Rye
40–47 City House, Cornhill Square, London EC1 4RT
0207 836 9368

PART I
WRITING AND DRAFTING

CHAPTER 1

Writing and Drafting

1.1	Introduction to writing and drafting	3
1.2	Preparation and research	4
1.3	Planning	4
1.4	Drafting	10
1.5	Checking	18
1.6	Practical and ethical considerations	18
1.7	Writing letters	23
1.8	Writing reports and memoranda	24
1.9	Spelling and grammar	26

> **LEARNING OUTCOMES**
>
> After reading this chapter you will be able to:
> - plan and draft a range of legal documents
> - identify and use different structures when drafting a clause
> - correctly use definitions within legal documents
> - identify and avoid using archaic language, jargon, tautology and other common errors
> - draft clear, precise and unambiguous documents
> - understand the critical importance of checking and proofreading documents.

1.1 INTRODUCTION TO WRITING AND DRAFTING

Much of your professional work will require you to communicate in writing. The ability to write clearly, concisely and professionally under time pressure is a core skill for every solicitor. Every type of written communication needs to be effective, unambiguous and well drafted, whether it is an e-mail, letter or formal legal document.

Modern working practices mean that we often send tens of e-mails every day. You will have to reply promptly to e-mails and letters, and will frequently be asked to draft legal documents quickly. Set out below are some of the fundamental rules of good writing and drafting practice, together with some of the most common errors. In each section, there are examples and exercises with recommended times for completion. The answers to exercises can be found in the **Appendix to Part I**.

Good writing and drafting requires a four-stage process:

(a) **preparation and research** take full instructions, undertake any further enquiries which are needed, identify the objective(s)/purpose of the document, research the law;

(b) **planning** decide on the best structure and necessary content;

(c) **drafting** clearly and concisely set out the information/points following your plan;

(d) **checking** cross-check your document to ensure that it is correct, unambiguous and meets the objectives you identified.

1.2 PREPARATION AND RESEARCH

1.2.1 Taking instructions

The first step will always be to take instructions from your client. You must have a clear understanding of what your client wishes to achieve and of all the relevant facts. Part of your role at this stage will be to ensure that you identify everything you need to know. Your client may not be aware of all the information you might need.

> **EXAMPLE**
> Your client instructs you to impose an obligation on a buyer of part of her land to put up a 2.5 metre fence along what will become the common boundary. You must identify the need for further information as to:
> (a) the type of fence required (eg, materials, purpose);
> (b) the time limit for construction of the fence;
> (c) requirements for maintenance; and
> (d) who will obtain planning permission and what happens if planning permission is not granted.

1.2.2 Researching the law

Before you can decide how best to advise your client and/or how to draft any necessary documentation, you must research the relevant law.

1.3 PLANNING

Once you have full instructions and have mastered the current legal position, you can begin to plan your advice.

Identify your client's objectives and decide how they can best be met. You will then need to select the most appropriate structure.

1.3.1 Common document structure

Many documents will contain the following elements:

- commencement;
- date;
- parties;
- recitals;
- operative part;
- testimonium;
- schedules;
- execution and attestation.

1.3.1.1 Commencement, date and parties

A document will normally begin with a 'commencement' which describes the nature of the document, for example 'This Agreement', 'This Conveyance'. Alternatively, the document's title can simply be set out as a heading. Deeds may also use the word 'deed' in the title, for example 'This deed of Conveyance'.

A space should be left for insertion of the date when the document is completed.

The full names and addresses of the parties should be inserted. (In the case of a company, the address of its registered office should be inserted.)

> **EXAMPLE**
>
> SERVICE AGREEMENT
>
> DATE:
>
> PARTIES: (1) Weyford Products Limited whose registered office is at 32 Bridge House, Wharf Road, Milton, Berefordshire.
>
> (2) Joan Alice Bennet of 8 High Street, Milton, Berefordshire.
>
> A long and complicated document can benefit from an index or table of clauses (preferably at the front).

1.3.1.2 Recitals

Recitals clauses are not essential and you should consider carefully whether or not to include them. You can use them to set out the background facts to the document and so make it more self-explanatory. For example, in a conveyance of land by a personal representative, the date of the deceased's death and the date on which a grant of representation was obtained could be recited.

Recitals are also sometimes used to introduce and summarise the contents of the operative part of the document but, except in complicated documents, this is generally not necessary and increases the risk of introducing ambiguities.

1.3.1.3 Operative part

The operative part of a document is the part which creates the legal rights and obligations.

The contents of the operative part of a document depend on the nature of the document. For example, a commercial agreement will generally contain:

(a) conditions precedent (conditions which have to be satisfied before the agreement comes into force);

(b) agreements (the rights and obligations of the parties);

(c) representations and warranties (ie, statements about factual and legal matters which one of the parties requires to be made to them in a legally binding way);

(d) 'boiler-plate' clauses (ie, standard clauses inserted into all agreements of such a type and dealing with, for example, the service of notices under the agreement, or the jurisdiction for action where the agreement has an international element).

1.3.1.4 Testimonium

A testimonium clause is not essential but, if used, it introduces the signatures of the parties and may describe a particular method of executing where, for example, a company is using its seal as part of its execution, or an attorney is signing on behalf of a party.

1.3.1.5 Schedules

Use schedules where appropriate to avoid breaking the continuity of a document with too much detail. The operative part of the document then refers to the schedule, and the schedule contains the detail.

> **EXAMPLE**
>
> TENANT'S COVENANTS
>
> The Tenant covenants with the Landlord to observe and perform the covenants set out in Schedule 1.

> **SCHEDULE 1**
>
> 1. To pay the rent ... etc.

Note that the obligation or right is created in the operative part of the document. Only the detail of the obligation or right is put in the schedule.

1.3.1.6 Execution and attestation

A document will end with an execution clause. This will refer to the signatures of the parties and any other formalities necessary to give the document legal effect. The wording of this clause will vary depending on the nature of the party executing, whether the document is executed as a deed, and whether the party's signature is witnessed ('attested').

For a document executed by an individual and not intended to take effect as a deed, the clause could read:

Signed by ALAN JONES)   (Alan Jones signs here)
in the presence of:)
(Witness signs here)

If the document is intended to take effect as a deed the clause could read:

Executed as a deed   )   (Alan Jones signs here)
by ALAN JONES   )
in the presence of:)
(Witness signs here)

1.3.2 Order of clauses in the operative part

It is difficult to lay down rules as to the order of clauses. It will vary according to the nature of the document, but it is often a matter of common sense and logic.

1.3.2.1 Common structures for operative clauses

Deciding on the best structure to adopt when drafting the operative clauses of a document is the most important stage in planning your document.

1.3.2.2 Chronological order

One possibility is to list topics in chronological order. This is often particularly suitable for a document that deals with one simple transaction.

Imagine a contract for the hire of a car. The order of topics could be:

- parties;
- definitions;
- agreement by Owner to hire out car to Hirer on the terms set out in the agreement;
- payment;
- insurance;
- promises by Owner as to the state of the car at the start of the hire;
- duration of hire;
- what the car can be used for;
- who may drive;
- Hirer's promises as to the return of the car;
- remedies for breach of the agreement.

For a contract such as this, a chronological structure will produce a simpler and less repetitious document than if you try to divide topics into Owner's Obligations and Hirer's Obligations.

1.3.2.3 Categorical order

A categorical structure sets out the duties and responsibilities in categories. An example of this is a lease.

The structure of a typical lease is:

- parties;
- definitions;
- the grant of the term by Landlord to Tenant;
- Tenant's covenants;
- Landlord's covenants;
- provisos, eg, the Landlord's power to forfeit the lease.

Here, the division into landlord's obligations and tenant's obligations is essential. The obligations have to be performed throughout the entire term of the lease. There is no chronological order to them.

1.3.2.4 Order of importance

This could be the order used in a simple contract, where the obligations are not to be carried out in any chronological order. An example could be an agreement between employer and employee on severance of employment.

1.3.2.5 Combinations

A document may use a combination of the above structures. A contract with a firm of furniture removers could list the firm's obligations in chronological order, for example:

- to pack the contents of the house;
- to transport to storage;
- to store;
- to transport to new house;
- to unpack;

and then list the owner's obligations.

In a lease, all the tenant's covenants will be put together, but will appear in order of importance.

1.3.3 Structuring a clause

1.3.3.1 Structuring clauses and sub-clauses within the operative part

(a) Use a separate clause for each separate matter.
(b) Use sub-paragraphing to avoid long, cumbersome clauses and provisos.
(c) Number each clause and sub-clause.
(d) Give each clause or group of clauses a heading that correctly defines the subject matter of the clauses, eg:

Tenant's Covenants

Look at the following two examples and decide which you think is easier to understand.

> **EXAMPLE 1**
>
> The Licensee shall purchase exclusively from the Grantor all materials used in making the Invention provided that the licensee shall be entitled to relieve itself of its liability to observe this obligation upon giving the Grantor three months' notice in writing.

> **EXAMPLE 2**
>
> 1. Subject to Clause 2, the Licensee must purchase exclusively from the Grantor all materials used in making the Invention.
> 2. The Licensee may end the obligation contained in Clause 1 by giving the Grantor three months' notice in writing.

Both examples contain the same provisions, but the second is easier to understand because it uses separate numbered clauses for each point.

1.3.3.2 Structuring a clause according to Coode

Read the following clause and think about the structure. Do you think the structure adopted helps to make the meaning clear?

> **Clause X**
>
> The Company shall reimburse the Replacement Value of lost or damaged goods provided that the value of the claim does not exceed £1,000 and the Policyholder notifies the loss within 7 days from (but excluding) the date of its occurrence PROVIDED ALWAYS THAT the above shall not apply to claims made under Clause 10 of this Policy.

This clause starts with a statement of a legal obligation which at first sight appears absolute. The conditions and exceptions attaching to the obligation are not stated until afterwards, so that it is necessary to reconsider the obligation in the light of them. This kind of clause construction is very common in legal drafting, but it is not the most logical way to structure a clause and it makes it more difficult to understand.

In 1843, George Coode wrote a treatise on 'Legislative Expression'; or, 'The Language of The Written Law'. His general principle is that a clause should be structured in the following order:

- circumstances/exceptions (ie, circumstances where the right or obligation does or does not exist);
- conditions (ie, conditions on which the right or obligation depends);
- obligation or right (ie, who **must** do what or who **may** do what).

Words suitable for introducing an exception are 'except where ...'.

Words suitable for introducing circumstances are 'where ...' 'if ... then' or 'when ...' or 'on ...'.

Words suitable for introducing conditions are 'if ...' or 'provided that ...'.

These are two examples of Coode in legislation:

> Section 2(1) of the Land Registration and Land Charges Act 1971
>
> **If** any question arises as to whether a person is entitled to an indemnity under any provision of the Land Registration Act 1925 [*circumstance*] [...] **he** [*person*] **may apply** to the court to have that question determined [*the right*].
>
> Section 23(1) of the Matrimonial Causes Act 1973
>
> **On** granting a decree of divorce ... [*circumstance*] **the court** [*person*] **may make** any one or more of the following orders ... [*right*].

This is an example of Coode in a document:

15 Compensation on termination of contract

Except where otherwise provided [exception], if before 1 December 2020 this contract is terminated by the Buyer [circumstance], then provided the Seller is not in breach of any of his obligations under this contract [condition] the Buyer must pay the Seller the sum of £5000 [obligation].

The rule produces a logical and, to lawyers, a familiar structure, but it does not have to be followed invariably.

Imagine that an owner of land has employed consultants to design and build an amusement park. The consultants want to control the use of their name in any advertising material issued by the landowner. Their name is to be used only if certain conditions are met.

If the clause were drafted using Coode's rule, it would read:

Only where
(a) the Landowner has given the Consultants advance details of any advertising material it plans to use; and
(b) the Consultants have given their express written approval; and
(c) the Consultants have not ended this Agreement under subclause 11(1)

may the Landowner use the Consultants' name in advertising material.

The clause could make the point in a more natural and in a stronger manner if Coode were ignored and the clause were drafted to read:

The Landowner may only use the Consultants' name in advertising material where:
(a) the Landowner has given the Consultants advance details of any advertising materials it plans to use; and
(b) the Consultants have given their express written approval; and
(c) the Consultants have not ended this Agreement under subclause 11(1).

> **EXAMPLE**
>
> Coode's structure can be a useful tool in preparing documents. The clause set out at the start of **1.3.3.2** has been redrafted below using Coode's structure and other techniques to improve its clarity.
>
> **Clause X   Claims for lost or damaged goods**
>
> Where:
>
> (a) a claim does not exceed £1,000; and
> (b) the Policyholder notifies the loss within 7 days from (but excluding) the date of its occurrence; and
> (c) the claim is not one made under Clause 10 of this Policy
>
> the Company shall reimburse the Replacement Value.

1.3.4 Use of precedents

Using a precedent can help in the planning of your document by giving an example of:

(a) suitable structure;
(b) provisions that you have not thought of and that will benefit your client;
(c) suitable wording; and/or
(d) legal problems you had not considered.

However, precedents should be used with caution.

1.3.4.1 Guidelines for using precedents

(a) Look for a precedent only after you have researched and planned your document.
(b) Always check that the precedent is up to date and legally correct.
(c) Adapt the precedent to your transaction, not your transaction to the precedent.
(d) Do not copy words from a precedent unless you are sure of their legal effect.
(e) Do not change words in a precedent unless you are sure that the change will not have an unexpected legal effect. This is particularly true of precedents for wills.
(f) Never assume a precedent cannot be improved.
(g) Do not copy clauses that are irrelevant or, worse, are to the disadvantage of your client;
(h) Do not adopt inappropriate or archaic wording.

1.4 DRAFTING

Having carefully planned the content and structure of your document, you can confidently begin to draft. Your document should be as easy as possible to read and understand. It is essential that everything you draft is precise and unambiguous. You should try to be as concise as possible. Concise documents are easier and quicker to read. Set out below are a number of rules and guidelines which can help you to keep your documents precise and concise.

1.4.1 Use definitions

A definition can do two things.

First, it can create a 'tag' or 'nickname'. This avoids repetition of lengthy names or phrases. This use is often seen in the description of parties to a document.

> **EXAMPLE**
>
> This agreement is made between
>
> (1) Everett Kingdom Finance plc ('Everett')
> (2) Samuel Luke Stowe ('SLS')

In the rest of the document it is only necessary to refer to Everett and SLS.

> **EXAMPLE**
>
> In this agreement
>
> 1. 'the Period of Hire' means from 9am on 1 November 2009 until noon on 23 November 2009.
>
> A subsequent clause might then say something such as 'if the Hirer does not return the Car at or before the end of the Period of Hire ...'.

Secondly, a definition can also create a private dictionary for the document by giving a word something other than its ordinary meaning, or by giving a word an unusually extended or restricted meaning.

> **EXAMPLE**
>
> In this agreement
> 'Boat' includes a sailboard.

> **EXAMPLE**
>
> 'Notified' means notice is given in writing by the insured, or its insurance agent, to the insurer.

1.4.1.1 Where to put the definitions

Definitions that are to apply throughout the document should be put in alphabetical order in a definitions clause at the start of the operative part of the document.

> **EXAMPLE**
> Definitions
> In this Agreement
> (1) 'Arbitration' means ...
> (2) 'Balance Sheet' means ... etc.

If a definition will be used only in one part of a document or in one clause, you can put the definition at the start of the relevant part or clause.

> **EXAMPLE**
> 4.1 In this clause, 'Promotional Material' means ...
> 4.2 The Landowner must ensure that all Promotional Material is ...

In a simple document, a 'tag' may be given to a name or phrase the first time that it is used, and the tag may then be used throughout the rest of the document. For example, in a contract for the sale of land, a clause may say:

> The Seller, for the benefit of his adjoining property, 10 Smith Avenue, Morton, N. Yorks ('the Retained Land') reserves a right of way on foot ...

Later clauses can then refer to the Retained Land.

This method should be used only for simple short documents. In a long document, it wastes time to have to search through the clauses to find the one in which the tag was first adopted.

1.4.1.2 Guidelines for using definitions

(a) It is usual to give the definition a capital letter and to use it with the capital letter throughout the document. This alerts anybody reading it to the fact that a particular word or expression has been given a particular meaning by the document.

(b) A definition should only define. It should not be used to create a substantive right or obligation. The right or obligation should be created in the clause that uses the definition.

(c) If you have a definition, do not forget to use it when you are drafting the rest of the document.

(d) When you use a defined term in a clause, check that it makes sense within the clause.

(e) In a definition, do not define by reference to other, undefined terms.

1.4.2 Padding/superfluous words

Cut out unnecessary phrases which lengthen the sentence while adding nothing to its meaning. For example:

- 'in the circumstances';
- 'in this instance';
- 'the fact that';
- 'of course'.

1.4.3 Tautology

Tautology or saying the same thing twice using different words should be avoided. For example:

- 'unfilled vacancy';
- 'true facts';
- 'now current'.

Similarly, avoid excessive use of adjectives which do not make the meaning more precise. For example:

- 'grave and fatal error';
- 'careful and detailed consideration'.

1.4.4 Compound prepositions

Use single prepositions instead of compound prepositions. For example:

Avoid	Use instead
'in accordance with'	under/by
'by reason of'	by/through
'with reference to'	about
'in order to'	to

1.4.5 Nouns derived from verbs

Use the verb itself rather than a noun derived from it. This helps create a more immediate effect:

Avoid	Use instead
'make an admission'	admit
'give consideration to'	consider
'effect a termination'	terminate or end

1.4.6 Archaic language

Twenty-first century documents should be drafted using contemporary language. Delete or replace archaic words and phrases such as:

- 'crave leave';
- 'the said';
- 'hereinbefore';
- 'aforementioned';
- 'whereof'.

1.4.7 Adverbs and adjectives

Only use adverbs and adjectives when essential to achieve your purpose. Their use is often unnecessary and can be detrimental. Consider for example:

> It was very wrong of you to take a copy of the document.
>
> It was wrong of you to take a copy of the document.

By including the adverb 'very', the level of the allegation is raised from 'wrong' to 'very wrong'. This can raise expectations of the proof required to satisfy the allegation. Be as precise as possible and remove emotive or inflating terms such as extremely, obviously, really, clearly and very unless you have a specific reason for using them.

1.4.8 Keep sentences and paragraphs short

In long sentences, the verb, subject and object may be separated by too many subclauses. This places a strain on the reader's memory and understanding. Always try to keep the sentence core together.

> **EXAMPLE**
> The evidence, including evidence from independent surveys as well as that gathered personally by the writers of this report and the results of investigations formally commissioned by this department, suggests that the public, while acknowledging an overall increase in the actual level of government spending on health, by which is meant on health care both at the doctor–patient level and in hospitals, still views the problems and defects in the National Health Service and in particular in National Health hospitals as the result of a general lack of funding.

The subclauses break up the main thought of the paragraph so that it is difficult to follow. The paragraph would be better rewritten in separate sentences with the main thought first, even though this may increase its length. Brackets may be used for subsidiary points where appropriate. For example:

> The evidence suggests that the public still views the problems and defects in the National Health Service and in particular in National Health hospitals as the result of a general lack of funding. This is so even though the public acknowledges an overall increase in the actual level of government spending on health care both at the doctor–patient level and in hospitals. (Evidence on this issue includes evidence from independent surveys, that gathered personally by the writers of this report and the results of investigations formally commissioned by this department.)

1.4.9 Use the active and not the passive tense where possible

In a sentence where the verb is in the active voice, the subject of the sentence acts upon the object of the sentence. Where the verb is in the passive voice, the object of the sentence is acted upon by the subject. Compare:

> The defendant struck the claimant (active voice).
>
> The claimant was struck by the defendant (passive voice).

1.4.9.1 Problems with the passive

Over-use of the passive voice lengthens a sentence and can make it sound weak. In the worst cases, it obscures meaning. For example:

> It is hoped that resources will be relocated so that changes may be made in the methods by which the system is administered.

Where the verb is in the passive, you may accidentally omit the phrase which indicates who or what is doing the acting. For example:

> The claimant was struck.

In a legal context, the effect of this omission may be important. For example:

> Notice will be served. By whom?

> **EXERCISE 1**
> Try rewriting the following using the active tense.
> (i) A final warning letter is to be written by the line manager.
> (ii) The matter will be considered by the committee at the next meeting.
> (iii) Notice was given by the solicitor.

1.4.9.2 Some uses for the passive

The passive can sound more objective and detached, and therefore more appropriate in certain legal contexts. For example:

> The allegations are denied

sounds better than:

> Our client denies the allegations (which introduces a personal note).

It is correct to use the passive where the subject of the legal action is irrelevant. For example:

> The common seal of X Co was affixed ... It does not matter who affixed it.

The passive may also be used in a legal context to cover the possibility of action by a number of different persons, some of whom are unknown. For example:

> If the goods are damaged we will refund the cost. This could cover damage by the supplier, the carrier, or any third party.

1.4.10 Precision

It is particularly important to ensure that what you write is not ambiguous and expresses exactly your client's objectives. An ambiguous document may at best cause your client to have to make further enquiries; at worst it can result in an expensive dispute and litigation.

1.4.10.1 Ambiguity

Take care with word order

Words or phrases in the wrong place may create ambiguity. Consider the sentence:

> We undertake to repair or replace goods shown to be defective *within six months of the date of purchase.*

It is not clear whether the phrase in italics governs the repair/replacement or the notification of defect. It could be rewritten as:

> Where, within six months of the date of purchase, goods are shown to be defective, we will repair or replace them.

(assuming this was the intended meaning).

Do you mean 'and' or 'or'?

Consider:

> The Seller may serve notice of termination, recover goods already delivered and retain all instalments already paid.

The use of 'and' in this sentence suggests that the list is conjunctive, ie that the seller may do all of the things in it. But can the Seller choose to do only some of them?

Compare:

> The Seller may serve notice of termination, recover goods already delivered or retain all instalments already paid.

The use of 'or' here suggests that the list is disjunctive, ie that the seller may do only one of the things in the list. But it could also mean that the Seller might both serve notice and either recover goods or retain instalments.

To avoid such ambiguity, consider (depending on the meaning required) using phrases such as:

> The Seller may do all or any of the following:
>
> or
>
> The Seller may exercise one only of the following rights:

The 'undistributed middle'

Take care with provisions 'before/after' a particular date or 'over/under' a particular weight or measure. Consider the following examples:

> Where the company delivers the goods before 1 January ... /Where the company delivers the goods after 1 January ...

What happens if it delivers them *on* 1 January?

> Goods over 20kg must be sent by rail ... /Goods under 20kg may be sent by air

What about goods weighing *exactly* 20kg?

Expressions of time

Take care to avoid ambiguity. Consider:

> The Buyer must pay a deposit within 7 days of today's date.

Does the 7 days include or exclude today?

For legal and practical reasons, avoid expressing periods of time in the following ways:

- from [a date];
- by [a date];
- within [so many days of] or from [a date];
- until [a date].

It is safer to be clear by using one of the following:

- from but excluding/not including;
- from and including;
- on or after;
- on or before;
- within a period of 7 days commencing with;
- until but excluding/not including;
- until and including.

Are you creating an obligation or a discretion?

An obligation is created by the phrase:

> The Customer shall pay a deposit on signing this Agreement.

A discretion is created by the phrase:

> The Company may retain the deposit if the Customer does not collect the goods on or before 30 June.

Take care when using 'shall'. It is grammatically correct to use it in the third person to indicate an obligation ('the Tenant shall pay the Rent'), but it is also used in the first person to indicate simple future ('I shall go to London'). Alternatively, you could use 'must' to create an obligation.

Avoid words of similar sound or appearance

Words of similar sound or appearance are easily confused and may also confuse a lay client. For example:

Avoid	*Use instead*
'mortgagee/mortgagor'	'lender/borrower'
'lessor/lessee'	'landlord/tenant'

Ambiguous pronouns

Consider:

> Where the Supplier fails to deliver the Goods to the Customer in accordance with Clause 9 or the Goods delivered do not correspond with the sample he may terminate this Agreement.

Who may terminate the agreement?

Where it is not clear to which noun a pronoun refers, the noun should be repeated.

The ejusdem generis rule

Consider:

> In consequence of war, disturbance or any other cause.

Unless a contrary intention appears, 'any other cause' will be construed as meaning only causes in the same category as those previously listed.

To avoid ambiguity, add (as appropriate):

> whether of the same kind as [the causes] previously listed or not

or

> or any other [cause] provided it is of the same kind as the [causes] previously listed.

1.4.10.2 Shall/will

In the first person, 'shall' simply looks to the future. In the second and third person, 'will' looks to the future.

> I shall interview the client tomorrow. I hope that you will sit in. Afterwards we shall discuss the problem and consider the next steps.

In the first person, 'will' expresses determination. In the second or third person, 'shall' expresses determination or obligation.

> I will make you do this.
> The Buyer shall pay £500 on 1 December.

This means that you create problems if your document says 'the Buyer will pay ...'. Is this what the Buyer intends to do, or is it what they are obligated to do?

Many documents use expressions such as, 'If the Company shall breach this term ...'. The clause is looking to the future but is using 'shall' incorrectly. It could be redrafted to say, 'In the event of the company breaching ...'. Better still, 'If the Company breaches ...'.

1.4.11 Layout and presentation

Use the layout and presentation of your document to enhance its readability and usefulness. Use headings and bullet points to break up text. Use diagrams, tables, colours and different fonts where they are necessary or helpful. Where a document is likely to be annotated, leave wide margins and use double spacing. For many court documents there are very detailed requirements as to how you should present your document. Check that you have followed any relevant rules/guidelines. For example, under the Civil Procedure Rules (PD 32) it is recommended that witness statements should be 'produced on durable quality A4 paper with a 3.5cm margin'.

1.4.11.1 Paragraphs

Using paragraphs makes prose more readable and helps to avoid cumbersome clauses and subclauses. Always number your paragraphs if possible as this aids navigation and will help anyone using the document.

1.4.11.2 Tabulation

Tabulation aids clarity and can help to avoid ambiguity. Consider the sentence:

> Any trainee solicitor is entitled to paid leave to attend a conference, lecture, or seminar *provided by The Law Society*.

How much of the sentence is the phrase in italics intended to qualify? Does it apply only to 'seminar', or to 'conference' and 'lecture' as well?

Compare:

> Any trainee solicitor is entitled to paid leave to attend:
> (a)   a conference; or
> (b)   a lecture; or
> (c)   a seminar,
> provided by The Law Society.

Care should be taken, however, not to indent the final phrase 'provided by The Law Society' to the same margin as 'a seminar' or the ambiguity would remain.

A useful basic rule is that any sentence longer than three lines is a good candidate for tabulation if it includes a compound or series.

1.4.11.3 Numbering

Where a series of points is being made, numbering may improve clarity and aid later cross-referencing.

Examples of numbering systems:

4.5.1   The system adopted in this book and known as the decimal system.

4(5)(a)(i)   A system based on the legislative approach and known as the alphanumeric system.

4.5(a)(i)   A combination system using elements of both decimal and alphanumeric systems.

1.4.12 Jargon

Jargon is a broad term and may include specialised language of a professional, occupational or other group which is often meaningless to outsiders. It may also include slang. While jargon can be a useful professional shorthand, it should never be used where it might obscure meaning.

> **EXAMPLE**
> - *Bilateral probital hematoma*   medical terminology for a black eye
> - *Ab initio*   Latin/legal terminology for 'at the beginning'
> - HTH, *web cookie*   computer/Internet jargon for 'Hope this Helps', and the name for a small text file that is sent to your computer via your web browser when you visit certain websites

Similarly, avoid using acronyms which might be unfamiliar or have several different meanings, eg CPR (Civil Procedure Rules, cardiopulmonary resuscitation, Canadian Pacific Railway, etc).

If appropriate, consider providing a plain English translation of any legal or technical terms. It is worth noting that in June 2006 the Coroner Reform Bill became the first Bill to feature a plain English explanation of every legal clause.

1.5 CHECKING

Always check your work.

(a) If possible leave the document for a while and then come back to it.
(b) Ideally get someone else to check it.
(c) Reading the document aloud can be a good way of identifying mistakes/poorly-drafted material.
(d) Print out your work and read from hard copy rather than trying to check it on screen.
(e) Do not read from the beginning of the document. Try starting from the middle or towards the end. The later parts of documents tend to be less familiar and less well checked.
(f) Always confirm names, figures, dates, addresses and page numbers.
(g) Do not rely on automated spelling or grammar checks.
(h) Check all cross-references in the document to other clauses or to schedules.
(i) Above all check that your document reflects your client's objectives.

1.6 PRACTICAL AND ETHICAL CONSIDERATIONS

1.6.1 Good practice when submitting a draft

Out of courtesy, you should always supply to the other side an additional copy of any draft sent for approval.

1.6.2 Good practice when amending the other side's draft

Make sure that all amendments are clearly identifiable.

1.6.3 Ethical considerations when negotiating a draft

The SRA Standards and Regulations set out the principles of professional conduct which apply to all aspects of practice and include the requirement to act:

(a) in a way that upholds public trust and confidence in the solicitors' profession and in legal services provided by authorised persons;
(b) with honesty;
(c) with integrity.

Breach of these rules renders the solicitor liable to disciplinary action.

Do not attempt to mislead the other side by concealing amendments you have made to their draft, for example by writing a covering letter which draws attention to some amendments and not to others. Any deliberate attempt to mislead could be criminally fraudulent as well as amounting to professional misconduct.

Do not attempt to take advantage of a mistake made by the other side. Point it out to them. They may otherwise be able to claim rectification of the document to incorporate an omitted provision or to allege that the agreement is a nullity, so enabling them to resist specific performance.

1.6.4 Inclusive language

Use language that is inclusive and respectful. Only refer to personal characteristics if necessary and relevant. Take an individual approach and ask about preferences. Using inclusive language is an ethical obligation as well as good practice. Inclusive language avoids use of words, expressions or assumptions that would stereotype, demean or exclude people.

Choice of language can be a sensitive area, and preferences are not necessarily universal. There are some forms of language which are generally unacceptable, and examples of these are set out below. Best practice and terminology have changed and will continue to evolve. You should not assume that etiquette regarding inclusive language is international, and what is acceptable will vary according to location and culture.

If you have concerns or questions about the most appropriate form of language, ask those you are dealing with what their preferences are. Engage in open discussion where necessary about the choice and use of language, particularly in some of the areas set out below.

1.6.4.1 Forms of address

Always use the preferred form of address etc when known. If addressing a woman when their preference is not known, you should use Ms rather than Mrs if you wish to use a courtesy title. Ms is more inclusive and can refer to any woman regardless of marital status. The new gender neutral title 'Mx' is now recognised by the Government and many businesses in the UK and can be used as a courtesy title regardless of gender. As an alternative, some writers use the addressee's full name, eg Dear Olivia Willis.

When you do not yet know which pronouns someone goes by, it is generally a good idea to use 'they/them' where necessary. The use of 'they/them' is gender neutral and has been commonly used for a long time. Many organisations encourage employees to include their pronouns on ID badges and email signatures to make preferences easier for others to adopt. The use of pronouns is discussed further at **1.6.4.3** below.

Be consistent in how you address people, for example if you refer to one person by their name, last name, courtesy title or profession then others should be referred to in the same way.

> **EXAMPLE**
>
> Professor Rajesh Singh and Hester will both be attending the settlement meeting.
>
> While the man has been given his first name, surname and professional title, the woman has been referred to by first name only.
>
> Professor Rajesh Singh and Dr Hester Rowe will both be attending the settlement meeting.
>
> In this example both people attending are consistently referred to using the same forms of address.

1.6.4.2 Characteristics

Careful consideration of language should always be made when reference to any of the following characteristics is necessary:

- age;
- disabilities, medical conditions and mental health;
- race and ethnicity; and
- sex, gender and sexuality.

Age

Only refer to age if it is necessary to do so. Where possible, refer to specific ages, eg 'The benefits listed in 12(1)(a) are only available to people aged 65 and over.' Avoid terms such as elderly, senior, middle aged, OAP/old age pensioner. Avoid terminology that risks stereotyping or assumptions.

Disabilities, medical conditions and mental health

Use positive language and avoid phrases such as suffering from, afflicted by, victim of, confined to a wheelchair, handicapped, sick, diseased etc. Instead refer to the factual situation without words which impute value or judgement, eg people with cancer, wheelchair user. Use a people first approach to writing. Rather than referring to people as mentally ill, you should refer to people with mental health conditions or problems.

Race and ethnicity

Race and ethnicity are often used interchangeably, and while there is some overlap in meaning they are distinct terms. Race is a categorisation based on mainly physical characteristics or traits such as skin colour. Race has no genetic basis and is a social construct. However, the social concept of race continues to affect human experiences and can be used as a basis for unity and action.

Ethnicity is a wider term and has been used to refer to long shared cultural experiences, national origins, religious practices, traditions, language etc. There are numerous terms for different ethnicities and nationalities, and people have different preferences. People can have multiple racial and ethnic identities which may not be obvious. Do not make assumptions about nationality or cultural background based on appearance. Do ask about preferences. Racism, racial bias and racial prejudice continue to be serious problems, and you must work to ensure that the language you use is anti-racist and as inclusive as possible.

In the UK, the terms BAME (Black, Asian and minority ethnic) and BME (Black and minority ethnic) should be avoided. It is usually best to avoid umbrella terms or grouping large numbers of very different people together. Refer to specific individual national and ethnic groups when necessary, eg people from a black Caribbean background, people from a white British background.

Use of the term 'global majority' is an increasingly common term and is a shortened version of 'people of the global majority'. It is used to refer to all ethnic groups, except white British and other white groups, who might previously have been referred to as 'ethnic minority groups'.

People of mixed ethnic background should be referred to as people from a mixed ethnic group or people from a mixed ethnic background. As in every category, ask about personal preferences where possible.

Sex, gender and sexuality

Only refer to sex, gender or sexuality when it is necessary to do so. A person's sex (sometimes referred to as biological or anatomical sex) is comprised of chromosomes, body parts, hormones etc and is distinct from gender. Sex can refer to male, female or intersex.

Gender identity is a psychological sense of self, based on how you see and describe yourself. Individuals may see themselves as being of male, female or non-binary gender or being in between genders. Genders may be fixed or fluid, and some people identify with a gender opposite to the sex they were registered with at birth.

Cisgender is the term used to describe people who identify with the gender assigned to them at birth. The term transgender is an umbrella term commonly used to describe people who identify with a gender opposite to the sex they were registered with at birth. For those not identifying as either male or female, the term non-binary is used. As always, ask about preferred forms of address.

Sexuality or sexual orientation is a person's physical, romantic and or emotional attachment to others, eg bisexual, gay, lesbian, straight. Transgender people may identify as any of these.

1.6.4.3 Gender neutral language

As part of ensuring that you use inclusive language, you should aim to use gender neutral language where possible. Avoid gender biased words and expressions which may reinforce gender stereotypes.

Examples:

- chairman, statesman etc

- mankind
- manmade
- manpower.

The use of some gendered nouns referring to job title or position such as actress, manageress etc is outdated, and words such as actor, manager etc should be used regardless of sex or gender.

There are many techniques that may be used to achieve gender neutral language, and the choice you make should be determined by identifying the most effective, clear and concise in each circumstance. If redrafting documents to ensure they are gender neutral, take particular care that meaning and clarity are not compromised.

Repeat the noun

One of the simplest options is to repeat the noun rather than using a pronoun. This can work well but tends to add length and detract from fluency. You can also use a defined term.

> **EXAMPLE**
>
> Annual salary, in relation to a person, means sums payable to him in connection with his employment over the course of a calendar year.
>
> Annual salary, in relation to a person, means sums payable to a person in connection with the person's employment over the course of a calendar year.

Pairing

Pairing is the use of both male and female pronouns ('she/he', 'her/his'). It is the best choice when you want to explicitly include both women and men or draw attention to the inclusion of both. It is not a generally recommended practice as it adds length and is distracting to the reader, particularly in texts where narrative is important. It may also risk creating inconsistencies and inaccuracies.

Some writers alternate placement of male and female pronouns in order to avoid giving precedence to either male or female. Again, while this may be a useful technique in some circumstances, it also risks confusing or distracting. Another disadvantage of pairing is that it is not fully inclusive.

> **EXAMPLE**
>
> When an apprentice accepts an offer of employment, he or she must be able to provide proof of address and identity. To qualify for overtime payments, she or he must provide written authorisation from a manager.

Change the pronoun

There are several ways in which you may change the pronoun used. The most common is to use 'they/them'. Care needs to be taken that using the plural form does not change the meaning or lead to ambiguity.

> **EXAMPLES**
>
> It is an offence for a person to carry a prohibited article into the building unless he can prove that he has a valid reason as set out in 5.3 below.
>
> It is an offence for a person to carry a prohibited article into the building unless they can prove that they have a valid reason as set out in 5.3 below.

> A judge is required to familiarise himself with the rules on equality and diversity.
>
> A judge is required to familiarise themselves with the rules on equality and diversity.

Use the pronoun 'one'

> **EXAMPLE**
>
> A member of staff located outside London earns less than he would in London.
>
> A member of staff located outside London earns less than one would in London.

Use the relative pronoun 'who'

> **EXAMPLE**
>
> A person commits a breach of the terms of the agreement if he does not comply with the provisions of paragraph 5.2 of this agreement.
>
> A person who does not comply with the provisions of paragraph 5.2 commits a breach of this agreement.

Use the gender neutral pronoun 'ze'

The gender neutral pronouns 'ze/hir' or 'ze/zir' are also available and have the advantage of not adding length. Their use is increasing but is not currently standard practice. Use of these gender neutral pronouns avoids many of the problems associated with other gender neutral solutions in drafting.

Omit the gendered word

> **EXAMPLE**
>
> An officeholder may be removed from office if he is convicted of a criminal offence.
>
> An officeholder may be removed from office if convicted of a criminal offence.

Use the passive voice

While using the passive voice has disadvantages and can lead to a lack of clarity (see **1.4.9.1** above), it is another way in which you can avoid including gendered language. When using the passive voice, make sure that it is clear who has to do what.

> **EXAMPLE**
>
> A complainant must supply written evidence of the situation he is complaining about.
>
> A complainant must supply written evidence of the situation complained about.

> **EXERCISE 2**
>
> Rewrite the following using inclusive language. There may be more than one correct answer. One or two suggested answers can be found in the Appendix to Part I.
>
> (i) Before he is formally appointed, the candidate must have written approval from the Chairman.
>
> (ii) A person must be a permanent employee at the firm for 20 years before he may apply for a long-term service benefit.

> (iii) In the event of an absence, mothers should contact the receptionist before 09:00 and give her details of the child's cause of absence.
>
> (iv) The Managing Partner may remove a Committee Member from office if he has failed to attend a meeting for a period of six months or more. The Managing Partner may, at his discretion, appoint a replacement Committee Member for the remainder of the calendar year.
>
> (v) The appellant is a middle-aged man who is suffering from cancer. Since the accident in 2020, he has been confined to a wheelchair and has been diagnosed as epileptic.

1.7 WRITING LETTERS

1.7.1 Who is the addressee?

Consider the needs of the reader and try to adapt your style accordingly.

1.7.1.1 The lay client

Avoid jargon and legalese when writing to a lay client. Explain all unfamiliar terms, but do not patronise. How familiar is the client with the subject?

1.7.1.2 The business client and other professionals

The business client will generally be familiar with solicitors' letters. Avoid padding and get to the point quickly. Where necessary, explain legal terminology or process.

1.7.1.3 Other solicitors

What kind of matter are you dealing with? Are you writing from a position of strength or weakness? Do you want to adopt a conciliatory or non-conciliatory stance? Consider which is more likely to persuade the addressee. Remember that the other solicitor may send a copy of your letter to their client.

1.7.2 'Ghosting'

You may be asked to write letters to be signed in a partner's name. Read the file and consider the partner's style. Check how well the partner knows the addressee; for example, if you are writing to a client, is the partner on first-name terms with them?

1.7.3 Starting and ending the letter

Letters beginning 'Dear Sirs/Sir/Madam' all end 'Yours faithfully'.

A letter addressed to a person by surname, for example 'Dear Mr Smith', ends with 'Yours sincerely'.

A letter beginning 'Dear John' may end with 'Yours sincerely' or 'Yours'.

1.7.4 Content

1.7.4.1 Consider overall structure

An initial heading identifying the matter is conventional. For example:

> Sale of 25 Acacia Avenue, Bristol

A complex letter will be easier to understand (and reply to) if you give each paragraph a number and a heading.

1.7.4.2 Form and style

If you are writing in the firm's name (eg, a formal letter to the other side), write in the first person plural ('we') and be consistent.

Acknowledge the addressee's last communication.

If it is your first letter to the addressee, explain your involvement.

State the purpose of the letter.

Carry out that purpose using:
- logical sequence;
- separate paragraphs;
- short sentences;
- active voice.

Write in a restrained tone. Avoid overemphasis (eg, unnecessary adverbs – 'totally unhappy', 'completely inaccurate'). Use exclamation marks sparingly. Do not express surprise, amazement, outrage, etc.

Avoid jokes and witticisms.

1.7.5 Some practical points

1.7.5.1 Second thoughts and editing

- Try to be detached about your document.
- How would it sound if read out in open court in the future?
- Try not to write in anger or when emotion is running high. If unavoidable do not send anything until you or a colleague have had a chance to review it.
- Consider giving a deadline for a reply (eg, if the matter is urgent or if the letter might be unwelcome).
- If you have asked a client to do something, make sure your instructions are clear. Consider ending with a list or table summarising the action points.
- Check the grammar and spelling.

1.7.5.2 Final checks

Check that the letter:
- carries the correct references (ie, yours and those of the other side);
- is dated;
- is signed;
- is accompanied by the right enclosures;
- is put into the right envelope, and is properly addressed.

1.8 WRITING REPORTS AND MEMORANDA

1.8.1 Reports

1.8.1.1 Purpose

Reports usually cover a specific subject and serve a particular purpose. In the office, you may have to write a report on some legal research or fact-finding you have been asked to undertake.

1.8.1.2 Is your research complete?

Consider whether you have all the necessary information and identify any gaps.

1.8.1.3 Edit your material

Consider how much information should go into the report. Brevity increases the likelihood of the report being read, but too little information and your conclusions may not be adequately supported and the document may be less persuasive.

1.8.1.4 Planning your report

Plan the text of your report carefully to produce a logical argument.

Consider what will be the most useful structure for the reader. For example, if you were asked to answer specific questions, could you use these to head paragraphs of your report?

Consider including:

- a contents page or an index;
- an introduction explaining why the report was commissioned;
- a brief summary of the report before the main text for quick reference;
- diagrams (if relevant);
- case or statute references (if relevant);
- a bibliography;
- appendices;
- acknowledgements of sources of information.

1.8.1.5 Style

For whom are you writing? Adapt your style appropriately.

Think about whether you should paraphrase or explain your source material, or whether you can reproduce it word for word.

1.8.1.6 Layout and presentation

Make sure the report is well set out, with clear headings and numbered paragraphs and subparagraphs if appropriate.

Is it to be used as a discussion document? If so, consider having it printed double-spaced with wide margins to leave room for annotation.

1.8.1.7 Final checks

Print the report and read it through carefully, amending and rewriting where necessary.

Check that you have:

- done what you were asked to do;
- identified any relevant options;
- reached a conclusion.

1.8.2 Memoranda

1.8.2.1 Types of memoranda

Solicitors generally have to write two types of memoranda:

- attendance notes (as a record of their meetings or telephone calls with clients, other solicitors, etc);
- internal memoranda (as a quick way of communicating with others in the firm).

1.8.2.2 Attendance notes

Attendance notes are put on a file as a record of an oral discussion, transaction or agreement and must be clear and accurate in case of any later dispute.

They are essential for anyone who takes over a file and was not present for the meeting, telephone call, etc.

They may also be needed when a client's bill is prepared as part of the record of chargeable time spent on the matter.

Write your attendance note as soon as possible after the event when everything is fresh in your mind and you are less likely to have forgotten something.

Always try to take contemporaneous notes – in a simple case, you can put them straight on the file. For more complicated matters, you can use your notes to compile your attendance note, but do not destroy them: they are important additional evidence in any dispute.

An attendance note should normally contain the following:

- the client's name;
- the subject matter;
- your reference;
- the date;
- the place (of any meeting);
- the people present (at a meeting);
- the starting and finishing times (of the meeting or phone call);
- a summary of what was discussed or agreed;
- any follow-up action to be taken by you or others.

If your attendance note records an important decision or agreement, always confirm it by letter to avoid misunderstandings.

1.8.2.3 Internal memoranda

Keep internal memoranda brief and business-like, but take care with the tone. If a memo sounds curt, you may cause offence to the recipient.

The format required is generally as follows:

MEMORANDUM

From:
To:
Fee earner's reference:
Date:
Client's name:
Client's matter:

Most firms use printed forms on which these headings already appear.

1.9 SPELLING AND GRAMMAR

Poor spelling and grammar will undermine the authority of anything that you write. Poor grammar is at best distracting and likely to leave a poor impression. At worst it may alter the meaning of a document and render it ineffective. The following exercises allow you to test your grammar. If you find that you have scored poorly then refresh your understanding using any of the books contained in the further reading section or using one of the many Internet resources on grammar which are freely available (eg, www.bbc.co.uk/skillswise/topic-group/word-grammar).

EXERCISE 3
Spelling

Which one of the following is correctly spelt?

(i)	acomodation	accommodation	accomodation
(ii)	unneccessary	unneccesary	unnecessary
(iii)	privilege	priviledge	privelige
(iv)	embarrass	embarras	embarass
(v)	professor	proffessor	profesor

Apostrophes

Add apostrophes where necessary in the following sentences:

(i)   Whos likely to be delayed by a few minutes of rain?
(ii) Weve always valued both the local Gardening Institutes lectures.
(iii) Im sure he said its a ten oclock train we need to catch.
(iv) The childrens enjoyment of the fair was greater than ours.
(v)   The girls football shirts hung on pegs in the cloakrooms main aisle.

Other punctuation

Add a comma or full stop beneath the *:

(i)   MARY DAVENPORT WRITES WELL * HOWEVER, LUCIEN GRANT HATES WRITING.
(ii) MY PRINCIPAL AREA OF SPECIALITY IS TAX * MY SECOND SPECIALITY IS FINANCE.

Add full stops and capital letters to:

(iii) The trainee was quite clear that he needed to work harder if he wanted to get taken on it was quite possible for the firm to hire all the trainees that year his friend had already been given an indication that he would be offered a job and he had been working really long hours.

Add commas to:

(iv) Edward O'Grady however always wanted to surf the Internet rather than do his work.
(v)   The solicitor walked up to her office opened the door took off her coat and slumped into her chair.
(vi) For business meetings the firm offered tea coffee water fruit juices biscuits and sandwiches.

Add semi-colons to:

(vii) I read the Legal Times before work every day it keeps me on top of changes in the law.
(viii) The employer wrote to the employee to complain about his time keeping workers ought to know that starting work on time is essential.

> **EXERCISE 4**
>
> (a) Identify the errors in the following paragraph.
>
> (b) Then try rewriting the paragraph using the rules and recommendations set out in this chapter.
>
> I am writing with reference to your enquiry concerning the use of the entrance area and hallway at the gallery for the purpose of displaying informational materials and presenting visual displays on the subject of recycling. In the circumstances the central question will be whether the internal content origins and visual qualities of the material hereinbefore mentioned are to be felt to be appropriate after due consideration has be given by the Gallery Board, such permissions are at the sole dicretion of the board. The Boards decision concerning any such request will be made after it has met in session on the first Thursday of each calendar month and notification will be sent within 14 days of the said meeting.

APPENDIX TO PART I

Answers to Exercises

Exercise 1

Answers

(i) The line manager will write a final warning letter.
(ii) The committee will consider the matter at the next meeting.
(iii) The solicitor gave notice.

Exercise 2

Answers

(i) Before being formally appointed, the candidate must have written approval from the Chair.
(ii) A person must be a permanent employee at the firm for 20 years before applying for a long-term service benefit.
   or
   A person must be a permanent employee at the firm for 20 years before they may apply for a long-term service benefit.
(iii) In the event of an absence, parents/guardians should contact the receptionist before 09:00 and give details of the child's cause of absence.
(iv) The Managing Partner may remove a Committee Member from office if he/she has failed to attend a meeting for a period of six months or more. The Managing Partner has discretion to appoint a replacement Committee Member for the remainder of the calendar year.
(v) The appellant is a man aged [insert age] who has cancer. Since the accident in 2020, he has used a wheelchair and has been diagnosed with epilepsy.

Exercise 3

Spelling

Answers

(i) accommodation
(ii) unnecessary
(iii) privilege
(iv) embarrass
(v) professor

Apostrophes

Answers

(i) Who's likely to be delayed by a few minutes of rain?
(ii) We've always valued both the local Gardening Institutes' lectures.
(iii) I'm sure he said it's a ten o'clock train we need to catch.
(iv) The children's enjoyment of the fair was greater than ours.

(v) The girls' football shirts hung on pegs in the cloakroom's main aisle.

Other punctuation

Answers

Add a comma or full stop beneath the *:

(i) MARY DAVENPORT WRITES WELL. HOWEVER, LUCIEN GRANT HATES WRITING.

(ii) MY PRINCIPAL AREA OF SPECIALITY IS TAX. MY SECOND SPECIALITY IS FINANCE.

Add full stops and capital letters to:

(iii) The trainee was quite clear that he needed to work harder if he wanted to get taken on. It was quite possible for the firm to hire all the trainees that year. His friend had already been given an indication that he would be offered a job and he had been working really long hours.

Add commas to:

(iv) Edward O'Grady, however, always wanted to surf the Internet rather than do his work.

(v) The solicitor walked up to her office, opened the door, took off her coat and slumped into her chair.

(vi) For business meetings, the firm offered tea, coffee, water, fruit juices, biscuits and sandwiches.

Add semi-colons to:

(vii) I read the Legal Times before work every day; it keeps me on top of changes in the law.

(viii) The employer wrote to the employee to complain about his time keeping; workers ought to know that starting work on time is essential.

Exercise 4

Answers

I am writing <u>with reference to</u> your enquiry concerning the use of the entrance area and hallway at the gallery for <u>the purpose of displaying informational materials and presenting visual displays</u> on the subject of recycling. <u>In the circumstances</u> the central question will be whether the internal <u>content origins</u> and visual qualities of the material <u>hereinbefore mentioned</u> are <u>to be felt to be</u> appropriate after due <u>consideration has be given</u> by the Gallery Board, such permissions are at the sole <u>dicretion</u> of the <u>board</u>. The <u>Boards</u> decision concerning any such request will be made after it has met in session on the first Thursday of each calendar month and notification will be sent within <u>14 days of the said meeting</u>.

- The structure of the paragraph is confusing and illogical, eg we are told the criteria for decisions before we are told who has authority to make them.
- The provision relating to time is ambiguous.
- Sentences are too long, use archaic terminology and unnecessarily complicated words and phrases, eg 'informational materials', 'hereinbefore mentioned'.
- There are numerous padding words and phrases and compound prepositions, eg 'with reference to'.
- There are spelling and grammatical errors.
- The paragraph uses archaic terminology.
- The paragraph uses the passive tense.

The overall effect of these errors is to make the paragraph difficult to understand and pompous in tone.

Set out below is an example of how the paragraph might be rewritten.

'I am writing about your request to use the entrance area and hallway at the Gallery for a display about recycling. Permission to mount a display is given by the Gallery Board ("the Board") which meets on the first Thursday of each month. The Board will decide whether the quality and content of the material is appropriate. The Board will let you know its decision within 2 weeks of and including the date of the meeting.'

The original paragraph was 120 words. The paragraph above which contains the same information is only 76 words. It is also easier to read and understand.

PART II
PRACTICAL LEGAL RESEARCH

CHAPTER 2

INTRODUCTION TO PRACTICAL LEGAL RESEARCH

2.1	Why should I read this section?	35
2.2	The role of legal research in the office	35
2.3	Problem-solving	36
2.4	Principles of practical legal research	39

> **LEARNING OUTCOMES**
>
> After reading this chapter you will be able to:
> - explain how legal research is used in a practical context
> - understand how to approach a problem presented by a client
> - identify the key stages in analysing a problem
> - describe the importance of selecting appropriate search terms
> - understand the significance of recording your research methods
> - identify how to update your research in different sources.

2.1 WHY SHOULD I READ THIS SECTION?

In a nutshell, you should read this section because in the early stages of your legal career you are likely to spend a large proportion of your time engaged in legal research. Strong research skills are therefore highly valued by firms.

You may think that you can already carry out research effectively as a result of previous study. In an academic context, that may well be true. Undoubtedly at some time you will have located and summarised a primary source of law. You may also have compiled long and detailed essays on legislative history, or analysed opposing learned opinions on a contentious legal topic. These sorts of experiences are useful. But on their own they do not equip you to research the law effectively as a solicitor. The following chapters will build on your existing skills, by shifting the focus from academic to practical application.

2.2 THE ROLE OF LEGAL RESEARCH IN THE OFFICE

Law firms exist to make money. They generate fees by selling the time that lawyers spend on solving clients' problems. Practical legal research is a particularly important step in this larger process.

In a law firm, legal research entails the ability to produce work that is:

- accurate;
- timely;
- up-to-date;
- carried out efficiently;
- commercially aware;

- presented in an appropriate and succinct form.

The focus on timeliness and efficiency in the commercial world requires a shift in mindset from the academic environment, where students often have several weeks to complete a piece of research. For practising lawyers, time really is money.

In addition, many students expect that other support staff will be on hand to carry out the spadework of research when their careers get underway. The reality is very different. Bluntly, a principal task of trainees is to carry out legal research on behalf of other fee earners! So your ability to impress the people for whom you conduct research will be a key factor in whether you succeed or fail in your career as a solicitor. Therefore the time and effort you invest in learning how to research effectively on the LPC will pay dividends from the earliest stage of your career.

Over recent years, you will have become aware of the growth of artificial intelligence (AI) tools in all areas of life. Surely these can now assist with legal research tasks? As is often the case with AI, the answer is not straightforward. Certainly, the use of AI in the legal sector has expanded over recent years and is likely to continue to do so. This includes using AI to review and summarise large volumes of material which is part of the legal research process. However, there will still be a need for legal professionals to contextualise the research, check and review the results of any research carried out by AI tools and then apply this to the issue they are researching. This means that you must be able to carry out your own research in order to effectively use and assess any AI tools which might be available to assist you. We will consider the use of AI further in the next chapter (at **3.6**).

2.3 PROBLEM-SOLVING

The main purpose of a lawyer's skills and knowledge is to bridge the gap between a client's actual circumstances and what the client wants them to be: in other words, to solve clients' problems.

At any one time, a solicitor is likely to deal with a variety of case files presented by clients who are diverse in background and personality. Unsurprisingly, the problems that clients present to solicitors tend to be complex and difficult. They may have multiple strands. Often there will be a range of possible solutions, some legal and some non-legal. Each client's circumstances will generate a different set of time pressures. For all these reasons, especially for the novice, it is sensible to adopt a logical framework for problem-solving. The following model sets out such a framework.

2.3.1 Problem analysis model

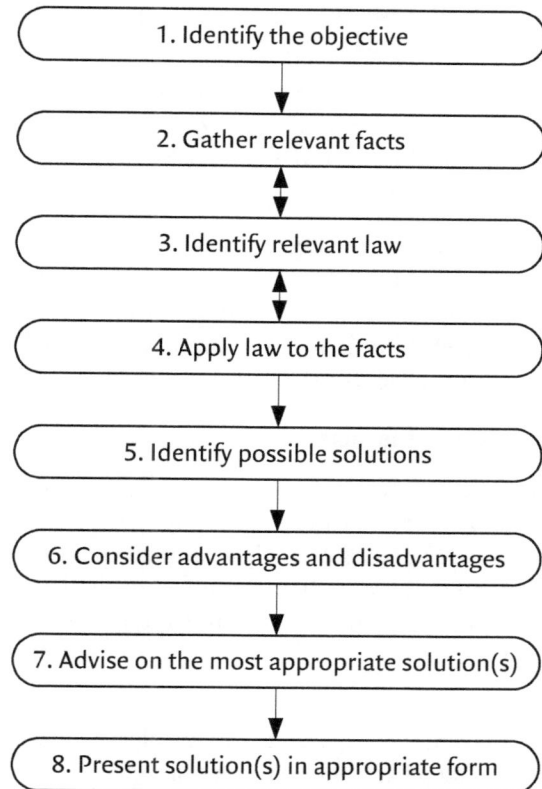

We shall now consider these steps in more detail.

Stage 1. Identify the objective

You must clearly establish the client's objectives by discussing the circumstances that prompted them to seek legal advice. It is important to remember that what the client wants to achieve must drive your approach to solving legal problems (in so far, of course, as regulatory and professional conduct rules allow). Focus your preliminary discussion on the client's objectives, and then keep them at the centre of your thinking.

Stage 2. Gather relevant facts

The client may begin with a brief explanation of their circumstances. You will then need to ask questions to obtain all the facts that may be relevant to tackle the problem in order to achieve the client's objectives. Lateral thinking is a useful technique at this stage: continually review in your mind any gaps in the client's account that might hamper a rigorous legal analysis.

You will often need to gather more facts from a range of other sources besides the client. This may include:

- other participants in the matter (such as witnesses or police officers);
- documents (such as witness statements, contracts or photographs);
- experts (such as surveyors, doctors or forensic scientists);
- other lawyers (perhaps more experienced colleagues or even the solicitor for the opposing party, for example if rules oblige them to disclose certain documents in the course of litigation).

This phase will inevitably generate large volumes of documents. It is vital to have processes in place at the beginning to manage this material in an orderly way.

Stage 3.   Identify relevant law

Now you should begin to narrow your focus by highlighting those facts that will help you investigate possible solutions to the client's problem.

A series of legal issues will arise from these key facts. These will tend to divide into issues of substantive law and issues of procedure. You may already have a good grasp of the issues in the area of law in question, or the area may be outside your usual field of practice. In either case, you are likely to need to undertake further research.

Note that double arrows link stages 2 and 3 in the model. This is because they are interdependent. Researching the relevant law may well prompt further questions, so that you may need to go back to the client to ask for more information. Retracing your steps is nothing to worry about. The key thing is to avoid jumping to conclusions on the basis of insufficient knowledge of either the facts or the law.

Stage 4.   Apply law to the facts

In stages 2 and 3 the aim has been to build a full picture of all the possibilities of both fact and law. Now the aim is to narrow the focus by applying the law to the material facts. This phase requires the same techniques of analysis and evaluation that judges use to decide disputes. However, remember that your client's interest in the law is limited to how it relates to their particular circumstances. The client is not interested in complex statements of the law in general.

Note once again in the model that a double arrow links this stage to the previous one. Reassess regularly and be prepared to be flexible as you work between facts and law; you may well need to take a step back before progressing.

Stage 5.   Identify possible solutions

When you have established clearly the relationship of facts and law, a range of potential solutions should begin to emerge. This phase is again one of expanding options: do not focus on the first option that emerges; you should try to ensure that no alternative is missed.

The technique of brainstorming can be useful: allocate a set period of time to thinking creatively and trying to generate as many solutions as possible, even solutions that seem impractical at first glance. This works well as a group activity.

Always consider the possibility of doing nothing. For example, it may be worth waiting to see what action another party may take first, or it may even be worth ignoring the problem if you have reason to expect that it will resolve itself. Sometimes a client will seek advice if they anticipate a problem, for example an employer may have dismissed an employee who has indicated that they intend to challenge the dismissal. In such a case it would be worth waiting to see if the employee actually does bring a challenge, rather than taking any immediate action.

Stage 6.   Consider advantages and disadvantages

Having listed all possible solutions, weigh each in terms of potential rewards and potential risks. The client's circumstances will clearly influence your analysis. Different options may carry different financial or emotional costs (for example the stress of going to court). The requirements of external regulators and the rules of professional conduct should also determine your thinking.

Some options you may eliminate at once as wholly unworkable or inappropriate. For others, this process of evaluation may be technically demanding and complex, calling for a high level of expertise and even some intuition. As a junior lawyer it will often therefore be necessary to confer with more experienced colleagues, either informally or as part of a practice team.

Stage 7. Advise on the most appropriate solution(s)

You should now be in a position to advise on which one or more solutions will best fulfil the client's objectives. Be prepared to outline the varying costs and benefits in detail, especially the risks of things going wrong, the consequences of that outcome, and options for limiting risk.

Stage 8. Present solution(s) in appropriate form

To end the process, you need to report your findings. Remember to tailor your report to the recipient. This may be the client in person. If so, the client will not need all the details of your research. They will want practical legal solutions. More likely early in your professional life, it will be your supervising solicitor to whom you will provide a written report. They will then use your analysis to advise the client.

It may be useful to involve the client as early as possible in the process of sifting different courses of action. The final decision on what to do, of course, lies with the client.

2.4 PRINCIPLES OF PRACTICAL LEGAL RESEARCH

The remainder of Part II of this book will focus on the mechanics of research in legal practice. The research process underpins all of the stages in the problem-solving model. It entails finding and reporting the material that is relevant to solving a legal problem in the quickest possible time. There is no magic formula that will enable you to do this. As with all skills, it has to be learnt, and practice is the only way to build competence. As a student, you have time and resources to explore and practice that will not be available to you after your career begins: make the most of this opportunity. It is also worth noting that reading about legal research is not the easiest way to learn it. When reading the next few chapters, if possible try the examples given, use the legal databases or practise using the printed sources if you have access to a law library.

The following general principles should guide your research.

2.4.1 Devise search terms carefully

In order to exploit any legal source, you must devise appropriate search terms. These are often known as 'keywords'. They are words or phrases that enable you to find the relevant law to help find a solution to your client's legal problem. You may need to look up these keywords in a printed index, or type them into a database search engine. It is worth spending time on getting the right keywords as effective keywords will help you pinpoint the relevant area of law, saving time and ensuring you find the correct information.

When starting their research, many people make the mistake of being too specific about the information they are searching for. A particularly common mistake is to attempt to find precedent which exactly matches the detailed facts of the problem.

> **EXAMPLE**
> Imagine that your supervisor has a client who is complaining that she has ordered a 3D television from a shop but the shop has delivered an inferior model. The supervisor asks you to investigate possible remedies. One way of tackling this problem is to do a keyword search using the word 'televisions'. This is not the best way of going about the search. A better approach is to think in legal concepts and to research the underlying law that might be relevant. So the more experienced researcher would probably start their search with keywords such as:
>
> - contract remedies;
> - sale of goods;
> - consumer contracts.

The published version of cases or statutes will use words preferred by the judge or draftsperson. These may be different from the words you would have chosen yourself in considering that area of law. Think along the lines of terms that lawyers might use; a legal dictionary may be useful in this respect. Be accurate. Beware slang, which is unlikely to appear in formal legal documents. Expand any abbreviations. Consider possible synonyms: all the alternative words that might describe the same concept or item or activity.

The following table lists possible alternative keywords that might arise out of different sorts of legal problems:

Problem	Example
Alternative expressions for the same legal concept or topic	**employment** or **labour**
Alternative English and Latin expressions	**stare decisis** or **precedent**
Synonyms used to describe non-technical terms	**buyer and seller** or **purchaser and vendor**
Broader and narrower terms which may have been used to construct the source (ie case or statute)	**tort – negligence – professional negligence – medical negligence – psychiatric damage**
Related terms	**immigration** and **nationality** **competition** and **monopolies**
Changes in terminology over time	**exclusion clauses** or **exemption clauses**
Abbreviations	**BBC** or **British Broadcasting Corporation**

2.4.2 Knowing where to look

You might now be thinking that you have to have considerable knowledge about the relevant areas of law before beginning a piece of research. This is not the case. The key to success lies not in knowing the law, but in knowing where to find it.

As a general rule, start with a source which gives a general overview of the law in a certain area. A useful starting point in this regard is *Halsbury's Laws of England* (see **4.2**) which is available both in print and online via the *Lexis+ Legal Research* database. Key practitioner texts and academic textbooks are possible alternatives. These texts which provide commentary on the law are often referred to as secondary sources.

Once you have a broad grasp of the relevant law, you should consider moving on to a second layer of research tools: those which contain the primary sources. Primary sources are the raw materials of the law, such as statutes, statutory instruments and case law. Many researchers are nervous about using primary sources. There is no need to be. Although sometimes the language is difficult, primary sources are essential to your research. This is because they contain authoritative statements of what the law actually is, rather than what a commentator thinks the law is, or what it should be.

It is worth remembering that there are hundreds of different sources of legal information. Some are in paper form; some are in online form; some exist in both. Each source has different strengths and weaknesses. The following sections of this book will familiarise you with some of the main sources. Think carefully about which source to use for a particular problem. If you choose the wrong information tool, the research job will take far longer and your results may be inaccurate.

2.4.3 Using indexes

The most effective way to access the information content in a source is to use an index. Most sources (paper and online) will have one or more 'tables of primary sources', and a 'subject index'. A table of primary sources is an index that helps you to locate cases, statutes or statutory instruments appearing in a work. It is also useful for completing or correcting a flawed citation. Arrangement may be alphabetical or chronological. A subject index helps you to locate commentary on specific areas of the law. Often this commentary will refer to primary sources, either in the text itself or in footnotes.

Using a subject index in a paper or online source can save you time by taking you directly to the information you need. Look at any index to see how it is arranged. There may be tiered entries in this form:

> **county court**
>> jurisdiction
>>> extent

The broad topic, **county court**, appears first. Subsequent entries are progressively more specific. To make best use of the index, you need to look up the most specific keyword that will lead to the answer to your problem. A good index will offer a variety of terms, including cross-references (that is, references between terms of similar meaning). However, choosing the right term will always involve a process of elimination and some inspired guesswork.

Online databases often allow you to search for terms appearing anywhere in a source. In other words, their 'subject index' is not a separate component as in a book. Instead it comprises every word appearing in the source. It is tempting to rely on this facility, known as a 'free text' search. However, it can generate large numbers of irrelevant results (for example, instances where your search term happens to appear in discussion of a different subject). For a better signal:noise ratio, it is usually more effective to search within a particular field of the search form in an online source, such as 'case name' or 'keywords' in a database of law reports.

Searching an online database also requires you to be alert to possible synonyms. For example, if you search for **employment law** but the preferred term used in the source is **labour law**, the database may return zero results even though there is actually plenty of coverage of the subject. If your initial search fails, think of alternative terms which may be preferred by the source you are using.

2.4.4 Record the research trail

When conducting legal research in practice, one or more of the following three things will often happen:

(a) The facts available to you might change, requiring the conclusions drawn from a piece of research to be reviewed.

(b) Your supervisor may want to check your work.

(c) The client or the court may want proof that the work you are charging for has actually been done.

For these and other reasons, it is vital to record the progress of your research and the methods used to locate information very carefully, and using the correct citations. So, for example, record the name of the resource used, keywords and the date you carried out the research – *Halsbury's Laws* on Lexis+ Legal Research, keywords 'party wall' and 'statutory definition', Vol 4, para 376, date accessed 05/03/25.

2.4.5 Update your information

The law changes constantly. A new Act of Parliament or a judgment by the Supreme Court can reverse lawyers' received wisdom on an issue overnight. You must therefore take steps to make sure that the law you cite in the course of your research is as up-to-date as possible.

Consider what sorts of developments are most likely to have occurred in your area of interest. For example, is it likely that relevant new legislation has recently been enacted? Is it an area that generates a large volume of case law, affecting the status of earlier decisions or affecting the interpretation of a statute? Is it an area where the law is liable to change by way of statutory instrument? A thorough update will encompass all these possibilities, but the efficient researcher will check the most likely developments first.

> **PROFESSIONAL CONDUCT POINT**
>
> Solicitors have a duty to base their advice to clients on legal knowledge that is current as well as thorough. In order to give sound advice, you must keep yourself abreast of recent developments. Updating your research must therefore become a matter of routine. Update even when a source seems to provide a satisfactory answer.

Subsequent chapters will outline the mechanics of how to update the information in particular sources. However, the following broad principles should be borne in mind:

(a) Different sources deal with the problem of currency in different ways. Many paper sources are published in 'looseleaf' format, for example, so that selected pages can be swapped on a regular basis. The title page at the front of the work will usually provide a publication date.

(b) Do not assume that online sources are wholly up-to-date – they can be subject to editorial delays. Usually, online resources on a database will have an information icon; click on it and it will give you details of how frequently the source is updated.

(c) Note the publication date of every source that you cite in your research (often online databases are continually updated and so have no static 'publication date'; in this case, note the date that you carried out your search).

(d) Check whether the source states a cut-off date (again this may not be explicit in relation to a database; again, look for links labelled 'information', or an 'i' icon).

(e) Stay with a source until you have exhausted its value (for example, if you find relevant information in a practitioner text, check whether an updating supplement exists).

(f) Learn how to use updating resources (for example, case and legislation citators covered further at **5.5** and **6.8**).

(g) When you switch from one source to another, always compare the scope of the content; look for an explanatory preface, a database user guide or an online help facility.

(h) Continue to make methodical notes of new information as the research progresses, including full citations and references.

2.4.6 Presenting your findings in an appropriate format

You should present your findings in writing where possible. It is important to remember that your supervisor is undoubtedly a busy person. You will soon learn how they like reports to be presented, but it is safe to assume that they will not thank you for producing armfuls of law reports and statutes without at least attempting to draw some conclusions from your research. Whatever structure you adopt, it is always a good idea to put a summary of your findings at the top of the report, and to reference your sources clearly and consistently. Reporting your findings is discussed in more detail in **Chapter 9**.

2.4.7 Know when to stop and ask

With so much law out there, it is sometimes very difficult to spot that you have found the correct answer when it is right in front of you. Remember what was said right at the beginning of this chapter about accuracy and efficiency. Getting the correct answer is very important; however, so is making the most efficient use of your time. If you think that you have found the correct answer, or if you are getting stuck, then stop the research and go back to your supervisor with what you have done so far. Do not be afraid to ask for guidance; it is what your supervisor is there for! Also bear in mind the expertise of any librarians or professional support lawyers in your organisation. They are there to help and will be happy to advise you about choosing sources, or about the mechanics of how to exploit a particular source.

> **SUMMARY – TIPS FOR SUCCESS**
>
> (a) Analyse the client's problem(s) carefully so that you are clear about their objectives.
>
> (b) Devise search terms based on relevant legal concepts.
>
> (c) Select the most appropriate research tool, and learn to use different tools and their indexes properly – do not cut corners.
>
> (d) Always update your information.
>
> (e) Present the information in an appropriate form.
>
> (f) Do not be afraid to ask for help.

CHAPTER 3

Online versus Printed Sources

3.1	Introduction	45
3.2	Advantages of online sources	45
3.3	Advantages of printed sources	46
3.4	Accessing online sources	46
3.5	Guidelines for searching online databases	46
3.6	The free Internet: Google, AI and beyond	48

> **LEARNING OUTCOMES**
>
> After reading this chapter you will be able to:
> - outline the advantages of both printed and online sources
> - understand how to access legal resources online
> - identify effective database search techniques
> - explain the pros and cons of legal information available via free Internet sites.

3.1 INTRODUCTION

Legal information is available in paper and online versions. Sometimes the same resource is available in both formats. When carrying out your research, the resources you choose to use and their format will depend upon what sources are available to you.

Increasingly, lawyers rely on online versions via subscription databases such as *Westlaw* or *Lexis+ Legal Research*, and these may be more up-to-date. They allow you to search quickly and print or download your results. Another advantage is that you can usually access them from anywhere, provided you have internet access.

However, printed materials continue to play a role in research carried out in legal practice. Cost may be a limiting factor, particularly for smaller firms (subscriptions to databases are expensive). Therefore, the chapters in this Part will cover using both online and print resources for your research.

Quality of information content is the most important consideration. If you do have a choice, you may find it useful to use both formats. Perhaps start with a printed secondary resource (such as *Halsbury's Laws of England* or a practitioner work) as an index can help you to structure your research, give you an overview of a subject and identify the key legislation and cases. Then move on to an online database to find and update those primary sources.

3.2 ADVANTAGES OF ONLINE SOURCES

(a) Usually accessible from anywhere with Internet access.
(b) Simultaneous access by many users to single source.
(c) High volumes of information can be stored efficiently.
(d) Speed of updating by publisher.

(e) Quick, flexible and efficient searching and retrieval.
(f) Ability to manipulate text (for example, to cut and paste key passages from a source).
(g) Rapid and customised current awareness in the form of e-mail updates and alerts.
(h) Material can be downloaded to personal devices (easier to transport phone/tablet than large books).

3.3 ADVANTAGES OF PRINTED SOURCES

(a) Straightforward to access (no need for passwords or training).
(b) Easy on the eye (many people do not like to read more than a couple of pages of information on screen).
(c) Costs associated with online access can be high.
(d) Not affected by technological failure.
(e) Convenience (for example, quick reference/to mark up a personal copy/not reliant on internet access).
(f) Easy to compare two or more sources at the same time.
(g) Easy to scan/browse by 'flicking through'.
(h) Indexes compiled by experts enable you to find relevant information quickly, rather than scrolling through pages of results.

3.4 ACCESSING ONLINE SOURCES

Legal information (including case law and legislation) may be accessed online via both freely available and subscription (paid for) sources. Freely available sources include government websites, such as www.legislation.gov.uk, and the website of the British and Irish Legal Information Institute, www.bailii.org. Reputable free sites can be extremely useful, but you do need to exercise caution and judgement when using some of these resources (we consider this further at **3.6**).

The two major subscription sources in the UK are the online databases *Lexis+ Legal Research* and *Westlaw*. There is some overlap between the content of the two (for example, both contain the full text of the authoritative ICLR *Law Reports*), but they are in competition so many journal and case reports appear in full text on one or the other. For advice on which titles are available from which source, ask library staff or search your library catalogue.

Note that, in practice, you will have access to subscription sources only if your firm is a paid-up subscriber. Due to the significant costs involved, this may not necessarily be the case. However, the main advantage of databases such as *Westlaw* or *Lexis+ Legal Research* is the amount of added value content they provide. For example, they update legislation to show any amendments and give guidance on whether cases are still good law. They also offer access to commentary on the law, through either journal articles or legal texts such as *Civil Procedure*, also known as *The White Book* (via *Westlaw*), or *Blackstone's Criminal Practice* (via *Lexis+ Legal Research*). As a consequence, many firms will decide that a subscription is a sound commercial investment, but they may subscribe to one, not both. For this reason, while you are studying, it is worth familiarising yourself with all the key legal databases available to you rather than picking a favourite.

3.5 GUIDELINES FOR SEARCHING ONLINE DATABASES

Searching online involves thinking of keywords that are likely to feature in documents relevant to a legal problem, then typing these keywords into a database search engine. It is not all that different from using the index to a book. However, other aspects are very different, so planning in advance how to formulate and carry out searches of databases is vitally important. Typing a string of words into a database is rarely an efficient use of time, and may well not get you the results you need.

To add to the problem, publishers of online databases use different versions of software, so the rules for searching them may differ. However, most databases feature an on-screen 'help' facility, and some even offer on-screen tutorials; working through such a tutorial is definitely a worthwhile investment of time. You may also have the opportunity to attend training sessions organised by your library or the database provider. These sessions can help you to get the most from the databases and improve your search technique.

A number of simple techniques will make your searching of online databases more structured and precise. For example, you may be able to use advanced search options which offer specific search fields to narrow your search using certain criteria, such as date range or level of court. In addition, certain symbols are widely understood across databases to stand for certain letters, or to combine or exclude words. These symbols can either widen your search or narrow it as you desire.

To search effectively, bear in mind the following techniques.

3.5.1 Truncation

A search with a truncated word will search for different word endings. Why is this necessary? In most databases, typing in the word **negligent** will retrieve only documents that feature exactly that word; it will not pick up occurrences of 'negligence' or 'negligently', words which might equally well be used in the case or statute you are searching for. To widen the trawl, use a truncated form of the word to perform the search.

The symbol used to truncate varies between databases; check the 'help' facility to make sure.

Truncation can be particularly useful for finding singulars and plurals. So, for example, searching *Lexis+ Legal Research* using **pollut!** will retrieve 'pollute', 'pollutes', 'polluting', 'pollution', 'pollutants', etc, in fact any word which begins with these six letters.

3.5.2 Wild card characters

These function within a word as a truncation symbol does at the end of a word. The symbol varies between databases; as with truncation, you should check the 'help' facility. So, for example, searching *Lexis+ Legal Research* using **wom*n** will retrieve instances of 'woman' and 'women'.

3.5.3 Connectors

The commands **and**, **or** and **not** are sometimes known as Boolean operators or connectors. They function as follows:

Connector	Effect	Function
and eg **Donoghue and Stevenson**	The computer will retrieve only those documents where both the first term and the second term appear	Narrows a search – to improve precision of results
or eg **fence or boundary**	The computer will retrieve all documents where the first term appears and also all documents where the second term appears	Expands a search – to search for possible synonyms, etc
not eg **pollution not air**	The computer will retrieve documents that contain the first term but do not contain the second term	Narrows a search – eliminates terms not relevant to your topic

3.5.4 Field searching

Most databases divide documents into a number of separate fields. Thus searches may be confined to a specified field or a combination of fields. For instance, if you are searching for cases on a particular topic, you could confine your search to the 'subject/keywords' field as you should get fewer, more relevant results than if you use the same term in a 'free text' search.

You can usually search across the entire database (cases, legislation, commentary, journal articles) using a 'free text' search from the home page. However, it is a scattergun approach: comprehensive, but likely to generate a large proportion of results that are irrelevant to your purpose. Use with caution. A more effective technique is to narrow your search to a particular area (cases, legislation, practice areas, journal articles) and then use links from your result to link to other relevant documents.

3.5.5 Phrase searching

How systems search for phrases varies. In some databases a phrase can be entered just as it is, eg **infringement of human rights**, and will be found; others, however, will assume that the **and** operator is to be placed between each word, and retrieve the words separately. This will probably undermine the effectiveness of the search.

The most common way of searching for a phrase is to include it within double quotation marks, for instance **"breach of contract"**.

3.5.6 Refining the outcome

If your initial search retrieves a glut of results, do not immediately go back to square one. Instead look for a way to edit the search, perhaps by adding an extra keyword and then searching again within the results. Or you may have the option to rearrange the results so the most relevant appear at the top of the results list.

> **CONCLUSION**
> Think before you type! Remember that computers cannot do the thinking for you. They can search only according to where you tell them to search, the words you feed into them and the way you combine those words. Planning your search strategy in advance using the methods described here will pay off.

3.6 THE FREE INTERNET: GOOGLE, AI AND BEYOND

So far our discussion of online research has revolved around commercial databases, which require payment of a subscription for access. A common, and dangerous, misconception on the part of students is that all the information they need for their legal research can be found on the free Internet, using a search engine such as Google. So why not rely just on Google, Wikipedia and so forth?

The answer may be summed up in one word: **quality**. Quality of information is a crucial consideration when you use free sites on the Internet. Anybody can publish there. Sites frequently change their appearance, or even disappear altogether. Unlike pay-to-access databases, nobody is responsible for ensuring currency, accuracy and impartiality of content. Instead, you must make an assessment against these criteria for yourself. Search engines such as Google do not search all websites or databases, so much online legal information is not accessible via this route. For example, Google Scholar provides this disclaimer on its site, *Legal opinions in Google Scholar are provided for informational purposes only and should not be relied on as a substitute for legal advice from a licensed lawyer. Google does not warrant that the information is complete or accurate.* Therefore, it is strongly recommended that you begin any legal research with an authoritative source such as an online legal database or printed legal resource.

> **PROFESSIONAL CONDUCT POINT**
>
> Solicitors are professionally liable for the quality of the advice that they give to their clients. Quality of advice depends upon quality of information. The following story from the *Law Society Gazette* underlines the risk to clients and to their own practices of solicitors relying upon Wikipedia, Google and other non-specialist search engines for legal research.
>
> ## Net-surfing lawyers warned of compliance risk
>
> *by Jonathan Rayner*
>
> Solicitors risk breaching conduct rules and could face insurance claims if they use non-specialist online sources for legal research, a leading QC solicitor has warned.
>
> Evidence has emerged that increasing numbers of solicitors, from trainees to senior partners, are putting clients and their own practices at possible risk by using collaboratively written online encyclopaedia Wikipedia, Google and other search engines for legal research.
>
> This is despite having specialist libraries and subscriptions to Lawtel, Justis and other authoritative on-line resources.
>
> Professional conduct solicitor Andrew Hopper QC said: 'Citing any authority in court other than the actual source is a recipe for disaster and an irate judge. Wikipedia and the rest are recognised and valued, but lawyers should use their common sense, filter and check everything by going back to the original.'
>
> Frank Maher, a partner at Liverpool risk management and law firm Legal Risk, said search engine results can get facts wrong.
>
> He added: 'They do not always update cases. An online press release, for example, might be out of date because the case has been appealed and the outcome changed. That's more than just embarrassing – you risk insurance claims and conduct issues.'
>
> Emma Harris, Law Society librarian, told the *Gazette*: 'Today's trainees, despite the best efforts of law school librarians, don't know the world outside the internet. We had a trainee come into the library who, when given the textbook that would answer his query, asked, "What's this list at the back and what do these little numbers mean?" That would be the index.
>
> 'Qualified lawyers are also vulnerable. Twice we've had practising solicitors contact the library looking for the full text of a statute that applied to their case. One statute turned out to be Swedish law, the other American. They had done their research through a non-legal search engine.'
>
> Harris pointed to a Wikipedia entry on intestacy rules that also highlighted the dangers of internet research. 'Whoever wrote it got the rules mixed up with inheritance tax. Anyone following its advice would make a very expensive mistake.'
>
> Amanda McKenzie, information services manager at City firm Olswang, said: 'A fee-earner or trainee needs to use authoritative material. This is a risk and a compliance issue.'
>
> (Reproduced with permission of the *Law Society Gazette*, 12 June 2008, vol. 105, no. 23, p. 1)

The same caution should be applied when considering using artificial intelligence (AI) to carry out legal research. The development and use of AI has increased significantly over recent years, and the legal sector, like others, is looking for ways it can be utilised without compromising accuracy and ethics. At present, the conclusion is that while there is nothing wrong in seeking to investigate how technology can assist with research tasks, legal practitioners and students are responsible for checking and verifying the accuracy of any information generated by AI tools. This is because these chatbots can be prone to inaccuracies (referred to in AI as 'hallucinations') and also because they will usually only be using free web resources to produce results. Some of these concerns are outlined in articles available via these links:

www.lawgazette.co.uk/commentary-and-opinion/lawyers-beware-ais-hallucinations/5115682.article

www.theguardian.com/technology/2023/jun/23/two-us-lawyers-fined-submitting-fake-court-citations-chatgpt

www.brettwilson.co.uk/blog/is-it-safe-to-use-ai-for-legal-research-not-yet/

www.lawgazette.co.uk/news/lip-presents-false-citations-to-court-after-asking-chatgpt/5116143.article

Law firms are highly competitive businesses. They spend large amounts of money on subscriptions to quality-assured commercial databases such as *Westlaw* and *Lexis+ Legal Research* (whose content is hidden from Google and AI tools). If there were a safe free alternative, you can be sure they would adopt it! However, there are useful free online resources available and there are times when you may need to use them. The guidance below is intended to help you find and evaluate the best sources.

3.6.1 Search engines

Search engines do not publish information on the Internet; they work as a finding tool. There are various search engines available, the most popular being Google (www.google.co.uk). The average Google search can return over a million results. Whilst it is convenient to rely on the results on the first page, be aware that these may not be the most relevant or authoritative as commercial sponsorship allows companies to pay to place their sites near the top of the results list. In order to produce fewer, more relevant results, there are various search techniques you can use. For example:

- enclosing search terms within inverted commas will find only that phrase, eg "litigation funding"
- site: searches only a particular site, eg site:www.law.ac.uk
- -site: excludes results from a particular site, eg -site:Wikipedia.org
- intitle: words in the title of the page, eg intitle:"environment act"

Alternatively, instead of using the general search box on the home page, use the advanced search screen which makes it easier to create a focused, accurate search.

To find this function, click settings in the bottom right corner of the Google screen and select Advanced search from the list.

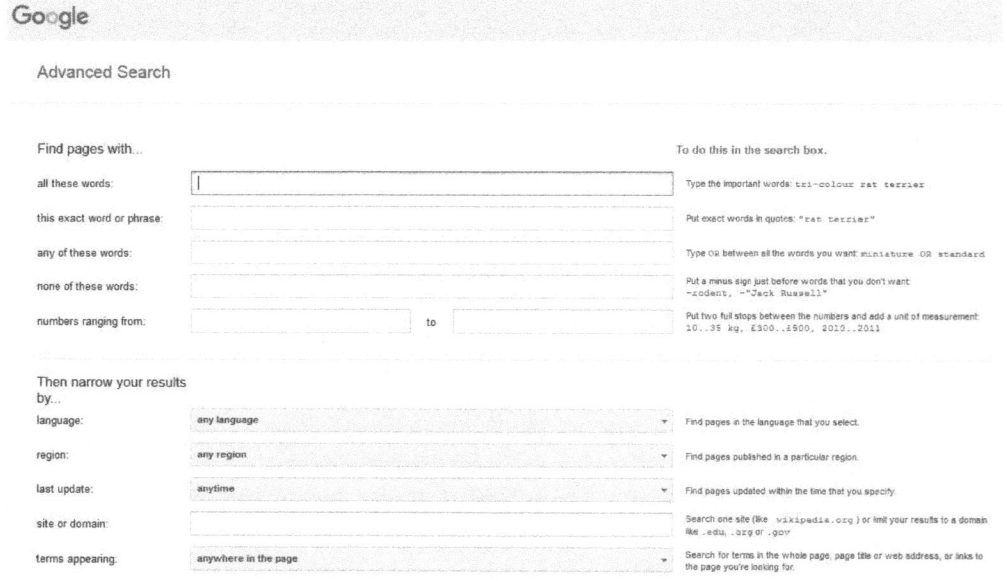

Google and Google logo are registered trademarks of Google Inc., used with permission

Another option for finding authoritative free resources is to use Google Scholar (https://scholar.google.co.uk) which specifically searches for academic material, including theses, articles, books, conference papers, etc. To use the advanced search facility, click on the menu icon in the top left of the screen.

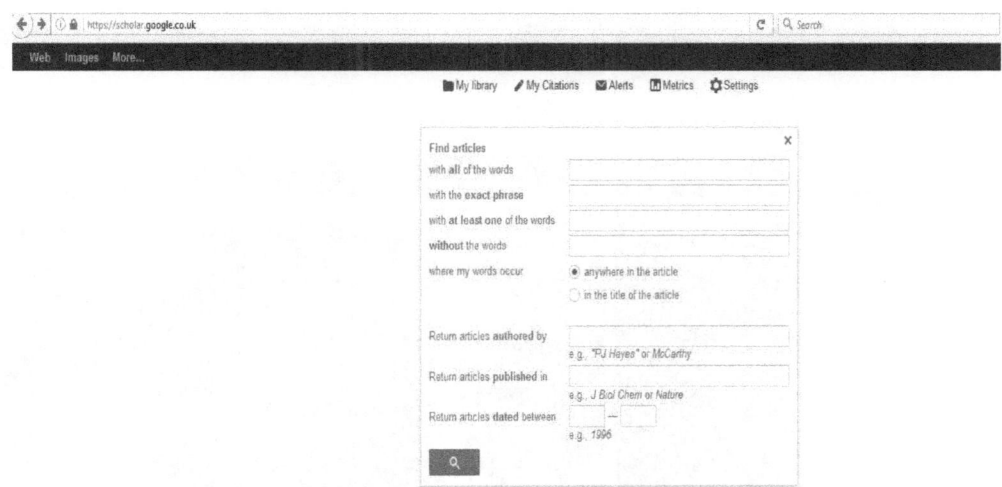

Google and the Google logo are registered trademarks of Google Inc., used with permission

3.6.2 Official websites

The EU, Parliament, the courts and government all publish authoritative information on their websites. Useful official websites are:

- British and Irish Institute of Legal Information (www.bailii.org)
- EUR-Lex (eur-lex.europa.eu/homepage.html)
- legislation.gov (www.legislation.gov.uk)
- Ministry of Justice (www.gov.uk/government/organisations/ministry-of-justice)
- UK Parliament (www.parliament.uk)
- UK Supreme Court (www.supremecourt.uk)

However, whilst the information on official sites can be treated as reliable and authoritative, caution may still be needed. For example, not all the legislation on the legislation.gov site is available in an updated form. If you have access to databases such as *Westlaw* and *Lexis+ Legal Research*, use them to find updated cases and legislation.

3.6.3 Portals and directories

Portals and directories are gateways to selected free online legal information. They are useful for helping to find authoritative sites and can provide a quicker, more efficient route than search engines. A good example is www.venables.co.uk.

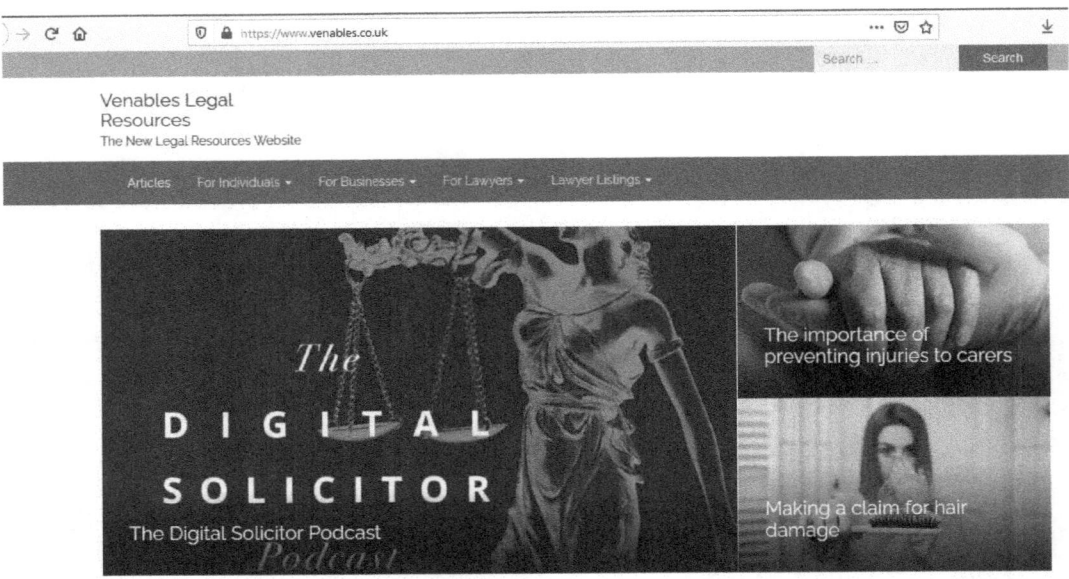

© Reproduced with kind permission of Infolaw

3.6.4 Social media and Web 2.0

Web 2.0 is an umbrella term used to describe collaborative Internet tools such as blogs, wikis and social media sites.

Wikis are collaborative websites, which allow users to create and edit information.

Blogs are online journals containing the personal opinions of the author. Over recent years many law firms, practising lawyers and law teachers have published blogs.

A useful directory of UK legal blogs is available at www.infolaw.co.uk/lawfinder.

Some content on blogs may be serious and useful (for example, a barrister may report recent developments in their specialist area of practice). Other content (even within the same blog) may be more frivolous. Therefore, while they may be worthwhile sources of comment about the law and legal practice, their content should not be relied upon uncritically when carrying out legal research. This same caution should be applied to all information found on social media and free websites.

3.6.5 Finding business information

Increasingly, both as part of your studies and in the workplace, you may need to find information on companies and markets. Whilst finding legal information may have become second nature, it can be difficult to know where to start when faced with this challenge. Fortunately there are some extremely useful and authoritative free resources you can use, such as:

- *The Financial Times* (www.ft.com): you can search the site for information on a specific company or on general commercial sectors such as banking or retail. Some of the content is freely available and some is restricted to subscribers. If you have a subscription you can find in-depth information on companies. Use the Markets tab and select Markets Data, search Securities using the company name. Select the company and you can see profile information, details of directors, financial data, share prices and news articles on the company published by the FT.

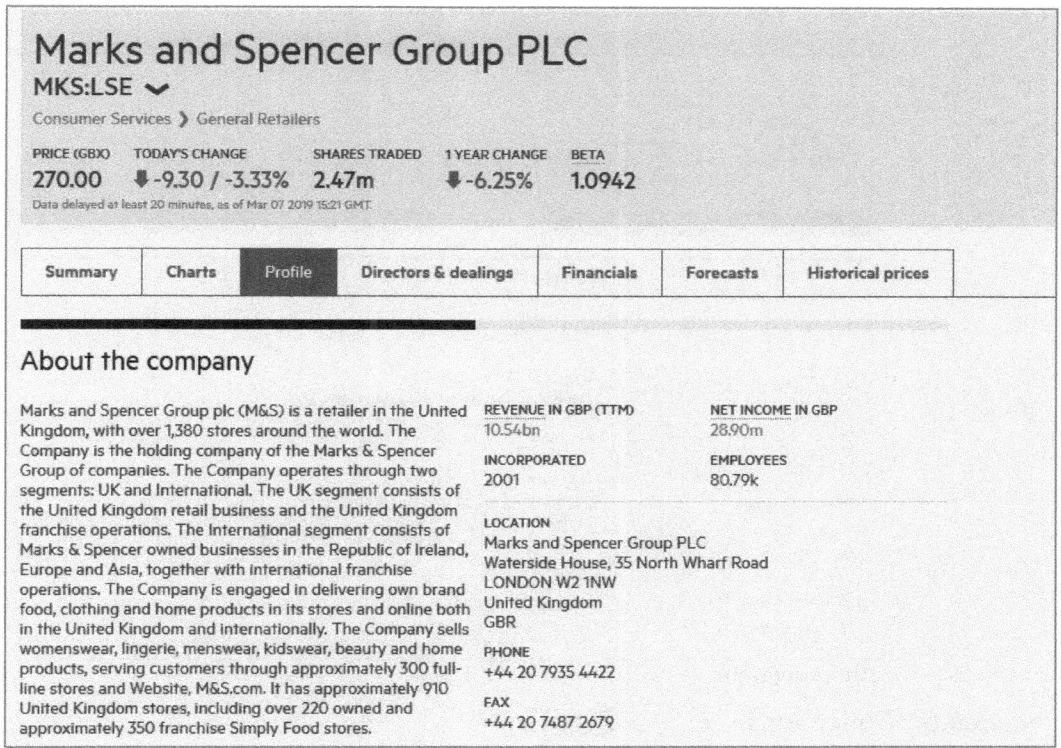

© Financial Times Ltd 2019. Used with kind permission. All rights reserved.

- Companies House (www.gov.uk/government/organisations/companies-house), a free website, allows you to search for a range of information on companies, forms and guidance.

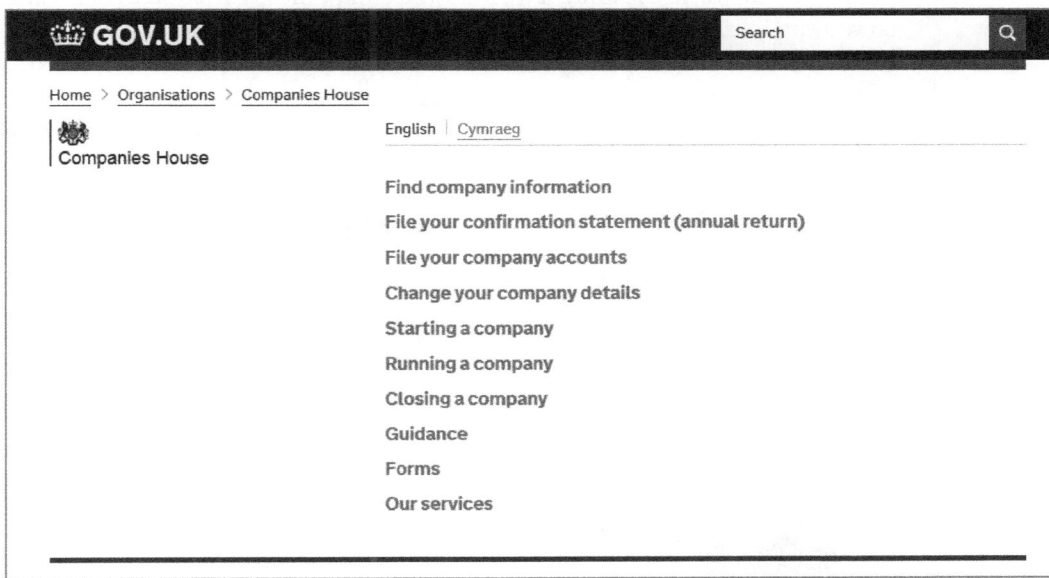

© Crown copyright

- *The Gazette* (www.thegazette.co.uk) is another free resource which publishes online profiles of every UK business registered with Companies House. It also contains a useful section called Companies Resources which includes articles and guidance on relevant topics.

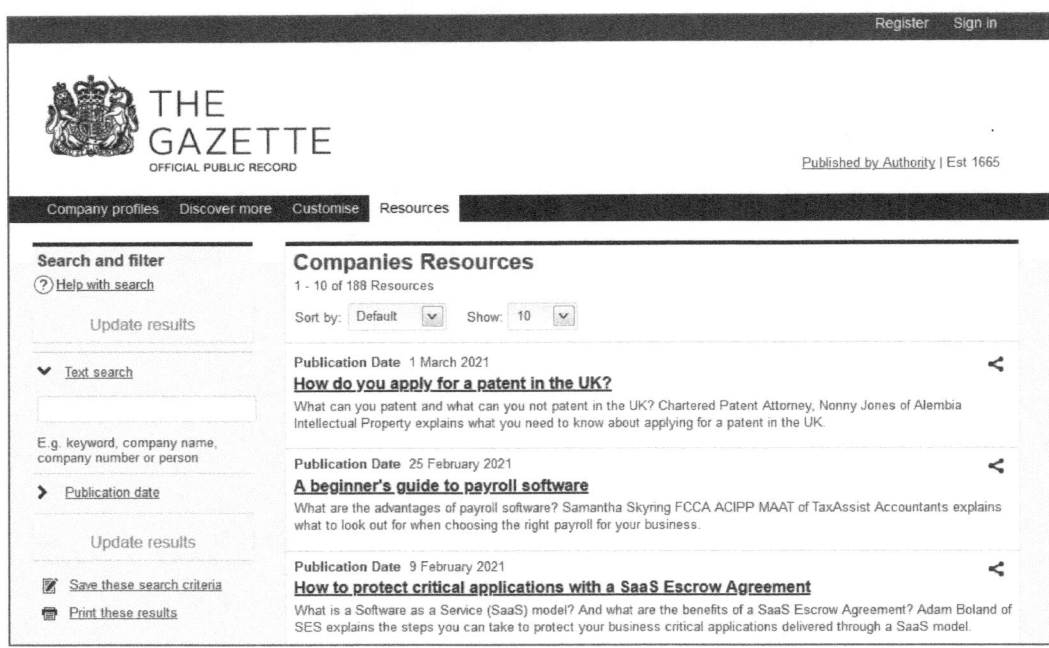

© Crown copyright

3.6.6 Collections

Some websites act as research collections, some of which you may find useful.

Law.com (www.law.com/resources/) is an extensive digital library of white papers, research, legal insights and press releases aimed at in-house and private practice lawyers. It provides access to a free digital library containing almost 10,000 executive insights, many of which are written by the world's leading law firms and companies. The content is organised by category, so you can locate information that is relevant to your practice area, sector or jurisdiction. You can also search the website by entering keywords into the search box located at the top of each page. In order to download resources you may need to complete a form which asks for work details; you can use a university email address and personal phone number and confirm that you are a student.

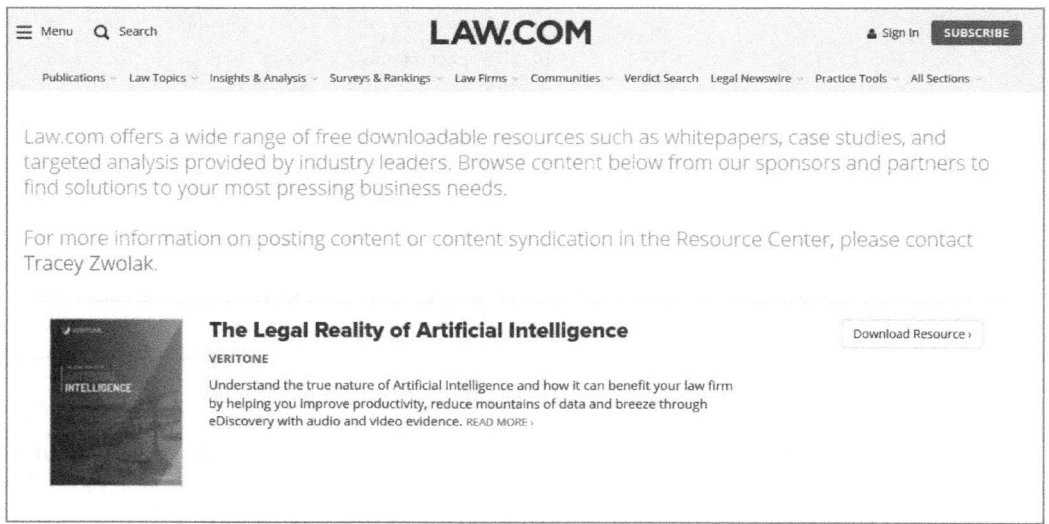

© Reproduced with kind permission of Law.com

ResearchGate (www.researchgate.net) is another collection with more of an academic focus. Again, you can register free and gain access to a wide range of business and legal research materials (www.researchgate.net/signup.SignUp.html). Once you have registered, you can access resources by clicking on the search box which then gives you options to search. You can search for publications on a particular subject. Results will appear with the most recent content at the top. Bear in mind that as it is a free site that contains international as well as UK materials, you should check the credentials of the author and use the guidelines for evaluating resources set out at **3.6.7**.

SSRN is another site providing access to research materials (www.ssrn.com/index.cfm/en/lsn/), covering over 30 disciplines including law and management. Use the advanced search facility to restrict your search to a particular discipline by ticking in the Network field. You also have the option to browse the collection.

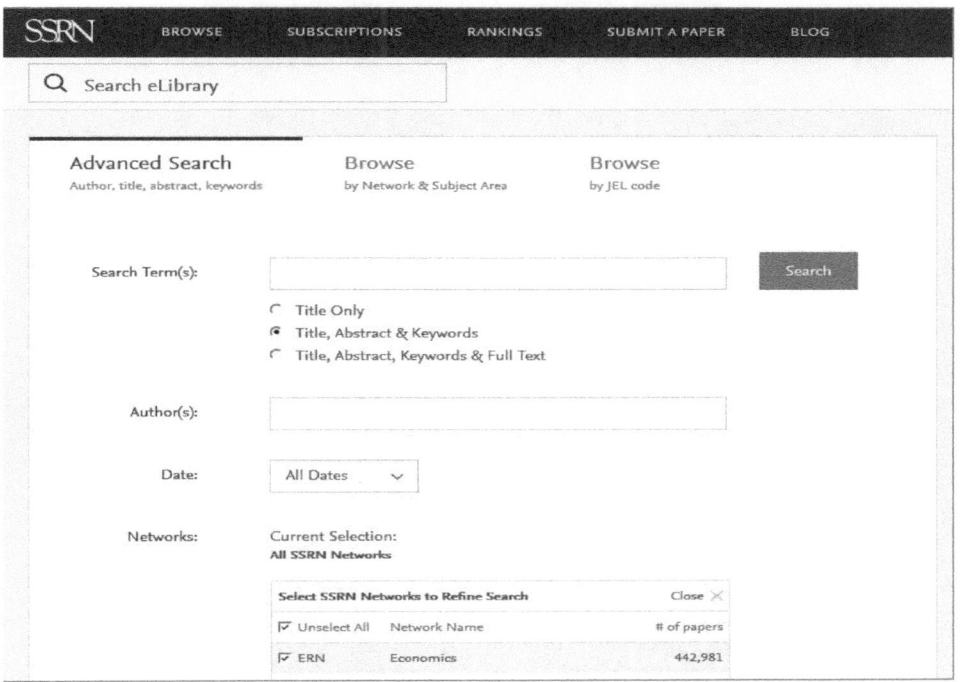

Reproduced with kind permission of SSRN

3.6.7 Evaluating websites

When using free online resources, it is vitally important that you establish whether the information you have found online is authoritative, accurate and up to date. To do so, consider the following:

- Who is the author or publisher of the material? Do they have expertise in this area?
- When was it published? Is the information current?
- What is the jurisdiction of the source – is it applicable to the UK? The domain name of the site can be useful in establishing this.
- Who is the intended audience?
- Is it objective? Is it published by a commercial organisation, a political party or an organisation with a specific objective?

If you consider these factors, it should enable you to determine whether the information you have found can be relied upon.

CHAPTER 4

Getting Started

4.1	Introduction	57
4.2	*Halsbury's Laws of England*	57
4.3	Practitioner databases	61
4.4	Practitioner books	65
4.5	Widening the net	66

> **LEARNING OUTCOMES**
>
> After reading this chapter you will be able to:
>
> - explain the difference between primary and secondary sources
> - understand how to use *Halsbury's Laws of England* in printed and online format
> - identify practitioner works and describe how to use them
> - select appropriate primary sources for your research.

4.1 INTRODUCTION

When you have completed your initial analysis of the relevant facts and identified the legal issues involved in your problem, you need to move on to the next step – researching the law in detail and applying it to the problem.

Rather than going straight to primary sources, it is often advisable to start with secondary sources such as a general legal encyclopedia (for example *Halsbury's Laws of England*) or a good practitioner text. These will give you an overview of the law and highlight any key legislation and case law.

4.2 HALSBURY'S LAWS OF ENGLAND

The printed version of *Halsbury's Laws of England* runs to around 100 volumes. The same content is available online on the *Lexis+ Legal Research* subscription database. It can help you answer day to day legal questions and answer any research questions you have. It provides the only complete narrative statement of the law in England and Wales.

Halsbury's Laws of England provides commentary upon the present state of all areas of English law. (Note that the word 'laws' in the title denotes laws of the land in a general sense; it is not limited to Acts of Parliament.) It is arranged alphabetically by subject. Each subject is divided into numbered paragraphs that summarise the law in a particular area. Footnotes direct you to related cases and statutes (the primary sources which you will also need to consult).

4.2.1 Using the paper version

To find out the law using the paper version of *Halsbury's Laws of England*, you must take four steps:

- index;
- main volume(s);
- Cumulative Supplement; and
- Noter-Up.

4.2.1.1 Consolidated index

The index volumes identify and give references to keywords. Think of subject terms that identify the problem you are researching. The index will refer you from those terms to discussion of the law in one or more of the main volumes.

> **PERSONAL INJURY CASE STUDY**
>
> For example, our road traffic case study involves a car whose driver was on the telephone at the time of a collision. Searching the Consolidated Index produces the following reference:
>
> MOBILE TELEPHONE
>
> driving while using, breach of construction and use requirements, **89** (5th), 61
>
> . . .
>
> vehicle, use in **90** (5th), 417

Each reference indicates the context in which mobile phones are being discussed, followed by the number in **bold** of the main volume where the discussion appears, and then the edition to which this main volume belongs, and then one or more paragraph (*not* page) number(s). If the paragraph number is followed by 'n', the reference is to a footnote to that paragraph.

Make an accurate note of the reference, so that you can find it again easily in future, then locate the relevant main volume and paragraph.

4.2.1.2 Main volumes

The 'main volumes' give statements of the law of England and Wales, arranged by subject. Each self-contained subject is known as a 'title'.

Each volume has its own subject index at the back. This may be useful if your main volume was reissued after publication of the annual Consolidated Index, since reissue of a volume may mean reordering of paragraph numbers.

4.2.1.3 Cumulative supplement

Over the years, the main volumes are reissued on a rolling programme. As time goes by, some information contained in older volumes will be superseded. For example, volumes 89 and 90, which deal with driving while using a mobile phone, were published in 2022. So you must always check that the information in your main volume is up-to-date.

This updating process involves two stages. To begin with, consult the annual, two-volume 'Cumulative Supplement'. There will be a note in the front which gives you the date to which the content has been updated. Any developments affecting your area of law since publication of the main volume and the date of the Cumulative Supplement will be noted. Entries appear under the same volume and paragraph references as in the main volumes.

4.2.1.4 Noter-Up

Finally, check the 'Noter-Up' booklet. Replaced monthly, this will alert you to any very recent changes in the law. Once again, look under the volume and paragraph number of your original reference.

How to use Halsbury's Laws of England

```
                    ┌─────────────────────┬─────────────────────┐
                    │                     │                     │
        ┌───────────┴──────────┐  ┌──────┴──────────┐  ┌───────┴──────────┐
        │ If you know the      │  │ If you are       │  │ If you are unsure│
        │ general subject of   │  │ looking for a    │  │ of the subject of│
        │ your research        │  │ topic relating   │  │ your research    │
        │                      │  │ to a particular  │  │                  │
        │                      │  │ Act or case      │  │                  │
        └──────────────────────┘  └──────────────────┘  └──────────────────┘
```

- **If you know the general subject of your research** → Turn to the *volume/title* which covers the general area – areas covered are listed on the spine of each volume → Turn to the table of contents at the front of the title, or the title index at the back of the volume, which will refer you to the relevant paragraph(s)

- **If you are looking for a topic relating to a particular Act or case** → Turn to the *Consolidated Table of Statutes* or *Consolidated Table of Cases*, which will refer you to the relevant volume and paragraph(s)

- **If you are unsure of the subject of your research** → Turn to the *Consolidated Index* volumes, which will refer you to the relevant volume and paragraph(s)

IS THE INFORMATION UP-TO-DATE?

Look in the annual hardback *Cumulative Supplement* for your volume and paragraph numbers. An entry means the law has changed between the publication date of the volume and the operative date of the *Cumulative Supplement*.

Then look in the Noter-Up booklet for your volume and paragraph numbers. An entry means the law has changed since the operative date of the *Cumulative Supplement*.

4.2.2 Using the online version

4.2.2.1 Scope

You can access the full text of Halsbury's Laws of England online via Lexis+ Legal Research. This also includes the updating material contained in the latest annual Cumulative Supplement and monthly Noter-Up. Content is updated twice a month.

4.2.2.2 Searching

From the Lexis+ Legal Research home page, look in the My Sources section for Halsbury's Laws of England. If it is not listed here, click the View All Sources link, then H, then you can click on the pin icon to add to your Lexis+ home page. You can just click on the title Halsbury's Laws of England to access the content.

There are two routes into the database: you can navigate by scrolling and selecting volumes or use the search option at the top of the screen.

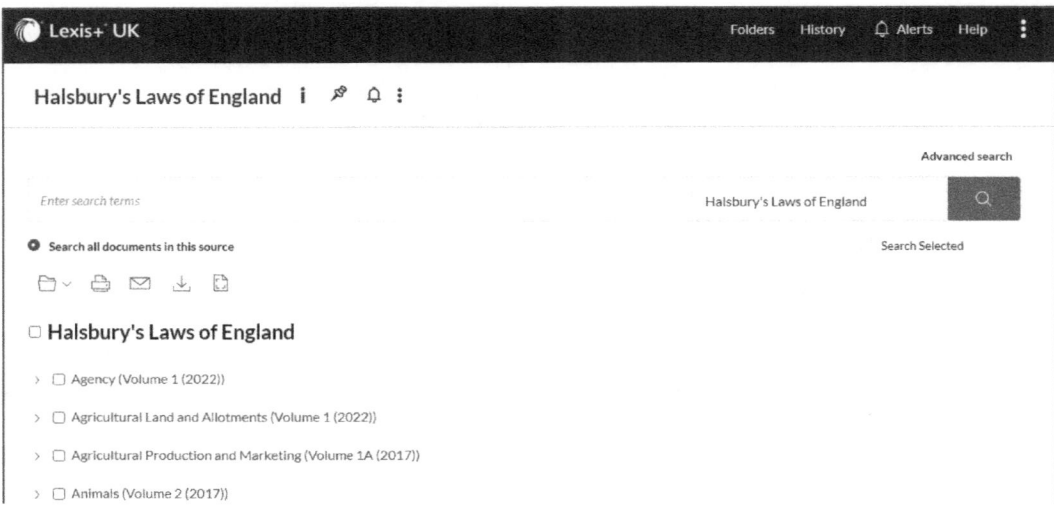

© Reproduced with kind permission of RELX (UK) Limited t/a LexisNexis

In either case, the basic building blocks of the content are set out in numbered volumes and paragraphs. Each describes the law in a narrow area and corresponds exactly to the numbered paragraphs in the equivalent printed volume of *Halsbury's Laws*.

To browse content, you can scroll down the list of volumes which are arranged by subject. Click on the title or the arrow next to the title to see sections within the volumes.

> **PERSONAL INJURY CASE STUDY**
>
> For example, thinking again of our road traffic case study, if you are looking for an explanation of the law surrounding use of a mobile phone while driving, you would work through the following sequence:
>
> *Halsbury's Laws of England*
>
> Road Traffic (volumes 89, 90 & 90A (2022))
>
> 6. Use of Vehicles
>
> (11.) Avoidance of Danger
>
> **417. Use of Mobile Telephones**

Alternatively, use the *Search* option to search the whole encyclopedia. Enter search term(s) to retrieve a list of paragraphs where they occur. If you enter two or more search terms they will be treated as a phrase, unless you link them using Boolean connectors (see **3.5.3**).

You are likely to get a list of results which contain your search terms. The results can be arranged by document title or relevance. The default is the relevance option, so the results which contain the most hits on your search terms will be listed first. Click on the appropriate paragraph heading to view the full text. The screen will split. On the left is the table of contents of the volume you are looking at, and on the right the text of the paragraph with relevant footnotes.

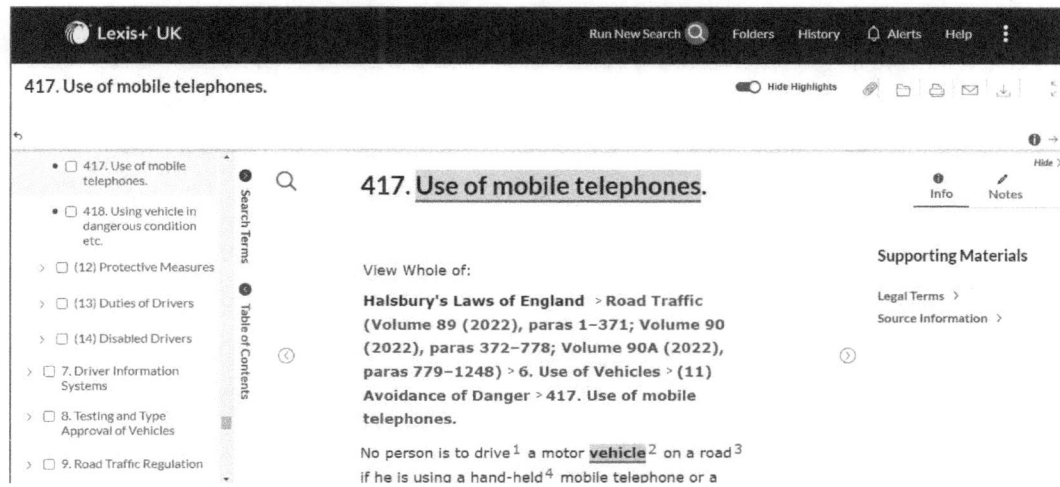

© Reproduced with kind permission of RELX (UK) Limited t/a LexisNexis

To jump to the previous or the next numbered paragraph of the encyclopedia, click on the backward and forward arrow buttons in the main body of the text. You might want to use the Reading Mode option available by clicking on the icon in the top right corner.

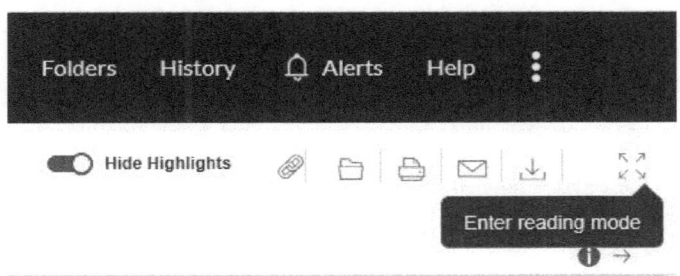

© Reproduced with kind permission of RELX (UK) Limited t/a LexisNexis

The online version of *Halsbury's Laws* is updated twice monthly. Lexis has started updating volumes online by integrating the legal changes into the core content in the numbered paragraphs, but as it has not yet completed this work, keep an eye out for an Update icon which is still used in some volumes. If you see the Update icon, click on the link for any updates to the law relating to the main paragraph. If there is no Update icon, you can assume that the law set out in the main paragraph is unchanged and up-to-date.

4.3 PRACTITIONER DATABASES

We have mentioned the two major academic legal databases, *Westlaw* and *Lexis+ Legal Research* (**3.4**), and we will look at using them in more detail to find cases and legislation (**Chapters 5** and **6**). Both of these databases are widely used in academic study, but there are also databases aimed more at legal practitioners, *Practical Law* and *Lexis+ Practical Guidance*. If you have access to these during your studies then it is worth familiarising yourself with them, and they can certainly help you when researching particular legal topics.

4.3.1 *Practical Law*

Practical Law is published by the same company that publishes *Westlaw*, so if you have access to both, you will be able to link between them.

From the home page you can use the search box, but you might find it easier to research a topic by browsing by practice area.

62 Skills for Lawyers

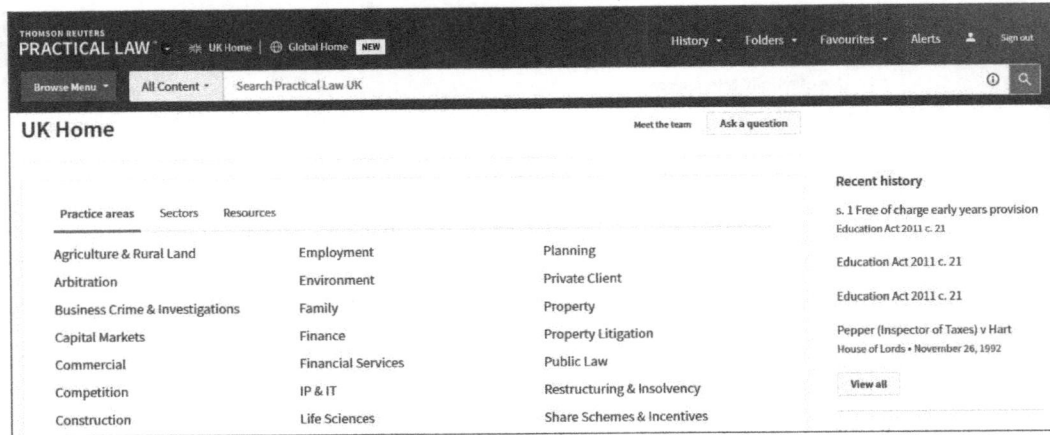

© Thomson Reuters

When you click on a practice area, you will then see all the topics covered and you can then click on the specific area you need to research.

© Thomson Reuters

Then in each topic, you can navigate to access different content.

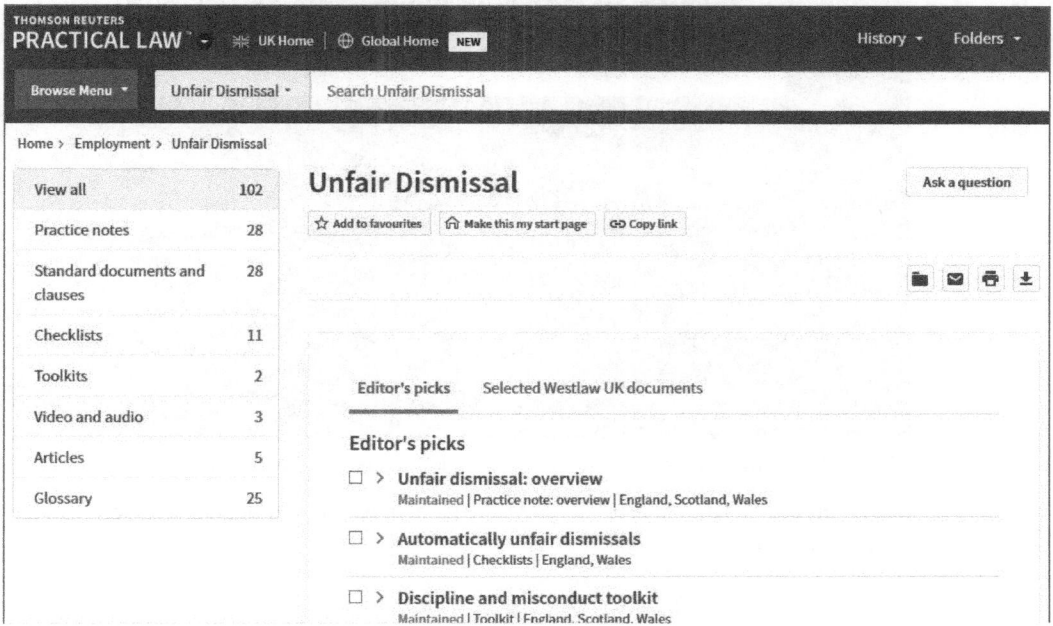

© Thomson Reuters

Overview documents are often a very good place to start your research as they will summarise the law. These documents provide a commentary, and so are secondary sources, but they will provide links to other relevant materials, including legislation and cases.

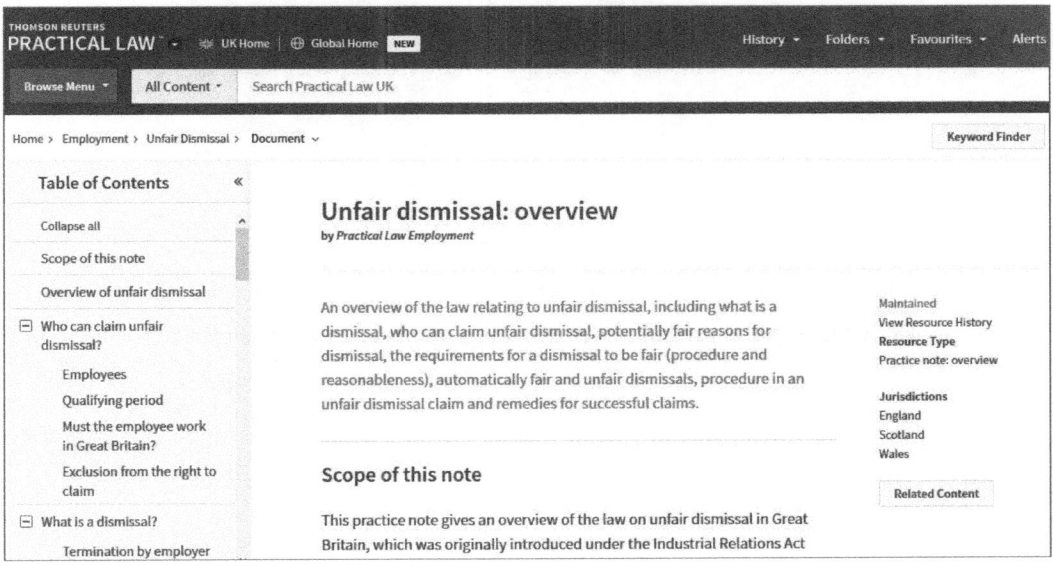

© Thomson Reuters

4.3.2 Lexis+ Practical Guidance

Lexis+ Practical Guidance is published by the same company that publishes Lexis+ Legal Research, and like Practical Law it is aimed at legal practitioners so arranges its content by subject area.

Click on the heading to select the area you want to research.

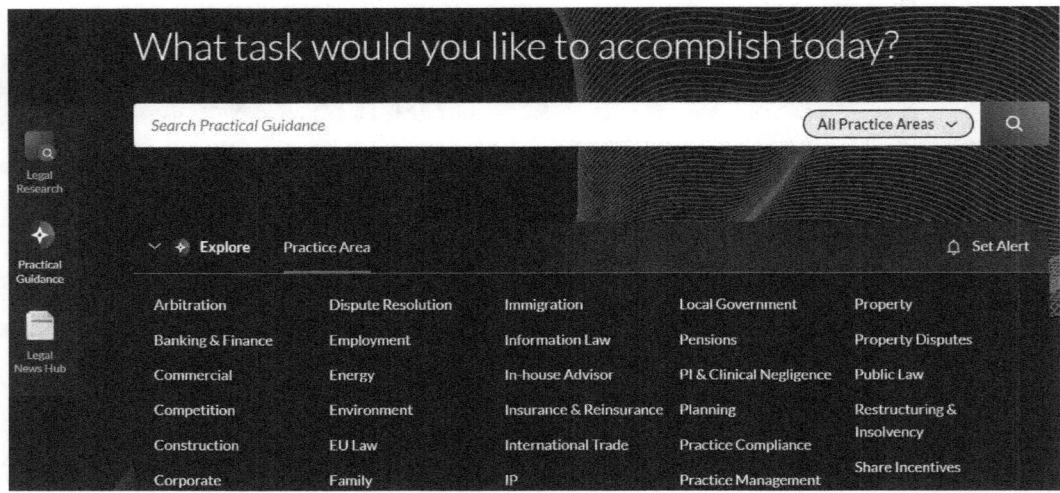

© Reproduced with kind permission of RELX (UK) Limited t/a LexisNexis

Once you are in the practice area, you can browse all the topics covered and select those that look relevant to your issue.

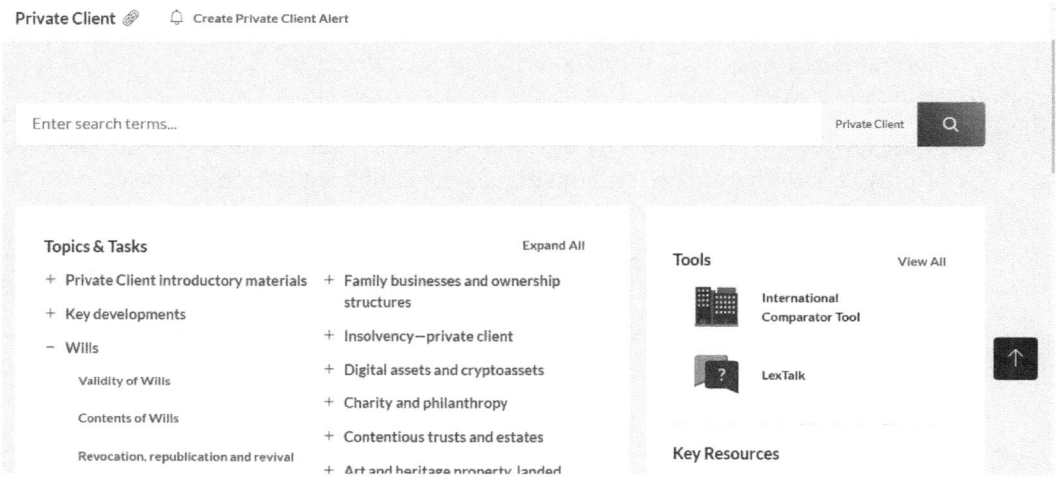

© Reproduced with kind permission of RELX (UK) Limited t/a LexisNexis

Each sub-topic is arranged in the same way. You can use the tabs to navigate to key content.

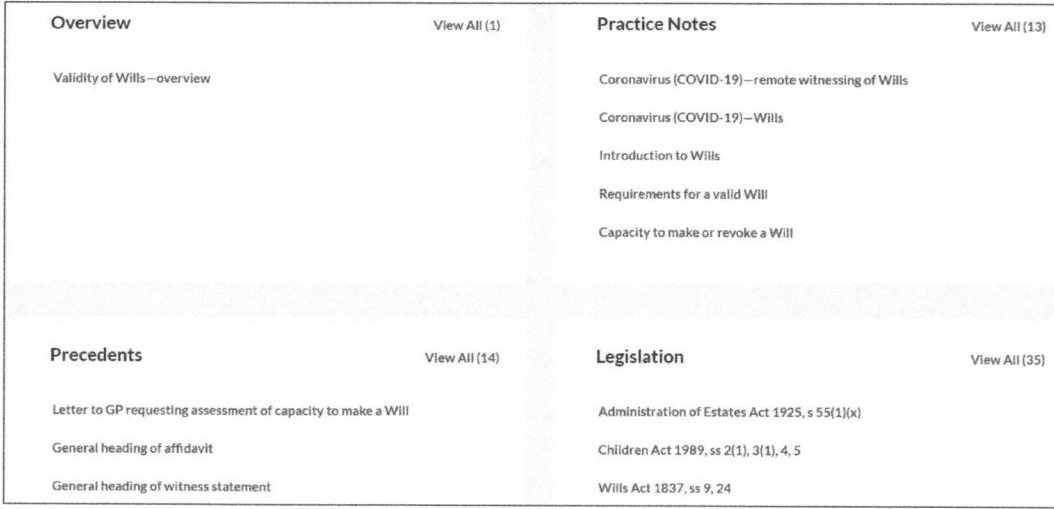

© Reproduced with kind permission of RELX (UK) Limited t/a LexisNexis

If you are unfamiliar with the subject, you can select the *Overview* document for a summary of the law.

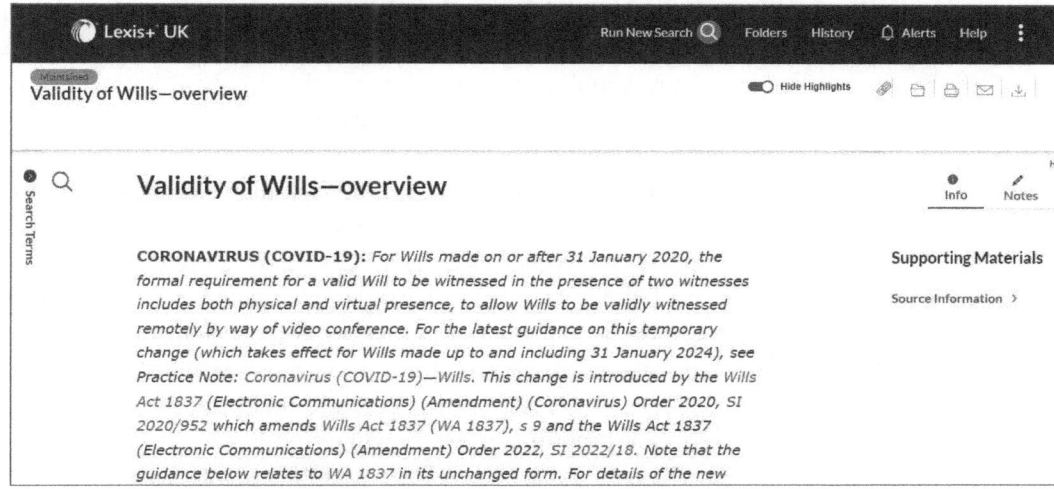

© Reproduced with kind permission of RELX (UK) Limited t/a LexisNexis

This overview document again contains links to key cases and legislation (primary sources of law). Or you can access these by using the boxes from the sub-topic page.

4.4 PRACTITIONER BOOKS

Lexis+ Practical Guidance and *Practical Law* are databases frequently used by practising lawyers, but again subscriptions to these can be costly so not all firms will have access. Therefore, what print alternatives are there?

Solicitors seldom refer to student textbooks or other academic works. These are not primarily intended to assist a thorough and pragmatic assessment of the law relating to a particular issue in hand. Practitioner books are intended to fulfil this role.

Practitioner books are written for, and usually by, practising lawyers. They give detailed and comprehensive coverage of an area of the law, with special emphasis on practice and procedure. Often they reproduce selected primary sources as well.

Although many practitioner books have online versions, printed versions are still used. So if you want to be a competent researcher, you should familiarise yourself with these texts.

4.4.1 Navigating practitioner works

The following guidelines will assist you to get the most from practitioner books:

(a) Although the original author may be long dead, their authority is such that practitioner works often continue to be known by their name rather than the name of the current editor. For example, *Chitty on Contracts*, now in its 35th edition and sometimes referred to as just *Chitty*, was originally written by Joseph Chitty (1796–1838).

(b) Choose between a variety of access points, according to the nature of your research query:
- an overall table of contents: use this to plot the layout of the work as a whole
- tables of cases and legislation referred to (usually towards the front): use these to jump to discussion of particular court decisions, statutes or statutory instruments
- subject index (usually towards the back): use this to jump to discussion of particular topics
- subject sections may be labelled by coloured divider cards (each such section may also have its own table of contents)
- for their own quick reference, individuals often add umpteen coloured page-tabs to personal or shared copies

(c) Keeping up-to-date is a challenge to publishers of practitioner works. Always take steps to establish how a source makes provision for currency:
- it may be replaced by a new edition every year (for example, *Archbold: Criminal Pleading, Evidence and Practice*)
- paperback supplements may appear during the lifetime of an edition; these accumulate updates to particular sections in the main work (for example, *Chitty on Contracts*)
- looseleaf format is another solution, as it allows individual pages to be replaced, so that changes to the law are integrated regularly into the text (for example, *Kemp and Kemp: Quantum of Damages*)
- titles in all these categories may be supplemented by a brief bulletin or newsletter, giving notes on recent cases or pieces of legislation

(d) Always check near the beginning for a note of the cut-off date to which the publisher affirms that the law expressed is current, and make a record of this. Where they exist, online versions of practitioner works will be updated as frequently as the editors can manage. This may be daily, but it may be monthly or even quarterly. Do not assume that the content is current to today! If you are using an online version of a practitioner work, you can find out the date to which it is up to date by clicking on the information icon.

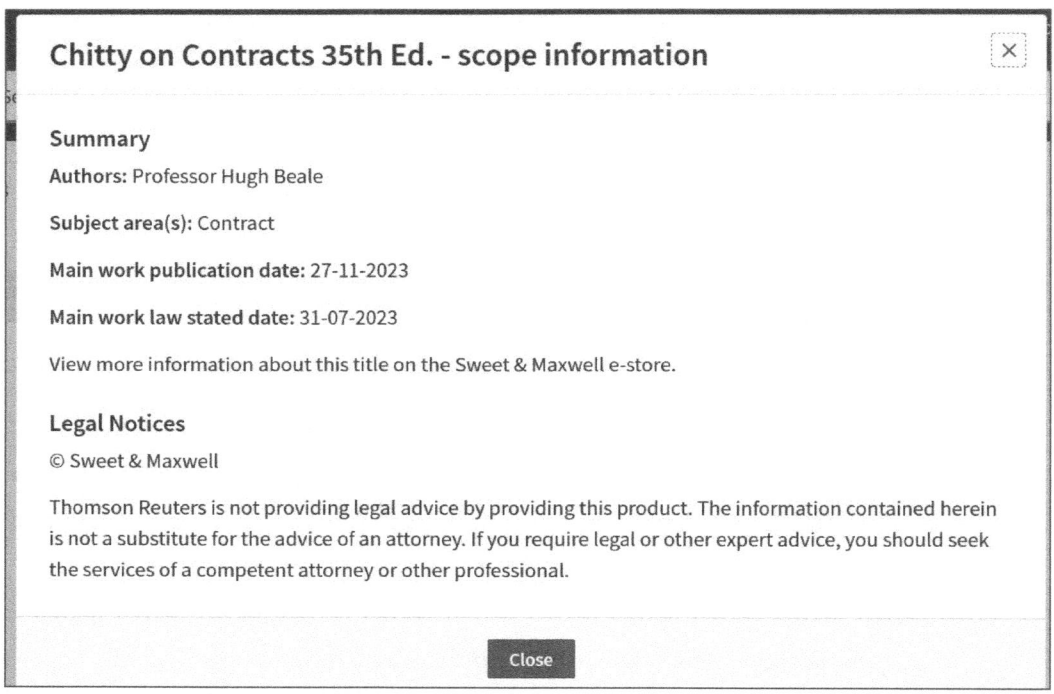

© Reproduced with kind permission of Westlaw UK

4.5 WIDENING THE NET

All of the sources described in this chapter are secondary sources. In other words they state what a commentator believes the law to be. They offer valuable introductions and summaries, written by authors who are experts in their field and whose names may carry authority; but the statements of law they contain are still secondhand.

Primary sources, that is cases and legislation, are the raw materials of the law. These are the foundation of sound legal advice, and therefore the mainstay of sound legal research. Having established a preliminary overview of your topic, you must shift your focus to primary sources.

The following table, which deals mainly with primary sources, is intended to save your time and build your confidence in linking particular types of research query with particular sources. Each group of sources is listed in order of preference, on the basis of extent of coverage and ease of use. You may not have access to all of these resources during your studies or in practice. The table provides a guide to what sources may be used to find particular types of information.

How to:	Online Route	Paper Route
(1) Find where a case is reported using party names only.	(a) *Westlaw: Cases* (b) *Lexis+ Legal Research: Content – Cases*	(a) Start with the *Current Law Case Citators*. Check most recent citator volume first and, if the case is not listed, work backwards through all the volumes until you find the case. (Covers cases reported or cited from 1947 onwards. The latest *Current Law Monthly Digest* also contains a cumulative table of cases) (b) Secondly, try the table of cases in a practitioner work such as *Palmer's Company Law*, or *Hill and Redman's Law of Landlord and Tenant*
(2) Find summaries of cases	(a) *Westlaw: Cases*: search for case, click *Case Analysis* (same summaries as *Current Law Year Books*) (b) *Lexis+ Legal Research: Content – Cases*: select *Case Overview* as source	(a) Use the *Current Law Case Citators* to find where your case has been 'digested', ie summarised in the *Current Law Yearbooks* (1947–) (b) *Halsbury's Laws Annual Abridgement* volumes, if case is referred to elsewhere in *Halsbury's Laws*
(3) Find cases on a certain subject	(a) *Westlaw: Cases*: search by *free text* OR *subject/keyword* (b) *Lexis+ Legal Research*: search by terms in *Case Overview* (c) *Lexis+ Legal Research: Halsbury's Laws of England*; search for subject – important cases feature in footnotes (selective)	(a) *Law Reports*: Consolidated Index (in 6 bound vols. 1951–2005, plus softback cumulations for recent years) (b) *Halsbury's Laws* (use footnotes) (c) *Current Law Year Books*: 1976, 1986, 1989 have cumulative subject indexes for the previous years. Then use the subject index in each succeeding volume
(4) Find cases featuring a piece of legislation	(a) *Westlaw: Cases*: from search screen use *More options*: search under *legislation title* and *legislation provision no.* (b) *Lexis+ Legal Research*: search via *Legislation* and then select *Cases* in *Supporting Materials – Related Documents* section	(a) *Current Law Legislation Citators*: Start with the volume covering the year of the legislation and work forwards through all subsequent volumes, and for recent coverage check the Citator section in the looseleaf *Current Law Statutes* Service File (b) *Halsbury's Statutes: Consolidated Table of Cases*; lists cases citing sections of Acts that feature in annotations to those sections

How to:	Online Route	Paper Route
(5) Track the judicial treatment of a case in subsequent proceedings	(a) *Westlaw: Cases*: search for case, click *Case analysis*; scroll down to *Key Cases citing* (b) *Lexis+ Legal Research: Case Overview: Cases referring to this case*	*Current Law Case Citators* volumes, cumulative table of cases in latest issue of *Current Law Monthly Digest*. Check most recent citator volume; work backwards if no reference found
(6) Find where very old cases are reported	(a) *Lexis+ Legal Research: Cases* (b) *Westlaw: Cases*	*English Reports: Table of Cases* (vols 177–178)
(7) Find information about very recent cases	(a) *Lexis+ Legal Research* (see *Judgments* source for transcripts – usually same day as decision handed down; see *All England Reporter* for summaries of recent cases) (b) *Westlaw*	Prefer online sources, otherwise try (a) *Current Law Monthly Digests* (b) *Times Law Reports* (monthly cumulative indexes) (c) Case reports in journals such as the *Law Society Gazette* or *New Law Journal*
(8) Find out the latest text of a Bill before Parliament, and what stage the Bill has reached	(a) Bills before Parliament (http://services.parliament.uk/bills): detailed coverage (b) Progress of public bills (www.parliament.uk/business/bills-and-legislation/current-bills/public-bill-list/)	Prefer online sources
(9) Find a statute in its latest amended form	(a) *Lexis+ Legal Research: Content – Legislation – Acts* (b) *Westlaw: Legislation*	*Halsbury's Statutes* (only if in force)
(10) Find out when a statute or sections of it came into force, and if any section has been repealed or amended by later legislation	(a) *Lexis+ Legal Research: Content – Legislation Status Snapshots* (only available from individual sections/provisions) (b) *Westlaw: Legislation: Legislation Analysis*	(a) *Is it in Force?* for commencement of Acts passed since 1 January 1960. *Halsbury's Statutes Citator* for details of amendments and repeals (b) *Halsbury's Statutes* (use footnotes) (c) *Current Law Legislation Citators*: volumes, and for recent coverage the Citator section in the looseleaf *Current Law Statutes Service File*

How to:	Online Route	Paper Route
(11) Identify which parts of a statute are later amendments	(a) *Lexis+ Legal Research: Content – Legislation – UK Parliament Acts*: within the text amended text appears enclosed by square brackets; footnotes give source of amendments (b) *Westlaw: Legislation; Table of Amendments* via *Legislation Analysis*	(a) *Halsbury's Statutes*: main volumes and Current Statutes Service binders: amended text appears enclosed by square brackets; footnotes give source of amendments (b) *Halsbury's Statutes* Cumulative Supplement and Noter-Up: list recent amendments not yet in main volumes
(12) Find annotated versions of the original Act, with background: Parliamentary debates, etc	For debates in Parliament: *Hansard* (https://hansard.parliament.uk)	*Current Law Statutes* (1949–)
(13) Find a statutory instrument by number, by title or by subject	(a) *Lexis+ Legal Research: Content – Legislation – Statutory Instruments* (b) *Westlaw: Legislation* (c) www.legislation.gov.uk/uksi; full text (1987–)	(a) *Halsbury's Statutory Instruments*: all SIs in force are listed – some in summary, many in full text (b) Text of some statutory instruments is reproduced in practitioner works such as *Palmer's Company Law*
(14) Find an account of the law on a particular topic, leading you to relevant legislation and cases	(a) *Lexis+ Legal Research: Content – Halsbury's Laws of England* (b) *Westlaw: Topics and overviews*	(a) *Halsbury's Laws* (use footnotes) (b) Looseleaf practitioner works (c) Textbooks (use footnotes and tables)
(15) Find EU primary legislation: Treaties	EUR-LEX (eur-lex.europa.eu/homepage.html)	*Blackstone's EU Treaties and Legislation* (selective full text; annual)
(16) Find EU secondary legislation: Regulations, Directives, Decisions	EUR-LEX (eur-lex.europa.eu/homepage.html)	(a) *European Current Law Year Books* and *Monthly Digests* (b) *Blackstone's EU Treaties and Legislation* (selective full text; annual)
(17) Check whether an EU Directive has been implemented in the UK	(a) *Westlaw: EU*: search for Directive; look for link to *National Measures* (b) EUR-LEX (eur-lex.europa.eu/homepage.html); from home page select National transposition from National law and case law section and then search for directive	*Halsbury's Statutory Instruments*: EU Legislation Implementator

How to:	Online Route	Paper Route
(18) Find EU cases (Court of Justice)	EUR-LEX (eur-lex.europa.eu/homepage.html)	(a) *Current Law Case Citators* and *Monthly Digests* (b) *European Current Law*
(19) Find European Court of Human Rights cases, citations, summaries, full text	(a) European Court of Human Rights (www.echr.coe.int): Case-law – HUDOC database for full text of cases (b) *Westlaw*: European Human Rights Reports (c) *Lexis+ Legal Research*: European Court of Human Rights Cases (1960–)	(a) *Current Law Case Citators* (b) Emmerson, *Human Rights Practice* (looseleaf)
(20) Find articles on topics in law, or case comment in periodicals	(a) *Westlaw*: Contents – Books and Journals: search includes Legal Journals Index (comprehensive; 1986–) (b) *Lexis+ Legal Research*: Content – Books and Journals: search across Journals Index which includes abstracts and full text articles	(a) *Current Law Year Books*: up to 1995, separate article index at back of volume; from 1996, references to articles under subject headings in main body of work (b) *Halsbury's Laws of England*: Monthly Review and Annual Abridgement volumes; arranged by subject (c) Publications such as the *Law Society Gazette* or *New Law Journal*, or specialist journals such as *Trusts and Estates Law and Tax Journal*
(21) Find out what abbreviations/citations stand for	*Cardiff Index to Legal Abbreviations* (www.legalabbrevs.cardiff.ac.uk/)	(a) Raistrick, *Index to Legal Citations and Abbreviations*, 4th edn (2013) (b) *Current Law Year Books* and *Monthly Digests* list abbreviations at the front of each volume

CHAPTER 5

RESEARCHING CASE LAW

5.1	How are cases published?	71
5.2	Which source of cases has the most authority?	72
5.3	How do I cite cases?	73
5.4	Finding cases	74
5.5	How do I update a case?	75
5.6	How do I find cases on a subject?	79

> **LEARNING OUTCOMES**
>
> After reading this chapter you will be able to:
>
> - identify where you can find case reports
> - understand how to cite cases
> - explain which resources can be used to find case reports when you have incomplete information
> - describe how to update a case and check whether it is still good law
> - use online and printed sources to find cases on a particular subject.

5.1 HOW ARE CASES PUBLISHED?

Judgments delivered in court are published via a number of channels. You can access many online soon after the judgment is given. For example, the raw texts of judgments of the Supreme Court are published on the Court's free website on the day they are handed down (see www.supremecourt.uk/cases). Another useful free site that gathers judgments from a variety of UK courts is BAILII (the British and Irish Legal Information Institute – see www.bailii.org). A large archive of transcripts of judgments can also be accessed via subscription databases such as *Westlaw* and *Lexis+ Legal Research*.

5.1.1 Transcripts

Transcripts are simply a written and verbatim record of the court's judgment. There are two ways in which a court can give a judgment:

Handing down

This tends to happen in more complex cases. At the conclusion of argument, the court will indicate whether it is going to reserve judgment or give judgment straight away. If it is reserved, the court will return to give judgment at a later date, usually in the form of a written judgment. In these cases the transcript will generally be an exact copy of that which was handed down. Transcripts of handed down judgments tend to consist of:

- a Neutral Citation: ie [2025] UKSC 9
- the names of the parties (the case header)
- a list of the judges who heard the case
- the date of judgment

- the date the case was heard
- the names of counsel and the firms of solicitors instructing them
- the text of the judgments

Ex tempore judgment

In more straightforward cases, the court may be able to give judgment as soon as it finishes. The judge or judges will give a verbal judgment which is either recorded and/or taken down by a short-hand stenographer. In these cases the transcript of the judgment will not be available until it has been transcribed by the court stenographers. It is then sent to the judge who gave the judgment for approval. Transcripts of judgments given ex tempore consist of the same components as transcripts of judgments handed down (see above).

5.1.2 Law reports

Law reports have all the information contained in a transcript but also include a number of significant editorial enhancements. A law report of a case is usually produced when the case makes a change to or develops the law. Law reports are written by law reporters (barristers and solicitors) and are always published as a series. Examples include:

- The *Law Reports* (AC, KB, Ch and Fam)
- The *Weekly Law Reports* (WLR)
- The *All England Law Reports* (All ER)

Law reports contain all of the components that you will find in a transcript, along with a number of other important and useful elements of content. Their editors add value in various ways, such as provision of summaries ('headnotes') and tables of cases and legislation referred to. These series of reports, rather than transcripts, should be your preferred source of case law (**use transcripts only if a law report of the case is not available**). They are usually available in both paper and online formats.

Brief reports are published regularly in *The Times* newspaper. Case notes also appear in weekly practitioners' journals, such as the *New Law Journal* and the *Law Society Gazette*. Some series of reports are intended to cover cases in specialist areas (eg, the *Road Traffic Reports* and the *Family Law Reports*). Finally, three general series feature the most significant cases across the law: the *All England Law Reports*, the *Weekly Law Reports* and the (confusingly named) *Law Reports*.

Cases that are not selected for inclusion in such publications are termed 'unreported'. This applies to more than 95% of the 200,000 or so cases decided by the UK courts each year. The Internet has facilitated widespread access to unreported decisions, in the form of case transcripts. However, they should be treated with caution as foundations for legal advice. The courts will permit an advocate to cite an unreported case only if it 'contains a relevant statement of legal principle not found in reported authority' (*Practice Direction (Citation of Authorities) (Senior Courts)* [2012] 1 WLR 780).

5.2 WHICH SOURCE OF CASES HAS THE MOST AUTHORITY?

The *Law Reports* are published by the Incorporated Council of Law Reporting for England and Wales (ICLR). They are the nearest to an official series of case reports for this jurisdiction (the Council is in fact a charity rather than a government body).

Uniquely, they include arguments presented by counsel and are checked by the presiding judge before publication. For these reasons, and by direction of the judiciary, an advocate citing a case before a court is required to use the version in the *Law Reports* in preference to any alternatives (see *Practice Direction (Citation of Authorities) (Senior Courts)* [2012] 1 WLR 780).

The *Law Reports* have been published continuously in various parallel series since 1865. The names of these series have changed frequently over the years, in line with the shifting structure of divisions of the courts. There are currently four separate series: Appeal Cases (abbreviated to AC); Chancery Division (Ch); Family Division (Fam); and King's Bench Division (KB). These reports are available in printed format and online via *Westlaw* and *Lexis+ Legal Research*. If a case is reported in the *Law Reports*, it will usually be the first citation listed (after any neutral citation – see **5.3.1**). On *Westlaw* it is easy to identify the *Law Reports* case report as an ICLR logo appears in the screen.

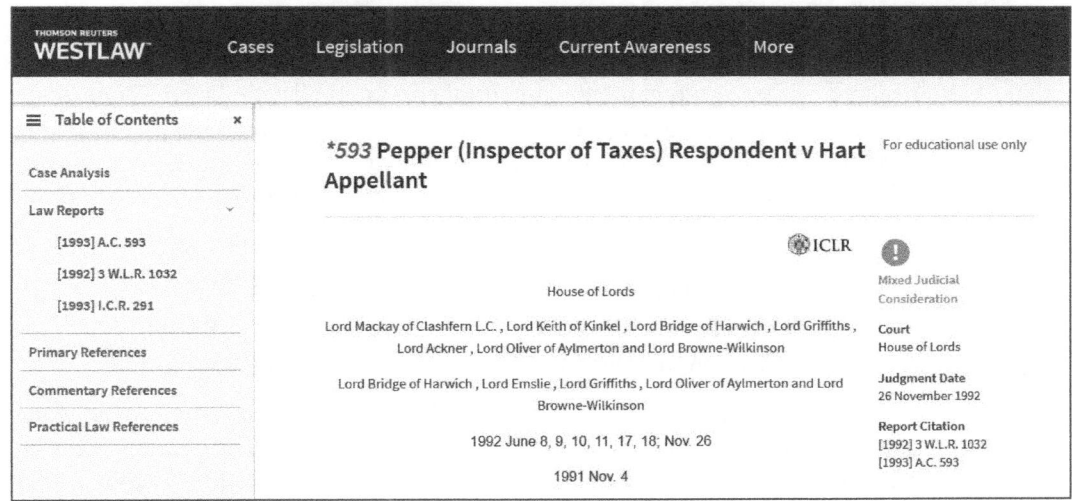

© Reproduced with kind permission of Westlaw UK

5.3 HOW DO I CITE CASES?

In order to locate the report of a case, you often need to interpret its citation. Citations identify cases by notation, referring to a volume and page in a particular series of law reports. A typical citation for an English case is:

Jordan v Burgoyne [1963] 2 QB 744

This tells you that the report of the case of *Jordan v Burgoyne* starts at p 744 of vol 2 of the Queen's Bench series of the *Law Reports* for 1963.

Certain conventions underpin the system of citation:

- Party names appear in italics.
- Year of publication appears in **[square]** or **(round)** brackets:
  - in the example above, the year appears in square brackets because it is essential for locating the case; volumes of the *Law Reports* are consecutively numbered within each year only, not from year to year;
  - by contrast, the case of *Bowker v Rose* is reported at (1977) 121 SJ 274; volumes of the *Solicitors' Journal* are consecutively numbered from year to year; therefore you can find this case simply by knowing that it is in volume 121; the year is strictly superfluous, so it appears in round brackets.
- The number of the volume in which the report appears comes before the (abbreviated) title of the series, and the number of the first page of the report comes after.
- References to different series of reports are ordered in a hierarchy: the neutral citation (if it exists – see below) comes first; then any reference to the *Law Reports*; the *Weekly Law Reports*; the *All England Law Reports*; other specialist series of law reports; newspaper law reports.

The convention of abbreviating titles of publications in the legal world is confusing. For a comprehensive list, see Raistrick, D, *Index to Legal Citations and Abbreviations* (4th edn, 2013). A useful free to access, online source is the database of abbreviations maintained by the University of Cardiff (www.legalabbrevs.cardiff.ac.uk).

5.3.1 Neutral citation

In January 2001 a new system of neutral citation of judgments was introduced (see *Practice Note (Judgments: Neutral Citation)* [2001] 1 WLR 194). The system is 'neutral' as regards format and publisher. In other words, it identifies cases by a unique reference, independent of the series of reports in which they are reproduced and independent of whether they appear online or in print. The purpose is to enable reports of cases to be published and accessed more easily online.

All cases heard in the Supreme Court, the Court of Appeal and the High Court are now covered by these arrangements. A neutral citation is allocated by the court to every judgment. This is intended to feature in every subsequent publication of that judgment. It takes the form of year (in square brackets), abbreviation of the name of the court, and running serial number (the serial number reverts to 1 at the start of each calendar year). Here are some examples:

Supreme Court	[2025] UKSC 1, 2, 3, etc
Court of Appeal (Civil Division)	[2025] EWCA Civ 1, 2, 3, etc
Court of Appeal (Criminal Division)	[2025] EWCA Crim 1, 2, 3, etc
High Court (Administrative Division)	[2025] EWHC 1, 2, 3, etc (Admin)

Since 2001, judgments have also been set out in numbered paragraphs, which are easier to locate within electronic law reports than page references. The citation of the authority from a particular decision might thus be in the form: *Smith v Jones* [2001] EWCA Civ 10 at [59], ie, paragraph 59 in the judgment of *Smith v Jones*, the 10th judgment of the year 2001 in the Civil Division of the Court of Appeal of England and Wales.

5.4 FINDING CASES

Trainees are often asked to track down a case on the basis of incomplete information. For example, your supervisor may say something like 'I'm advising a client who's considering suing her bank for the return of unlawful charges. I saw an article that mentioned a successful case along the same lines, I think the name was Curtis or something. Can you dig out the case for me?'

If you have a citation to a series of law reports, this should be enough to locate a case, even if you do not know the names of the parties concerned. However, how do you locate a report if all that you know is the name of one or more of the parties?

You could type the party name into an online database in the hope that the case features there. The more common the surname, the less efficient this approach is likely to be. However, where the subject matter of the case is known, you could also add this as a search term, or try checking the table of cases in a relevant practitioner book or student textbook.

5.4.1 Westlaw: Case Analysis

To search for a case using *Westlaw*, go to the home page and click on *Cases* then *Case Search* at the top of the screen. A search template will appear. If you know the name, enter one or more of them in the *Parties* box and click *Search*. A list of results will appear. To view the abstract of a particular case, click on the title. This *Case Analysis* document will give you a useful summary of the case. A list of citations (referring to where the case is reported in full) features on the right hand of the screen. If the full text of the case is available to view on *Westlaw*, one or more of these citations will appear in colour as a link.

Here is the beginning of the document on *Westlaw* for *Pepper v Hart*:

© Reproduced with kind permission of Westlaw UK

5.4.2 Lexis+ Legal Research: Case Overview

Case Overview is a case citator that is available in online form only, via *Lexis+ Legal Research*.

To access from the home page of *Lexis+* from the *Content* section, click *Cases*, then if you know the name of the case, type it into the general search box. The full citation for your case will appear at the top of the results screen. This includes references to a wide range of publications where the case is reported, including (if it features in full on *Lexis+*) links to the full text. Click on the *Overview* link to access a summary of the case.

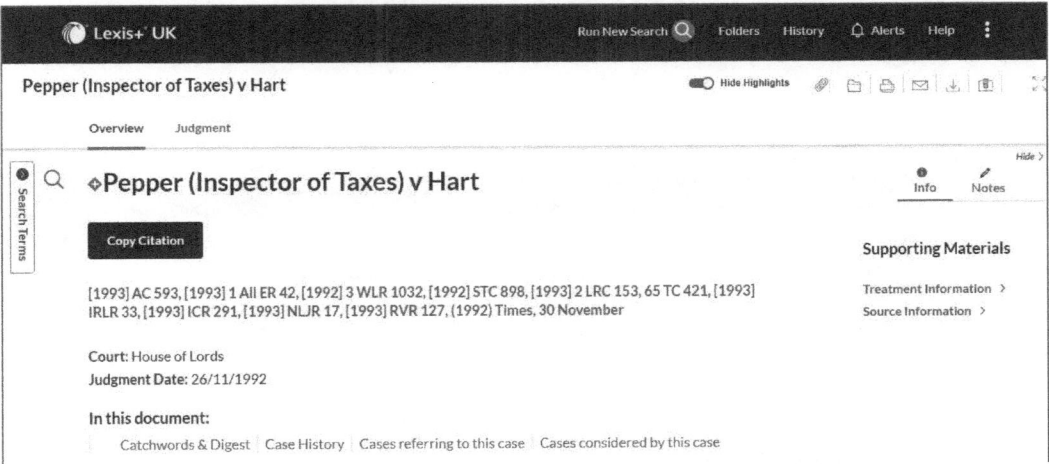

© Reproduced with kind permission of RELX (UK) Limited t/a LexisNexis

5.5 HOW DO I UPDATE A CASE?

Once you have found your case, you must **always** check if it is still good law. You can do so using printed or online resources.

5.5.1 Online resources

If you have access to a subscription legal database, such as *Westlaw* or *Lexis+ Legal Research*, checking for developments to a case is relatively straightforward. In *Westlaw*, from the home page, click on *Cases* then *Cases Search* at the top of the screen. Enter one or more names in the *Party Names* box and click *Search*. From the results screen you will see the name of your case, details of the court and date of the hearing and a symbol indicating the type of subsequent judicial treatment the case has received. For example, a no entry icon signifies negative judicial treatment and warns that at least one point of law in the case has been overruled or reversed.

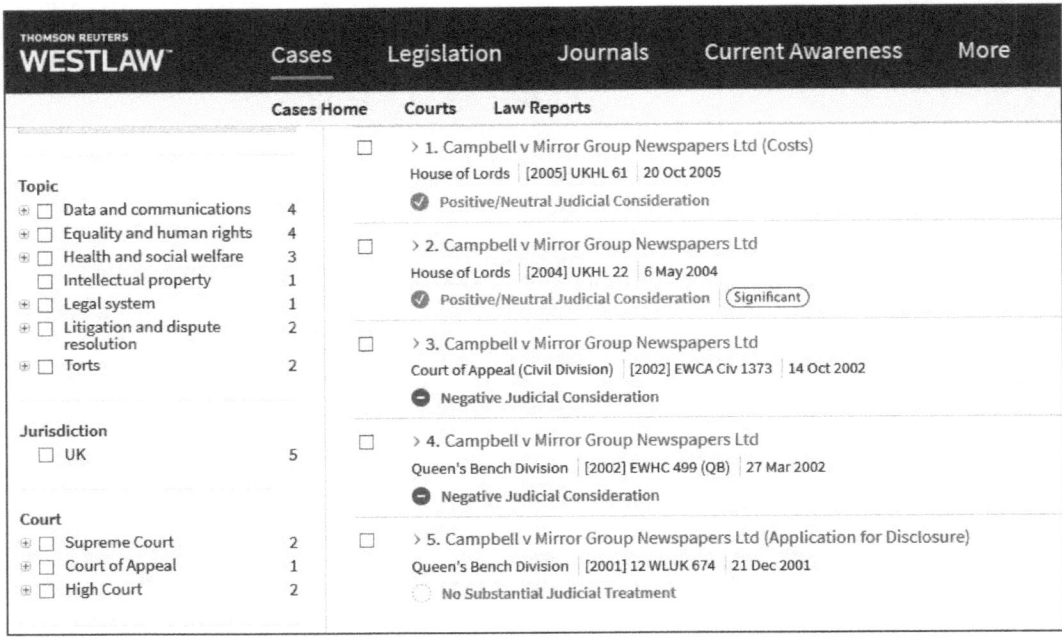

© Reproduced with kind permission of Westlaw UK

To find out more, click on the case name and scroll down to the *Appellate History* section to track the progress of the case. To check later judicial treatment in other cases, click on *Primary References* and *Key Cases Citing*.

© Reproduced with kind permission of Westlaw UK

Case Overview (part of *Lexis+ Legal Research*) is an alternative online citator for researching subsequent judicial consideration. Access it via *Content*, then *Cases*, then carry out your search. Use the Advanced Search option to allow you to search by case name. From your results, select the *Overview* link. The result will give you access to a list of cases which have referred to this case. You will also see status icons: green for positive treatment in subsequent cases; red for negative; yellow for mixed or cautionary; and blue for neutral.

Researching Case Law

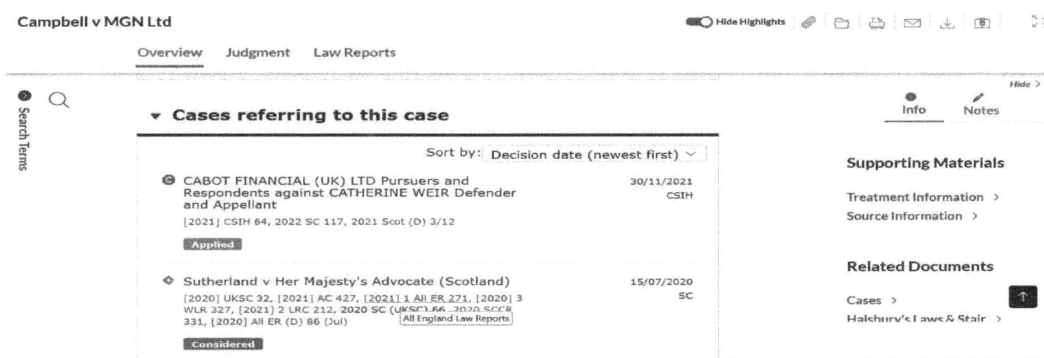

© Reproduced with kind permission of RELX (UK) Limited t/a LexisNexis

Both *Case Overview* on *Lexis+* and *Case Analysis* on *Westlaw* use a variety of symbols to flag the standing of individual judgments. (Westlaw also features symbols in connection with legislation.) It is important to understand the significance of these, especially because, unfortunately, the two publishers do not use the same symbols.

Within *Case Overview*, you will come across the following in the Help section:

Case Overview

This content is unique to LexisNexis

Citator

Case Overview is a daily updated comprehensive database of over 300,000 case records, dating from 1502, which provides procedural history, annotations, keywords, summaries and links to all subscribed versions of a case.

KEY FEATURES

A **traffic light** system takes into account both the procedural history and the subsequent judicial consideration of a case.

❌ - **Negative Treatment Icon:** This indicates that the decision has been subsequently reversed, disapproved or overruled.

⚠ - **Cautionary Treatment Icon:** this indicates that the decision has had some doubt cast on it.

➕ - **Positive Treatment Icon:** This indicates that the decision has received positive treatment: affirmed, applied etc.

◐ - **Neutral Treatment Icon:** This indicates that the decision has received neutral or ambivalent treatment: considered, explained etc.

ⓒ - **Citation Information Icon:** This indicates that no treatment has been given and that only citation information is available.

© Reproduced with kind permission of RELX (UK) Limited t/a LexisNexis

Within *Westlaw* search results, you will come across the following:

Case Status Icons	
ICON	**WHAT DOES IT MEAN?**
✓	Case has received positive consideration – a higher court has either affirmed the case, or it has been cited by another case in a positive way.
!	Case has received mixed consideration – subsequent cases have provided mixed treatment (good and bad) although the case should technically still be considered 'good law'
–	Case has received negative consideration – this can has been overruled or reversed in full or in part and should no longer be considered 'good law'
A ✓	Appeal Outstanding – there is currently an appeal going through or an appeal has been requested. This icon can appear in addition to any of the above.
○	No Substantial Judicial Treatment

© Reproduced with kind permission of Westlaw UK

5.5.2 Printed resources

If you do not have access to *Westlaw* or *Lexis+ Legal Research*, there is a print alternative that you can use. The best source for checking the subsequent judicial treatment of a case is a citator, such as the *Current Law Case Citator*. (If the case pre-dates 1947 it is still worth checking here, since consideration in a post-1947 judgment qualifies an older case for inclusion.)

Using the printed version, the procedure is to find the latest reference to the case in an annual volume (entries in these volumes are cumulative), so work backwards from the most recent citator until you find a reference to your case. Then check the case lists in the latest issue of the *Monthly Digest* for any recent developments. Here is an example of an entry in the 1977–88 citator:

> R v Blackburn (James) (1979) 1 Cr App R (S) 205, CA Digested, 81/**525**: Considered, 87/1035: Cited, 89/1071: Referred to, 84/880: Distinguished, 88/977

The case of *R v Blackburn* is summarised, or 'digested', in the *Current Law Year Book* of 1981 at para 525. It has been commented upon in various ways in subsequent decisions that are also summarised. The references 'considered, 87/1035', etc are to summaries of these other cases in later year books.

Certain conventional terms denote the effect of later decisions on the status of earlier decisions: terms such as 'applied', 'distinguished' and 'followed'. Their meanings are as follows:

- *distinguished* – outlines differences between a current case and an older case being referred to in a court hearing so that it cannot be used as a precedent
- *followed* – a case uses the same precedent as outlined in an earlier case quoted during the hearing
- *applied* – the same precedent set out in an older case is used again during another case
- *approved* – the original findings of an older case are 'approved', or agreed with, in a new case
- *disapproved* – in a case hearing, older cases referred to can be disapproved, ie the current court does not agree with the original decision but does not overrule it
- *mentioned* – brief mention in a court case
- *overruled* – to set a new precedent, overturning a precedent set out by another court

- *not followed* – a case does not use the same precedent as outlined in an earlier case
- *reversed* – to change a decision in the same case that has already been made by a lower court.

5.6 HOW DO I FIND CASES ON A SUBJECT?

Cases on a particular topic may be traced using a general source, such as *Halsbury's Laws of England* or a relevant practitioner book (see **Chapter 4**).

Online databases are very useful for subject searching, since they offer the facility to search for occurrences of keywords anywhere in the text of documents. However, beware of information overload! You may find that you generate large numbers of results, many of which are irrelevant to your purpose. If this does happen, try using the *'sort by relevance'* option, if available, to bring the most meaningful results to the top of your results list.

5.6.1 Using *Westlaw* to find cases on a subject

From the home page, click *Cases – Cases Search* at the top of the screen. Enter one or more keywords in the *Free Text* box and click *Search*. Try to be as specific as possible. If you generate too many results using *Free Text*, try the *Subject/Keyword* search. A list of judgments whose summaries contain your keyword(s) will appear. Click *Case Analysis* beneath the entry of any case that looks promising. Go to *Case Digest – Abstract* to make sure that the case concerns the area of law in which you are interested (as you may retrieve some cases where your keywords feature only incidentally). If you then wish to read a full report of the case, look to see whether any of the citations in the *Where Reported* section are in colour and underlined. If they are, the full report is available on *Westlaw* itself – just click the link. If they are not, make a note of the citation and look for the report elsewhere, either within another database or on the library shelves.

5.6.2 Tips for using legal databases to find cases on a subject

Most online versions of single series of law reports, such as *All England Law Reports* on *Lexis+ Legal Research* or *Weekly Law Reports* on *Westlaw*, permit free text subject searching using keywords. This is a thorough and powerful search facility.

However, it is important to understand the coverage of the database that you are using (for example, if you choose to narrow your case search on *Lexis+* to *All England Law Reports*, you will of course retrieve references to that single series only, when in fact the database features many other series in addition, including the authoritative *Law Reports*).

You may prefer to search across all case reports on a particular database. However, if you do this and use a general search term, you might generate a large volume of results, not all of which may be particularly relevant. Therefore, look for ways to make your results list more meaningful. For example, in *Westlaw*, from the Cases search screen, click on *More Options*. This will give you more search fields and enable you to restrict your search by limiting the date, or court or even cases heard by a particular judge. Consider searching by *Subject/Keyword*. These keywords are applied by the database editors, and if you use this field you will get fewer, more relevant results than if you use the same term in the *Free Text* field. If you are unsure of the appropriate keyword, either look at the *List of Terms* provided by *Westlaw* or, when you find a relevant case, look at the keywords applied to it and then re-run your search using that term. The *Advanced Cases* search screen in *Lexis+ Legal Research* also offers similar search options.

Another way of finding the most relevant cases from a large list of results is to use the *Sort by Relevance* option offered by both *Lexis+ Legal Research* and *Westlaw*. This works by reordering your results so that those cases with the most mentions of your search term are listed first. Look for the link to reorder (usually found at the top of your results list); you can also use other filters, for example to restrict the results to cases in a particular practice area.

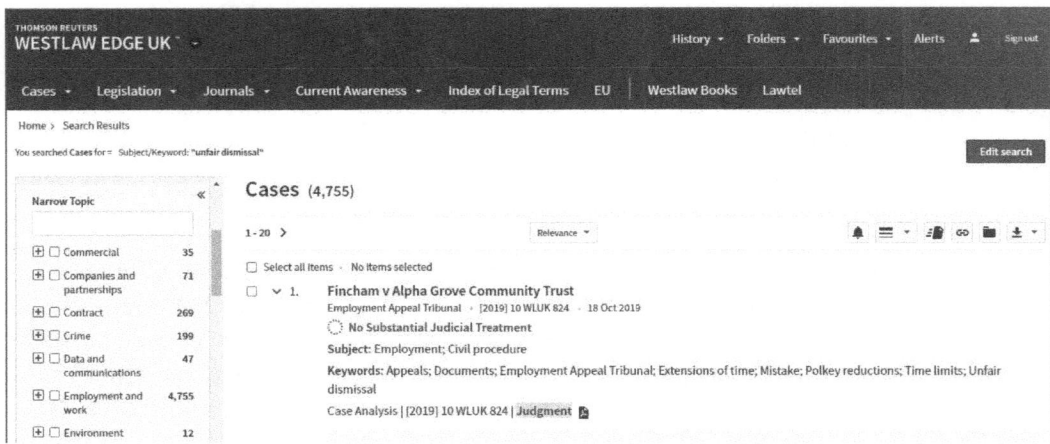

© Reproduced with kind permission of Westlaw UK

5.6.3 Chart of specialist law reports

The following selective chart identifies the leading series of law reports, their abbreviations which you will see in citations and where you can access them, across a range of practice areas:

Subject	Title	Abbreviation	Online Access
Business and Company	British Company Cases	BCC	Westlaw
	Business Law Reports	Bus LR	Westlaw
	Butterworths Company Law Cases	BCLC	Lexis+ Legal Research
Commercial	All England Law Reports. Commercial Cases	All ER (Comm)	Lexis+ Legal Research
	Commercial Law Cases	CLC	Westlaw
Consumer	Goode: Consumer Credit Reports	GCCR	Lexis+ Legal Research
Competition	Common Market Law Reports. Antitrust	CMLR	Westlaw
Crime	Criminal Appeal Reports	Cr App R	Westlaw
	Criminal Appeal Reports (Sentencing)	Cr App R (S)	Westlaw
	Justice of the Peace Law Reports	JP	Lexis+ Legal Research
Employment	Industrial Cases Reports	ICR	Westlaw
	Industrial Relations Law Reports	IRLR	Lexis+ Legal Research
EU	All England Law Reports. European Cases	All ER (EC)	Lexis+ Legal Research
	European Court Reports	ECR	EUR-Lex / Lexis+ Legal Research / Westlaw
	Common Market Law Reports	CMLR	Westlaw
Environment	Environmental Law Reports	Env LR	Westlaw
Family	Family Law Reports	FLR	Lexis+ Legal Research
Housing	Housing Law Reports	HLR	Westlaw
	Landlord and Tenant Reports	L&TR	Westlaw
Human Rights	European Human Rights Reports	EHRR	Westlaw

Subject	Title	Abbreviation	Online Access
Immigration	Immigration Appeal Reports	Imm AR	BAILII
Intellectual Property	Fleet Street Reports	FSR	Westlaw
Local Government	Butterworths Local Government Reports	LGR	Lexis+ Legal Research
Media	Entertainment and Media Law Reports	EMLR	Westlaw
Personal Injury	Butterworths Medico-Legal Reports	BMLR	Lexis+ Legal Research
	Personal Injuries and Quantum Reports	PIQR	Westlaw
Professional Negligence	Professional Negligence and Liability Reports	PNLR	Westlaw
Property	Estates Gazette. Law Reports	EGLR	EGi (Estates Gazette Interactive)/Lexis+ Legal Research
	Property, Planning and Compensation Reports	P&CR	Westlaw
Revenue	Simon's Tax Cases	STC	Lexis+ Legal Research
	HMSO Tax Cases	TC	Lexis+ Legal Research
Road Traffic	Road Traffic Reports	RTR	Westlaw
Wills and Probate	Wills and Trusts Law Reports	WTLR	Not available online

CHAPTER 6

RESEARCHING LEGISLATION

6.1	Introduction	83
6.2	How do I cite legislation?	83
6.3	Where can I find Acts?	85
6.4	How do I establish whether an Act has come into force?	87
6.5	Where can I find statutory instruments?	87
6.6	Legislation on *Lexis+ Legal Research*	88
6.7	Legislation on *Westlaw*	91
6.8	How do I update legislation?	95

> **LEARNING OUTCOMES**
>
> After reading this chapter you will be able to:
> - explain how to cite legislation
> - understand how to find legislation using printed and online resources
> - describe how to establish whether legislation is in force
> - identify the means of updating legislation.

6.1 INTRODUCTION

There are two major classes of legislation in the UK:

(a) *Primary legislation* is passed by Parliament in the form of Acts (also known as statutes); the number of Acts passed each year varies – over the last decade, the average annual figure is 36.

(b) *Secondary legislation* is made under powers delegated by Parliament, usually to government ministers; it almost always takes the form of statutory instruments (also known as regulations or orders); the number made each year can vary greatly but in recent years the average has been around 1,500.

It is vital to check that the version of any legislation that you refer to is in force. Some provisions do not come into force for some time after they have been passed by Parliament. Many are then amended over time, or even repealed altogether.

There are many different sources of legislation, in paper and online form. The first question to ask before you choose a source is this: do I need the original version of this provision, or do I need the version of the provision that is in force now? If, as is commonly the case in legal practice, you need the version in force now (ie, incorporating any subsequent amendments and repeals), the best printed sources are *Halsbury's Statutes* (see **6.3.4**) and *Halsbury's Statutory Instruments* (see **6.5.2**). Online alternatives for legislation in force are *Westlaw* (see **6.7**) and *Lexis+ Legal Research* (see **6.6**).

6.2 HOW DO I CITE LEGISLATION?

A statute is generally cited by its 'short title' (which should include the year it was passed), eg, 'Human Rights Act 1998'. You may also come across citations by 'chapter number' (the first statute passed in a given year is chapter 1, and so on). Thus the Human Rights Act 1998 may be cited as 'c 42 1998' (because it was the 42nd Act to be passed in 1998).

The present system of citing statutes by their calendar year and chapter number began in 1963. Prior to that, statutes were referred to by the year of the monarch's reign or the 'regnal year' (where each regnal year began with the anniversary of the sovereign's accession to the throne) and the running chapter number. The short titles by which many of these surviving pre-1963 Acts are informally known were invented subsequently for convenience. So, for example, the Act that lawyers refer to as the Criminal Libel Act 1819 is formally cited as: '60 Geo 3 & 1 Geo 4 c. 8'. That is, the eighth Act to be passed during the parliamentary session that spanned the sixtieth (and last) year of the reign of George III and the first year of the reign of George IV.

The body of a statute is divided into numbered sections, each containing a different rule of law. When you refer to a rule of law contained in a statute, you should identify where it can be found. It is usual to abbreviate 'section' to 's', so that 's 1' refers to section 1. Sections are subdivided into subsections, eg s 1(1); paragraphs, eg s 1(2)(a); and even sub-paragraphs. In larger statutes, sections may be grouped together into different parts, each dealing with a separate area of law.

Some statutes have one or more schedules at the end. The content of schedules varies: for example, some may contain detailed provisions which are not found in the main body of the Act, or they may expand or define phrases in the Act or contain detailed amendments of earlier legislation. The last schedule will normally say which earlier statutes the present Act repeals. References to schedules are often abbreviated as 'sched' or 'sch' and the divisions are known as 'paragraphs', often abbreviated to 'para'.

A statutory instrument is cited by its title and also by the form 'SI [year]/[serial number]', eg, SI 1998/3132, which was the first published form of the Civil Procedure Rules 1998. The serial numbering reverts to '1' at the start of each calendar year.

The body of a statutory instrument is divided. The names of these divisions depend on the form of the title. If it is called an 'Order', the divisions are known as articles. If it is entitled 'Regulations', the divisions are also known as regulations. If it is entitled 'Rules', the divisions are also known as rules. A subdivision is always known as a paragraph.

The following table summarises the conventions for citing divisions and sub-divisions of the various categories of legislation:

Category	First division (numbered 1, 2, 3 etc)	Second division (numbered (1), (2), (3) etc)	Third division (lettered (a), (b), (c) etc)
Primary Legislation:			
Act	section	subsection	paragraph
Bill	clause	subsection	paragraph
Secondary Legislation:			
Order	article	paragraph	sub-paragraph
Regulations	regulation	paragraph	sub-paragraph
Rules	rule	paragraph	sub-paragraph
Schedules:			
Schedule	paragraph	sub-paragraph	paragraph

6.3 WHERE CAN I FIND ACTS?

6.3.1 Official versions of Acts of Parliament

6.3.1.1 Chronological

Upon receiving Royal Assent, the official version of an Act is published by Her Majesty's Stationery Office (HMSO). It appears in paper form and also, within a chronological sequence, on the website www.legislation.gov.uk.

6.3.1.2 Consolidated

The legislation.gov.uk website is a very useful resource in that it also makes freely available official consolidated versions of Acts on the Internet (that is, versions that incorporate subsequent repeals and amendments). However, for the practising lawyer, there is a significant caveat:

- It may take time for changes to Acts to be incorporated within the text. The site states that it aims to incorporate new amendments into the text of the legislation within three months of those amendments coming into force. Updating gaps are flagged in two ways. A 'Changes to Legislation' message appears above the Table of Contents to each Act, stating either that there are no known outstanding changes, or that outstanding changes remain to be applied by the Editorial Team. In addition, any changes waiting to be applied are also listed at the top of each provision. It is also worth noting that most secondary legislation (statutory instruments) is not currently available with changes incorporated in the text.

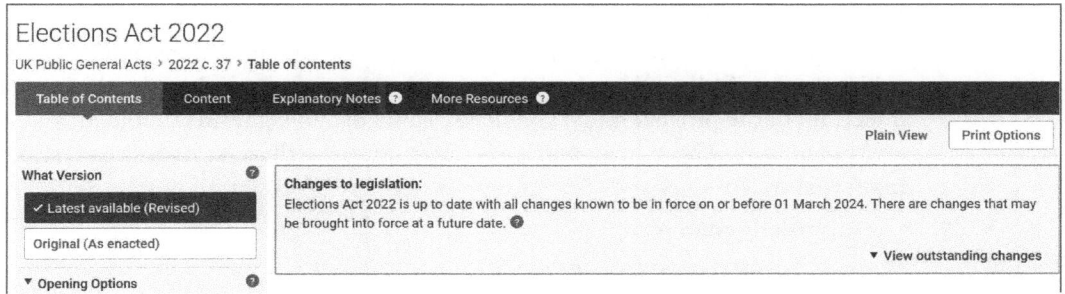

© Crown copyright

The legislation.gov.uk website is continually being enhanced and it is a very useful free source. However, for the practising lawyer (and law student) engaged in legal research, if you do have access to commercial databases of legislation, such as *Lexis+ Legal Research* (see **6.6**) or *Westlaw* (see **6.7**), you should use these as they will also provide added value by linking to commentary and cases relating to the legislation.

6.3.2 Current Law Statutes

If you do not have access to legislation online, there are still print options available. *Current Law Statutes* is a print resource which publishes statutes chronologically. They first appear as looseleaf booklets. These are later republished as several hardback volumes each year. This original version of the statute is then 'frozen' permanently: subsequent amendments and repeals are not incorporated.

The editorial annotations to *Current Law Statutes* are especially helpful in carrying out so-called 'Pepper v Hart' research. The decision of the House of Lords in *Pepper v Hart* [1993] AC 593 opened the way for the courts to consider what was said in Parliament during consideration of a Bill in circumstances where perceived ambiguity creates a need to clarify the intentions of the legislature. *Hansard* is the verbatim official record of proceedings in Parliament (the full text is available at www.parliament.uk/business/publications/hansard). The preface to each

Act in *Current Law Statutes* gives *Hansard* references to all debates in Parliament, as well as further background information on the events that prompted legislative proposals.

> **PROFESSIONAL CONDUCT POINT**
>
> The decision in *Pepper v Hart* creates a professional responsibility to take into account *Hansard* as a primary source of research to assist legislative interpretation, especially in areas of the law that are heavily statute-based (for example, tax).

6.3.3 Halsbury's Statutes

Halsbury's Statutes contains an annotated version of all statutes in force in England and Wales. Amendments are incorporated; repealed provisions are excluded. The arrangement is alphabetical by subject. It is the best printed source for consulting up-to-date versions of statutes. Although if you have access to legislation via *Lexis+ Legal Research* or *Westlaw*, it is quicker to use these to find up-to-date legislation, and you can also link to relevant related content (see **6.6** and **6.7**).

To find out the law using the paper version of *Halsbury's Statutes*, as you do when using *Halsbury's Laws*, you must take four steps:

- index;
- main volumes;
- Cumulative Supplement; and
- Noter-Up.

6.3.3.1 Consolidated index

This paperback volume contains an *alphabetical list of statutes*, a *chronological list of statutes*, and a subject index (called the *consolidated index*). The subject index should be used if you are uncertain of the provision that you need. Think of subject terms that identify the problem you are researching. The subject index will refer you from these keywords to relevant statutes in a main volume:

disorderly conduct
licensed premises, on, **13** [717]

The number in **bold** is the number of the volume in which the relevant statute appears. The following number in light type and square brackets is the paragraph number. If the second number is not enclosed in square brackets then it refers to a page number in the main volume. If the volume reference is followed by **(S)**, the provision is a recent one and will be found in one of the *Current Statutes Service* looseleaf binders. The volume and subject arrangements of these are the same as the main set.

6.3.3.2 Main volumes

The 52 'main volumes' feature statutes in force in England and Wales, arranged alphabetically by subject. In addition, these are supplemented by *Current Statutes Service* binders A–F. Each binder is clearly labelled to show the volume numbers that it supplements.

If a statute covers several subject areas, it may be split over several different volumes. The text is up to date to the year of publication of the volume (printed on the spine). Amended text appears in square brackets; text that has been repealed appears as "…"; text that will be amended or repealed at a future date appears in *italics*. Detailed footnotes provide useful commentary in relation to: parliamentary debates; amendments and repeals; derivation of older provisions in the case of consolidating legislation; commencement details; cross-references to other related provisions; judicial interpretation; linked subordinate legislation; and references to words defined elsewhere in the Act.

6.3.3.3 Cumulative Supplement

Over the years, main volumes are reissued on a rolling programme. Therefore you must always check whether the information in any main volume has changed since the volume was published.

This updating process involves two stages. To begin with, consult the annual hardback *Cumulative Supplement*. Check the first couple of pages for a note confirming the date to which the legislation has been updated. Any developments affecting your statute between the publication of individual main volumes and the cut-off date of the *Cumulative Supplement* will be noted. The *Cumulative Supplement* is arranged by subject. Look up the subject covered by the main volume, eg Employment, and then entries are listed chronologically, with the oldest Act still in force listed first.

6.3.3.4 Noter-Up

Lastly, check the looseleaf *Noter-Up* binder. This is updated monthly and will alert you to any very recent changes in the law. Here you should look for the subject area covered by the main volume, eg Employment. Then Acts are arranged chronologically, starting with the earliest statute in that area which is still in force. If the Act is not listed, there have been no amendments to it since the *Cumulative Supplement* was published.

6.4 HOW DO I ESTABLISH WHETHER AN ACT HAS COME INTO FORCE?

A statute that has passed all its parliamentary stages and received Royal Assent may not necessarily come into effect straight away. To complicate matters further, often some sections of statutes enter into force before others. Sometimes sections are brought partially into effect, for a limited purpose and period, before entering fully into force later. And just occasionally a statute is repealed before it enters into force at all (eg, the Antarctic Minerals Act 1989).

The last section of a statute usually deals with arrangements for its own commencement. A specific date may be given; a specific period after the date of Royal Assent may be stipulated; or the commencement may be delayed until such time as the Secretary of State makes a commencement order (usually by way of a statutory instrument).

If no commencement statement is made within the text of a statute (sometimes the case with older statutes), you may assume that it came into force on the date of Royal Assent.

6.4.1 Is it in Force?

The paperback volume, *Is it in Force?*, is reissued twice yearly as part of *Halsbury's Statutes of England*. It lists statutes passed since 1 January 1960, with commencement details. Arrangement is by year, then alphabetical by title of statute, then by section. A supplement dealing with the current year appears in the looseleaf *Noter-Up* binder of *Halsbury's Statutes of England*. The same content is also available on *Lexis+ Legal Research* (choose My Sources, View All Sources: H: Halsbury's Is It In Force?).

Note: The title 'Is it in Force?' is misleading. A more accurate title might be 'Has it Come into Force YET?', in the sense that this publication deals with commencement information only; it does not deal exhaustively with amendments and repeals that may affect the status of your statute since its date(s) of commencement. For sources of information on amendments and repeals, see **6.8**.

If your statute was passed by Parliament before 1960, you will need to consult the text of the provision itself for information about commencement. Alternatively, a practitioner book may give useful guidance.

6.5 WHERE CAN I FIND STATUTORY INSTRUMENTS?

The official version of a statutory instrument is published by Her Majesty's Stationery Office (HMSO). It appears in paper form and also on the website www.legislation.gov.uk. However, again, many of these texts are not subsequently amended to show the effects of later legislation.

If you look at a statutory instrument on the website, a status note will tell you whether amendments have been incorporated.

© Crown copyright

For this reason, if you have access to *Lexis+ Legal Research* or *Westlaw*, use them in preference to legislation.gov.uk.

6.6 LEGISLATION ON LEXIS+ LEGAL RESEARCH

6.6.1 Scope

Lexis+ Legal Research contains the full, amended text of UK primary and secondary legislation in force. Legislation that has been recently enacted but is not yet in force is also included. It also provides access to Acts passed by the Scottish Parliament and Welsh Parliament and EU legislation.

6.6.2 Searching

Within *Lexis+ Legal Research*, from *Content* select *Legislation* and then you can carry out a general or advanced search of all Legislation, or if you know you are looking for an Act or SI you can select *Acts* or *Statutory Instruments* as appropriate.

From *Acts* you can then select *UK Parliament Acts* and then either type the name of the Act or Browse to find it by opening up the alphabetical list under the search box.

Researching Legislation 89

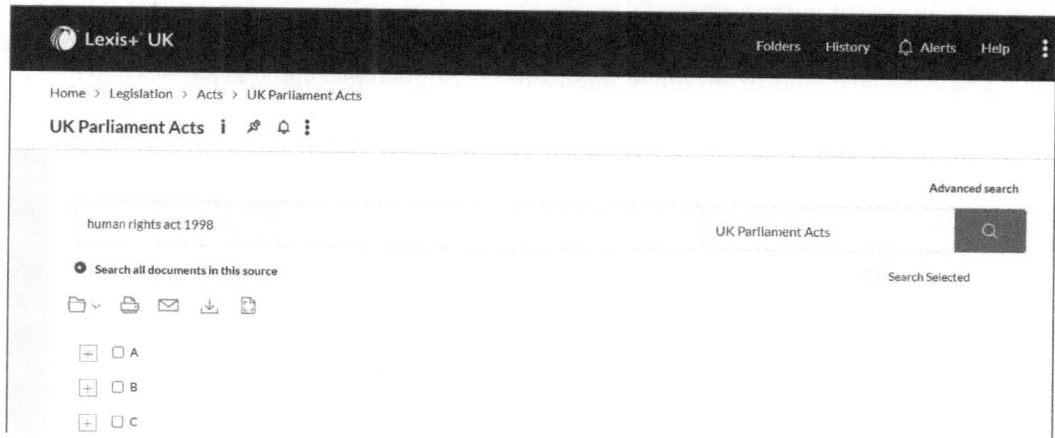

© Reproduced with kind permission of RELX (UK) Limited t/a LexisNexis

From the results, select the Act you need for your research.

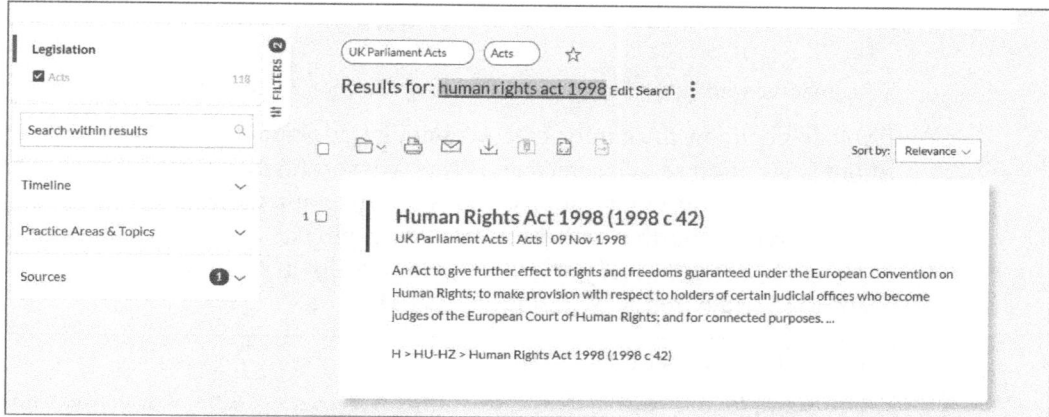

© Reproduced with kind permission of RELX (UK) Limited t/a LexisNexis

From the Act, you can use the Table of Contents to navigate to particular sections, and you will also see links to cases and commentary which are relevant to the legislation.

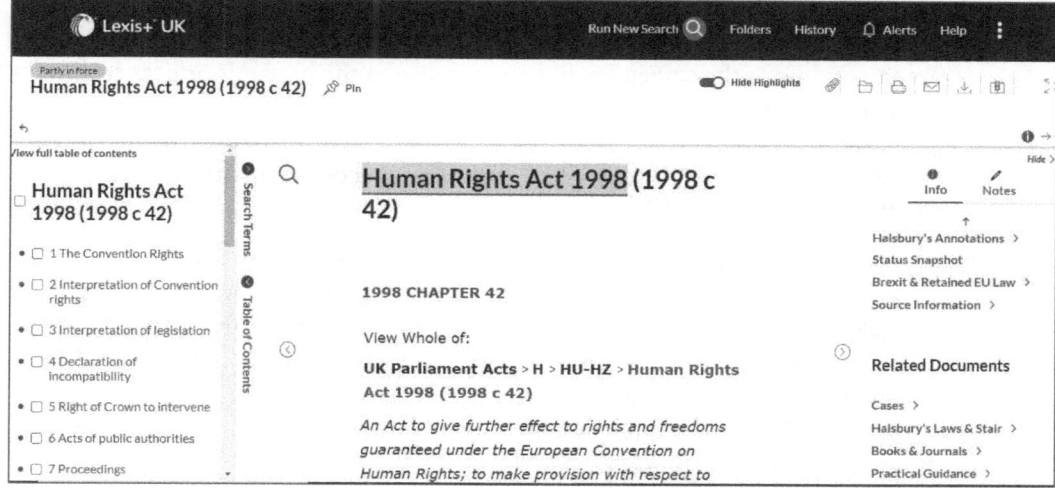

© Reproduced with kind permission of RELX (UK) Limited t/a LexisNexis

From the title section of the Act, you will see an icon in the top left corner which gives you the status of the Act, so in the screenshot for the Human Rights Act 1998 you can see that it shows as *Partly in Force*. This is because certain sections are in force but others are not. If, from the Table of Contents, you select a particular section, you will then see the same information but just about the particular section, so s 2 is showing as *In Force*, and if you scroll down from the text of the section to the *Notes*, you will see details of the date it originally came into force and also details of any amendments to the original text and when they were made.

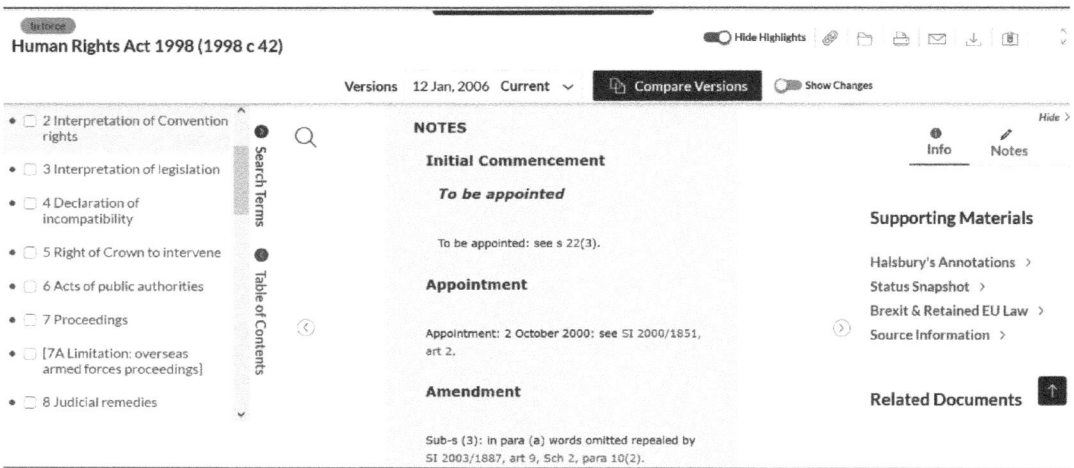

© Reproduced with kind permission of RELX (UK) Limited t/a LexisNexis

If you do not know the name of the Act but instead want to search for legislation on a topic, go to the Legislation search screen and enter keyword(s) in the box labelled *Terms*. Click the red *Search* button to retrieve a list of sections of legislation where these occur. If you enter two or more search terms they will be treated as a phrase, unless you link them using Boolean connectors (see **3.5.3**). If you get too many results, try sorting them by relevance or use the *search within results* option, entering another keyword.

> **PERSONAL INJURY CASE STUDY**
>
> For example, our road traffic case study involves a car whose driver was alleged to be on the telephone at the time of a collision. Searching *UK Parliament Acts* with the terms **"mobile telephone" and driving** retrieves s 26 of the Road Safety Act 2006, which creates an offence of driving while using a hand-held mobile phone.

From the list of search results, click on the appropriate heading to view the full text. Footnotes provide brief details about commencement and sources of amending legislation. Arrows in the middle of the screen enable you to move to the previous or next section of the legislation. The green in force button in the top left corner of the screen tells you that the section is currently in force. Click on the grey tab on the left to see a Table of Contents of the Act. The version currently in force will be showing; to access earlier versions, use the drop-down box above the text.

On the right of the screen, under *Supporting Materials*, you can also access information about commencement, repeals and amendments via links to *Is it in Force?* (see **6.4.1** above) and *Halsbury's Statutes Citator* (see **6.8.2** below). Note also the link to *Halsbury's Annotations*; this links to commentary drawn from *Halsbury's Statutes* (see **6.3.3.2**). The *Related Documents* section also allows you to link to commentary, cases or journal articles relating to the section on the screen. This added value content is one of the advantages of using subscription databases rather than legislation.gov.uk.

© Reproduced with kind permission of RELX (UK) Limited t/a LexisNexis

6.6.3 Statutory instruments

To find statutory instruments on *Lexis+ Legal Research*, from the home screen, under *Content*, select *Legislation* and then *Statutory Instruments*. If you know the year and number of the SI, you can just type these into the general search box.

© Reproduced with kind permission of RELX (UK) Limited t/a LexisNexis

If you do not know the SI number, you can type your search terms into the general search box, but you are likely to then get more results; remember to use the filters/relevance sorting to find what you need.

6.7 LEGISLATION ON WESTLAW

Westlaw is a good alternative to *Lexis+ Legal Research* for researching legislation.

On the home page, click *Legislation, Legislation Search*. The *Basic Search* screen allows you to search the text of UK Acts and SIs, as amended. It is possible to search either by *Title* and *Provision Number* or, to find material about a topic, by *Free Text*. Click on *More options* to see extra fields such as *Subject/Keyword*, *Jurisdiction*, and a *Statutory Definition* search option offers the facility to find definitions of a word or phrase within the text of different pieces of legislation.

© Reproduced with kind permission of Westlaw UK

Note that from the Legislation search screen, you have three tabs offering different search options. First, you have the option to search for primary and secondary legislation (ie Acts of Parliament and statutory instruments currently in force). The second tab allows you search for draft Bills currently before Parliament. Thirdly, you can search for policy and guidance material relating to legislation. This includes resources such as Codes of Practice, Consultations and HMRC Manuals which you may need to consider alongside relevant legislation.

As well as searching this content, you also have the ability to browse. This might be useful if your searches are not finding what you need. To browse, click on any of the headings under the *Legislation* tab.

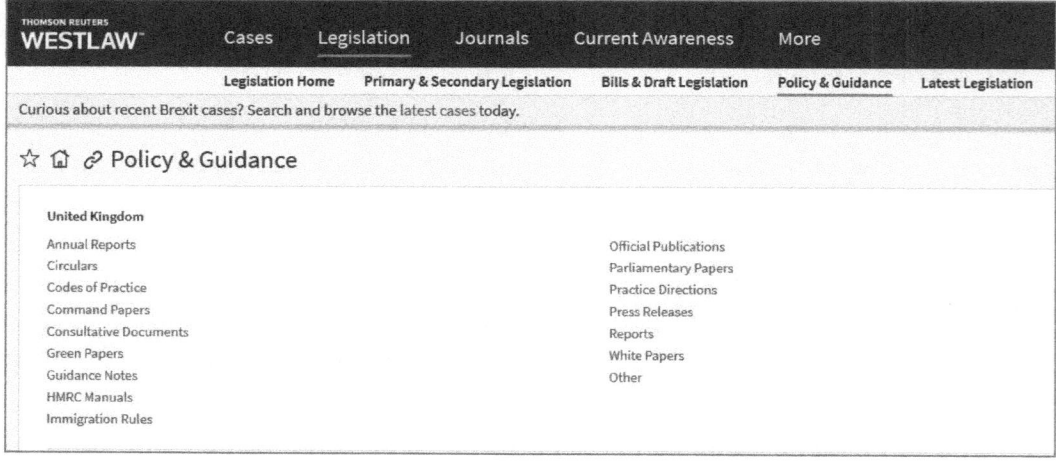

© Reproduced with kind permission of Westlaw UK

Then select the area you are interested in, and you can browse content arranged by year or title.

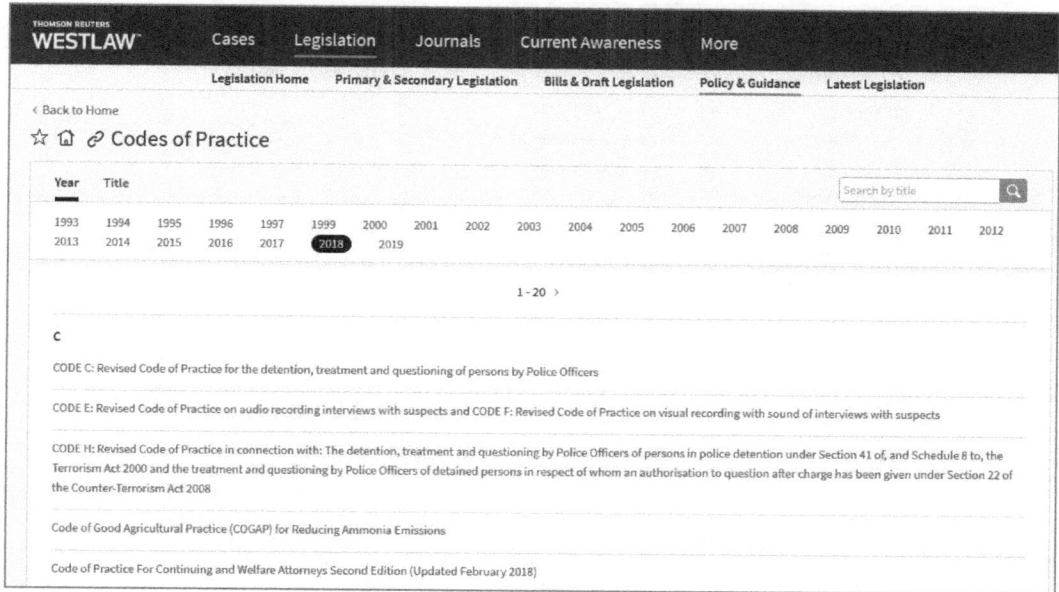

© Reproduced with kind permission of Westlaw UK

When you have found the legislation you are interested in either by browsing or searching, select it and you will be taken to a screen showing the arrangement of the Act (listing the individual parts, sections, Schedules etc). Note that each section will have a symbol alongside it which tells you the status of that section; hover over the symbol for an explanation.

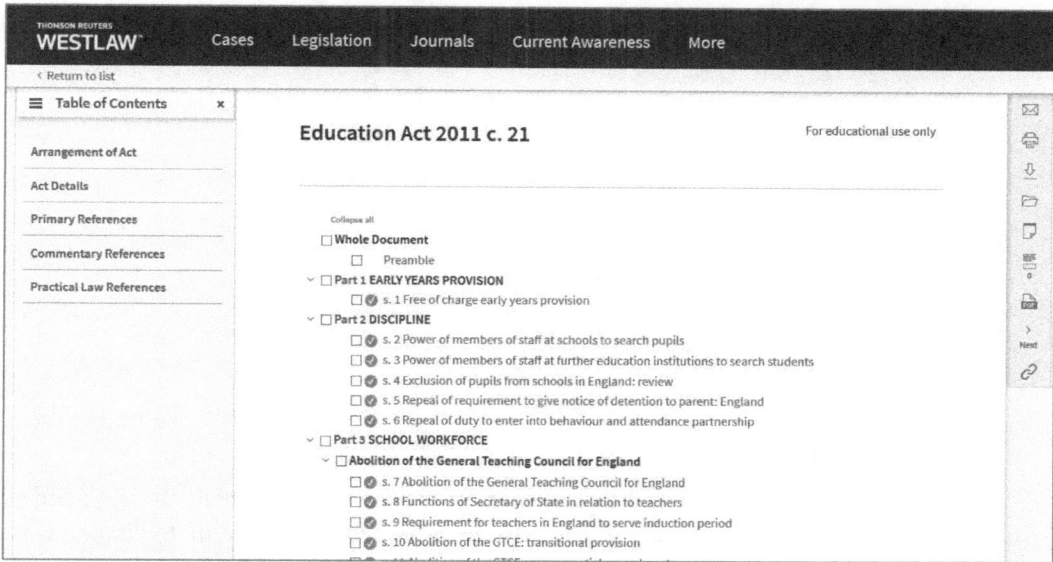

© Reproduced with kind permission of Westlaw UK

From the *Table of Contents* column, select *Act Details* for details of any changes which are planned, commencement information, details of any legislation which has already modified the Act, links to definitions of terms contained in the legislation and any statutory instruments which have been made under the Act.

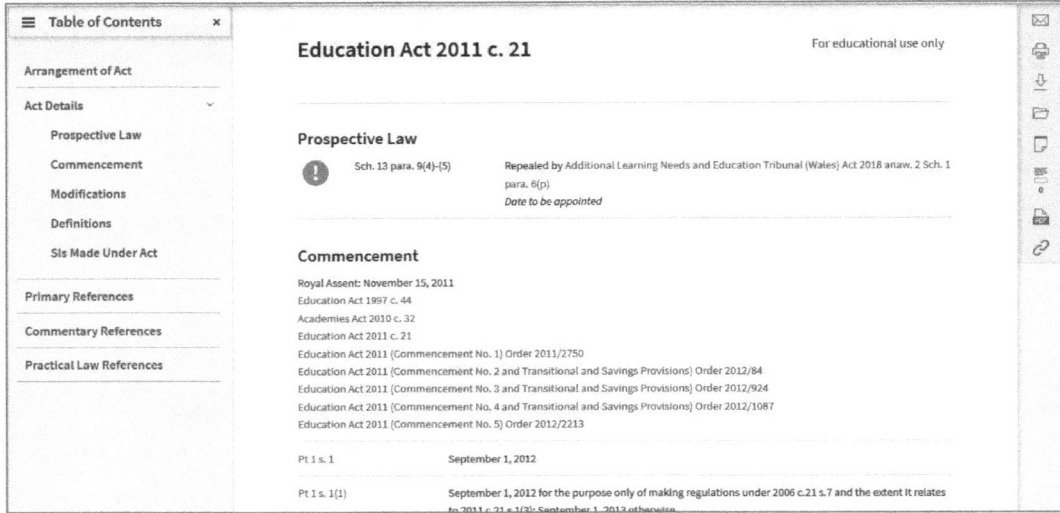

© Reproduced with kind permission of Westlaw UK

Select *Primary References* for details of any other legislation which mentions this Act. *Commentary References* will provide information on relevant journal articles and topic overviews available on *Westlaw*. These can be useful for putting the legislation into context. Finally, *Practical Law* references will link you to pertinent resources available on that database.

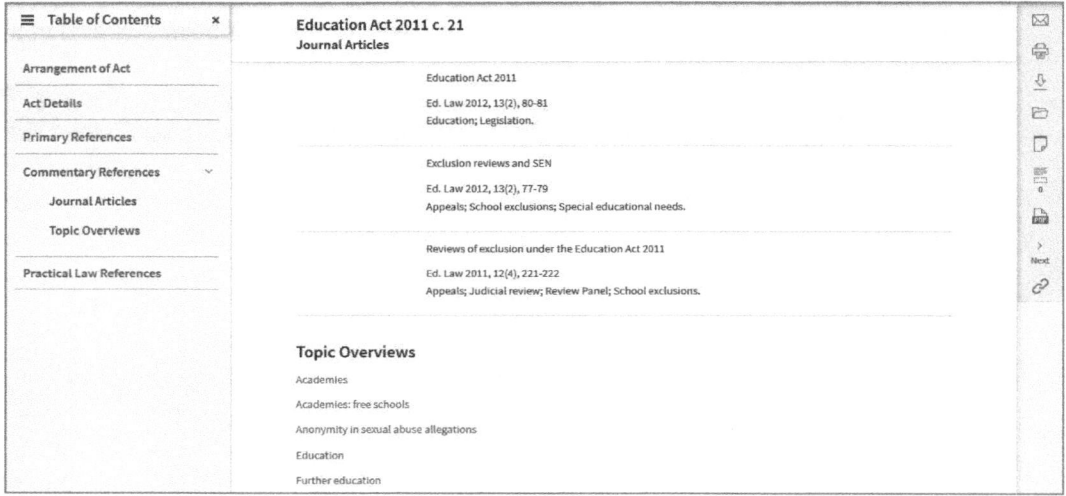

© Reproduced with kind permission of Westlaw UK

To look at a particular section, select it from the *Arrangement of Act* section, and you will see the text. The column on the right-hand side of the screen allows you to email, print, download or save the section. The arrows allow you to navigate through other sections of the Act. Again, you will see a status icon (such as a green tick) telling you that this provision is currently in force.

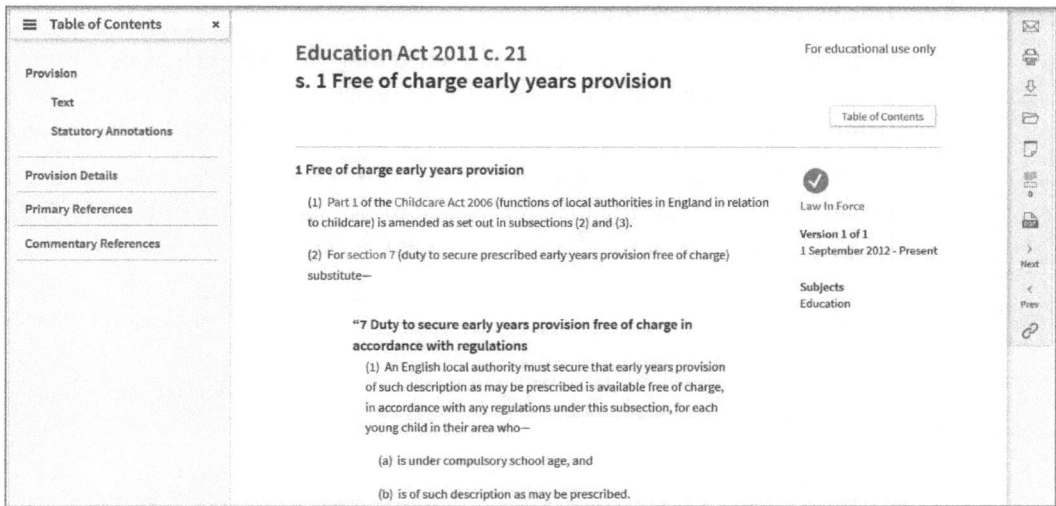

© Reproduced with kind permission of Westlaw UK

To see notes on each section, select *Statutory Annotations*, which provide additional context including from the explanatory notes and from Parliamentary scrutiny of the legislation. *Provision Details* will set out commencement dates for each subsection and give information on whether the section has been amended by later legislation. *Primary References* will contain links to any cases which have referred to this section. *Commentary References* will link to books or journal articles dealing with the provision.

6.8 HOW DO I UPDATE LEGISLATION?

It is vital to check for changes to the legal status of legislation that you use in the course of your research.

Legislative updates take two principal forms: later amending legislation, and statements of interpretation by judges in subsequent cases.

The issue of amending legislation is especially critical if the source you have consulted is a print title that publishes measures chronologically as enacted (for example, *Current Law Statutes*). You can rely on the consolidated versions in *Halsbury's Statutes* and *Halsbury's Statutory Instruments* in paper format being current to within a month or so, provided all the updating steps have been followed through properly.

6.8.1 Online resources

If you have access to legislation via a database such as *Lexis+ Legal Research* or *Westlaw*, use these in preference to print resources.

Legislation on *Westlaw* and *Lexis+ Legal Research* is generally updated daily, in the sense that the editors add new material every day. However, it does not follow that the content is current to today. Incorporating all the effects of new legislation is a complex and time-consuming task, and it makes it difficult for publishers of databases to state exactly how current the text of amended legislation can be relied upon to be. Within UK Parliament Acts on *Lexis+ Legal Research*, for example, the publisher states:

> Daily UPDATE INFORMATION Amendments made by new legislation are incorporated into the text of existing legislation. The NOTES segment at the end of each document indicates the changes that have been made to the text. A Stop Press icon on an enactment indicates that recently published amendments are pending, and provides a link to the amending enactment. The icon is removed once amendments are fully consolidated.

Again, this regular updating process is why you should prefer subscription databases to free resources if you have access to them.

6.8.2 Halsbury's Statutes Citator

Halsbury's Statutes Citator is a quick reference tool for tracing changes to Acts. This paperback volume is published twice yearly as part of *Halsbury's Statutes*. It will list amendments or repeals to individual sections or entire Acts. The arrangement is by year, then alphabetical by title.

The text of *Halsbury's Statutes Citator* appears on *Lexis+ Legal Research* as a free-standing source, which you can access from the home page via *My Sources, View All Sources, H*, then either search for or Browse for the title of the Act you want to check.

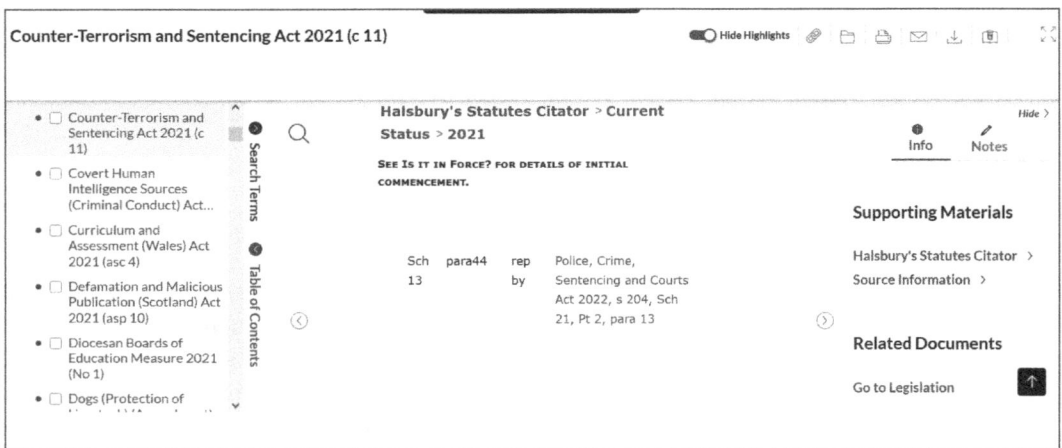

© Reproduced with kind permission of RELX (UK) Limited t/a LexisNexis

Or you can access it via the legislation itself (see **6.6.2** above). Remember that if you need further guidance on using the legal databases, they do have support available: in *Lexis+* this is available via the *Help* link in the top right hand corner of the home page, and in *Westlaw* via the *Product support* link at the bottom of the home page. Whilst you are studying, you can also take advantage of workshops and training arranged via your Library service. The time you spend on attending these will save you time during the rest of your studies and your career.

CHAPTER 7

RESEARCHING EUROPEAN UNION LAW

7.1	Introduction	97
7.2	General sources	98
7.3	Primary legislation	99
7.4	Secondary legislation	100
7.5	Case law	103

> **LEARNING OUTCOMES**
>
> After reading this chapter you will be able to:
> - identify which resources to use to research European Union (EU) law
> - find EU legislation on the *Europa* and *EUR-Lex* websites
> - explain how to check if an EU directive has been implemented in the UK
> - understand which sources to use to find EU case law.

7.1 INTRODUCTION

Following the result of the referendum on the UK's membership of the European Union (EU) on 23 June 2016 and the subsequent withdrawal from the EU, you might think there is no longer a need for your research to include reference to EU law. However, this is not entirely the case. There is a good explanation of how EU legislation impacts upon UK law both before and after the UK's exit from the EU at www.legislation.gov.uk/eu-legislation-and-uk-law:

> The Withdrawal Agreement between the UK and the EU set out the arrangements for the UK's withdrawal from the EU at 11.00 p.m. on 31 January 2020 ("exit day"). The withdrawal included a 'transition' or 'implementation' period, during which EU law continued to apply in the UK. The implementation period, which had effect in UK law by section 1 of the European Union (Withdrawal Agreement) Act 2020 (c. 1), expired at 11.00 p.m. on 31 December 2020 ("IP completion day"), by section 39 of the same Act.
>
> EU legislation which applied directly or indirectly to the UK before 11.00 p.m. on 31 December 2020 was retained in UK law as a novel form of domestic legislation known as 'retained EU legislation'. This is set out in sections 2 and 3 of the European Union (Withdrawal) Act 2018 (c. 16). Section 4 of the 2018 Act ensures that any remaining EU rights and obligations, including directly effective rights within EU treaties, continue to be recognised and available in domestic law after exit. After the end of 2023, 'retained EU law' became known as 'assimilated law', by section 5 of the Retained EU Law (Revocation and Reform) Act 2023 (c. 28).
>
> The European Union (Future Relationship) Act 2020 (c. 29) implements the arrangements for the relationship between the UK and the EU after the implementation period, as agreed on 24 December 2020. These arrangements include the Trade and Cooperation Agreement, the Agreement on Nuclear Cooperation and the Agreement on Security Procedures for Exchanging and Protecting Classified Information. The Act provides for the application of these, and any supplementary, agreements in domestic law. It also provides for the interpretation of domestic laws in light of these agreements.

Also, as the UK will continue to have close links with Member States of the EU, it is the case that EU law and its application will remain relevant for many years to come. Therefore, any researcher will still need to consider the potential impact of EU law on the area being considered, even if these considerations conclude that the area is now wholly covered by domestic legislation. If you do still need to research the law of the European Union (EU) then the following paragraphs will offer some guidance on using key resources to do so.

The *Official Journal of the European Union (OJ)* is the official publication of record for the EU. EU legislation only becomes legally binding in EU States once it has been published in the *Official Journal*. It consists of two main series: L (legislation) and C (information and notices). From 1 July 2013, the electronic version of the OJ is authentic (has legal force) – see Regulation (EU) No 216/2013. Generally, the paper version no longer has any legal value (https://eur-lex.europa.eu/oj/all/auth-direct-access.html).

The European Union itself also publishes a vast amount of information, including primary legal materials, freely on the Internet. The major sites are *Europa* (https://european-union.europa.eu/index_en) and *EUR-Lex* (https://eur-lex.europa.eu/homepage.html). There is a help section which includes tutorials on using *EUR-Lex* (https://eur-lex.europa.eu/content/e-learning/index.html), or try using *Google* for searching instead (see www.google.co.uk): type keyword(s) into the search box as usual, followed by 'site:europa.eu'. Alternatively, if you have access to a subscription database such as *Westlaw* or *Lexis+ Legal Research*, you may find it easier to use it if you need to find EU information.

If you have access to the *Practical Law* database, there is a comprehensive section dealing with all aspects of Brexit, which contains an extremely useful guide on researching EU law. From the home page, select *Beyond Brexit: the legal implications*, then scroll down to the section *Guides for navigating Brexit legislation*, and there you will find a link to a guide to assist research into post-Brexit divergence between UK law and EU law which provides information on how to identify the relevant law on *Westlaw* and other databases.

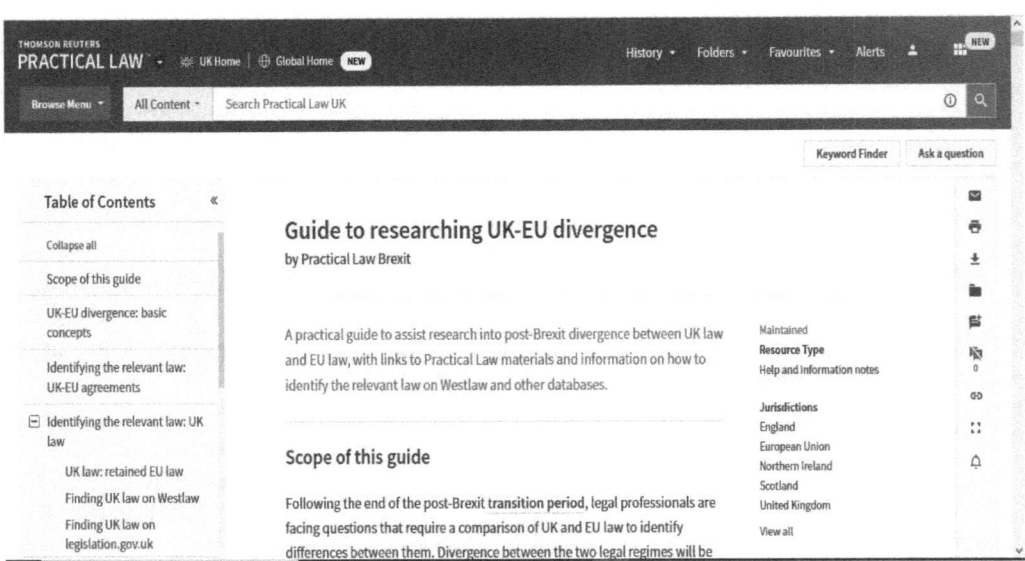

© Thomson Reuters

7.2 GENERAL SOURCES

7.2.1 EUR-Lex

If you are regularly carrying our research in areas which are still impacted by EU law, you will also need to familiarise yourself with *EUR-Lex*, which is the legal portal within the *Europa* website. It offers free access to EU law, including the *Official Journal of the European Union* L-series

(Legislation) and C-series (Information and Notices), treaties, legislation, international agreements, preparatory acts and parliamentary questions. Case-law coverage includes judgments of the Court of Justice and the General Court of the European Union. Also available are the Commission documents (the 'COM' series), a collection of consolidated legislation, and the texts of treaties. There are links to summaries of EU legislation – short, easy-to-understand explanations of the main legal acts passed by the EU.

We will now look at how to search for content (legislation and cases) on *EUR-Lex*. There are two options for searching from the home page. First, *Quick* search available from the home page gives you the ability to search across the entire database, but this option is likely to yield a large number of results, so you may not find this option particularly useful.

The second option, which you may find more useful, is to select the *Advanced Search* option.

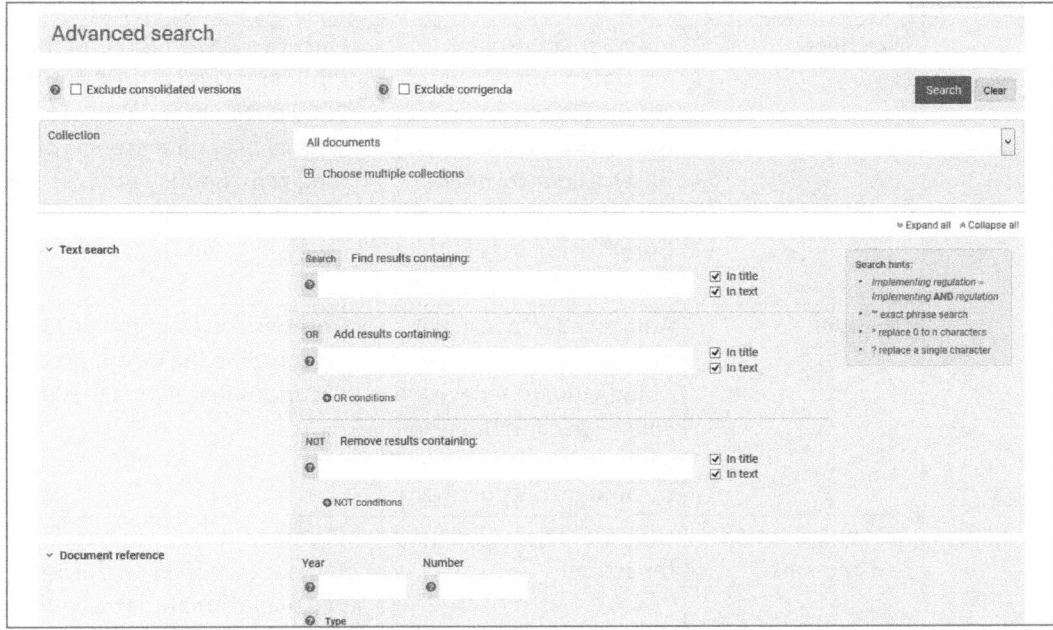

© European Union

This allows you to carry out a more focused free text search. You can limit your search to a particular collection on the database (eg, *EU case law*), search for words that only appear in the title of a document, select a date range, etc.

You can also use the option to search by *Document reference*. Select the document type (eg *Regulation, Directive* or *EU Court Case*), enter the year and number, and click *Search*. If you know the year and number of the legislation or case you are looking for, using this search option is the easiest way to find it.

7.3 PRIMARY LEGISLATION

The primary legislation of the EU comprises the founding treaties that established the three European Communities, along with later amending treaties. These documents lay out the aspirations and objectives of the Union. The accession treaties that admit new Member States also fall under the heading of primary legislation.

The official text of the treaties may be freely accessed via *EUR-Lex* (see https://eur-lex.europa.eu/collection/eu-law/treaties/treaties-force.html). Various paper sources also reprint the treaties, including the annual textbook, *Blackstone's EU Treaties and Legislation*.

7.4 SECONDARY LEGISLATION

7.4.1 Introduction

The secondary legislation of the EU sets out how the objectives expressed in the treaties are to be accomplished. Various categories of provision fall under this heading:

Category	Description	Example, as published in the *Official Journal*
Regulations	Directly applicable to Member States: no need for national legislation. They are binding in their entirety on all EU countries	Commission Regulation (EC) No 2/2009 of 5 January 2009 establishing the standard import values for determining the entry price of certain fruit and vegetables
Directives	Member States must legislate to implement within a fixed period (generally within 2 years). When a country does not transpose a directive, the Commission may initiate infringement proceedings	Directive 2008/122/EC of the European Parliament and of the Council of 14 January 2009 on the protection of consumers in respect of certain aspects of timeshare, long-term holiday product, resale and exchange contracts
Decisions	Addressed to particular Member States, companies or individuals. A decision which specifies those to whom it is addressed shall be binding only on them	Commission Decision of 23 January 2009 establishing the Committee of European Securities Regulators (2009/78/EC)
Recommendations and opinions	Non-binding suggestions for action	Commission Recommendation of 11 February 2009 on the implementation of a nuclear material accountancy and control system by operators of nuclear installations

In practice, you will mainly encounter regulations and directives. From 1 January 2015 the numbering of EU legislation changed. Previously, a regulation was cited by running number then year (ie, Regulation 1/99 was the first regulation of 1999); a directive was cited by year then running number (ie, Directive 99/1 was the first directive of 1999). The new method aims to harmonise and simplify the numbering system so the type of provision is always followed by the year and sequential number. For example, Regulation (EU) 2015/1, Directive (EU) 2015/2, Council Decision (EU) 2015/3. For more information, see https://eur-lex.europa.eu/content/tools/elaw/OA0614022END.pdf.

7.4.2 Sources of EU secondary legislation

7.4.2.1 EUR-Lex

EUR-Lex provides access to secondary legislation.

If you know the year and number of the Regulation, Directive or Decision, you can use the search *By document reference* option from the advanced search page.

Alternatively, from the *EU law* section on the home page, select *Legal Acts* and search from there.

© European Union

Or you can browse the *Directory of legal acts* to see all legislation on a particular subject, such as *Freedom of movement for workers*. The *Recently published* (legislation from the last 14 days) option is likely to be less useful.

The official text of all EU legislation is the text printed in the *Official Journal*. As with UK legislation, this is subject to amendment and repeal over time. A project to consolidate the vast body of EU legislation for free publication on the Internet is ongoing. To access this material, go to the *EUR-Lex* home page and select *Consolidated texts* from the *EU law* section.

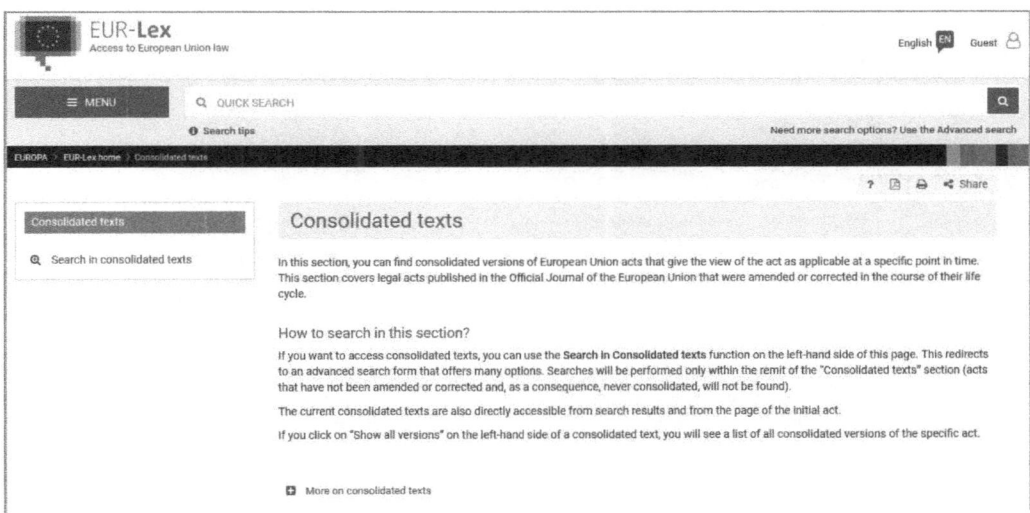

© European Union

If you need to carry out research into planned EU law (not currently in force), from the *EU law* section of the *EUR-Lex* home page you can link to *Preparatory documents* (used to prepare EU legislation).

7.4.2.2 Blackstone's EU Treaties and Legislation

If you want a print alternative, the annual text *Blackstone's EU Treaties and Legislation*, edited by Foster, reprints a convenient selection of the most useful and frequently consulted secondary legislation.

7.4.3 How to check if EU legislation is in force

As with UK legislation, European Union secondary legislation is subject to later amendments and repeals. Besides the collection of legislation in force on *EUR-Lex*, there are several ways of tracing the current status of a given provision.

The most straightforward option is to select the Advanced search option from the home page (https://eur-lex.europa.eu/homepage.html), select *Legal acts* as the collection to search and tick the box at the top of the screen to limit to legislation in force.

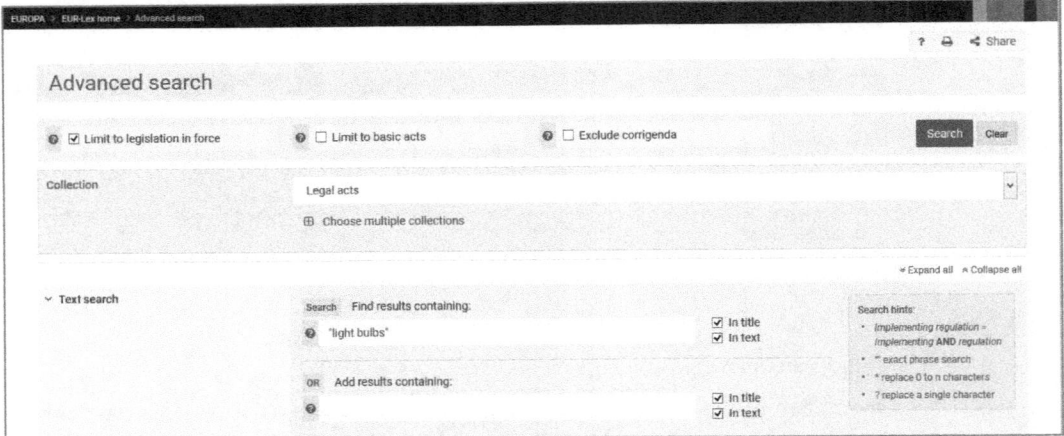

© European Union

Another option is to browse the Directory of European Union Legislation by subject (https://eur-lex.europa.eu/browse/directories/legislation.html).

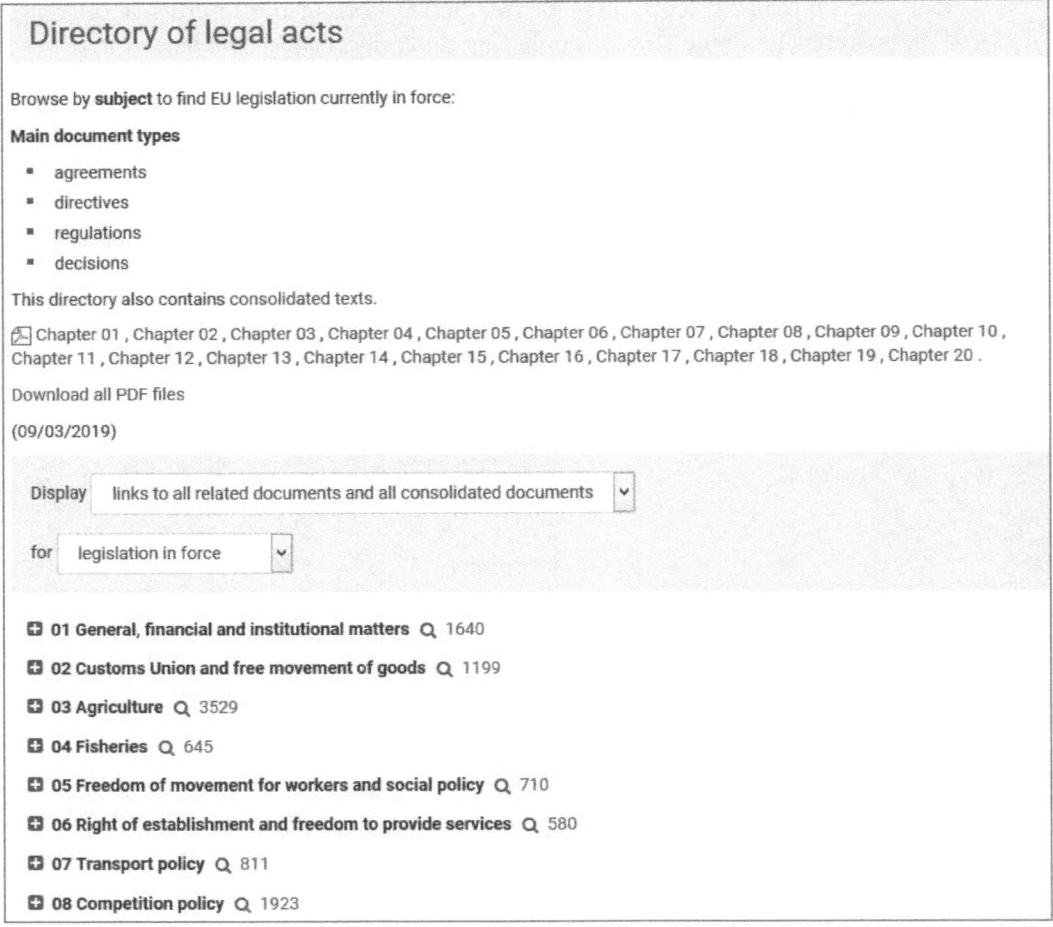

© European Union

However, be aware that browsing until you find what you need can be time-consuming.

If you are unsure whether a piece of EU legislation is in force, check whether the proposal has been adopted and published in the *Official Journal*. EU legislation does not have legal force until it has been published in the *Official Journal*.

7.5 CASE LAW

7.5.1 Introduction

European Union cases are heard before either the Court of Justice or the General Court. Before implementation of the Lisbon Treaty on 1 December 2009, these were known as the European Court of Justice and the Court of First Instance respectively.

The term 'Court of Justice of the European Union' refers collectively to the Court of Justice, the General Court and any specialist Judicial Panels created (such as the EU Civil Service Panel).

The UK practitioner will be unaccustomed to certain aspects of the procedure of EU courts:

(a) Judgments are preceded by an 'opinion' of the Advocate General; this is not necessarily binding on the court, but its reasoning is usually followed.

(b) Applications to the court that concern the same area of law may be joined together.

(c) The names of parties are often very long; some leading cases are therefore referred to by nicknames, which may or may not appear in electronic databases or indexes to paper sources.

(d) The court delivers one judgment only; there are no dissenting opinions.

Be careful to differentiate EU case law from the case law of the European Court of Human Rights (https://www.echr.coe.int/en/knowledge-sharing#). This court belongs to a separate institution altogether, the Council of Europe. It hears complaints concerning alleged violations by Nation States of the European Convention on Human Rights.

7.5.2 Citation

The case number is an important feature of citations for EU cases. A full citation gives the case number first, followed by the parties, then the citation of the authoritative report in the paper version of the *European Court Reports*. For example:

C-295/95 *Farrell v Long* [1997] ECR I-1683

The case number comprises a running serial number followed by the year of application or reference to the Court (note that application and judgment may be separated by several years). Since the creation of the Court of First Instance in 1989, all cases are prefixed by 'C-' (Court of Justice, or '*Cour*' in French) or 'T-' (General Court, or '*Tribunal*' in French).

7.5.3 Sources of EU cases

All judgments of the Court of Justice and the General Court are freely available on the *Curia* website within *Europa* (https://curia.europa.eu/). Click *En* to access information in English, then you can search from the home page using the *Search for a case* section if you know the case number or names of the parties, or select the *advanced search* option to use a more detailed search form.

The advanced search form permits free text searching (*Text*) or searching by the provisions of national law referred to. It also allows you to confine your search to material classed under one of 50 or so broad subject headings, via the *Subject-matter* drop-down menu.

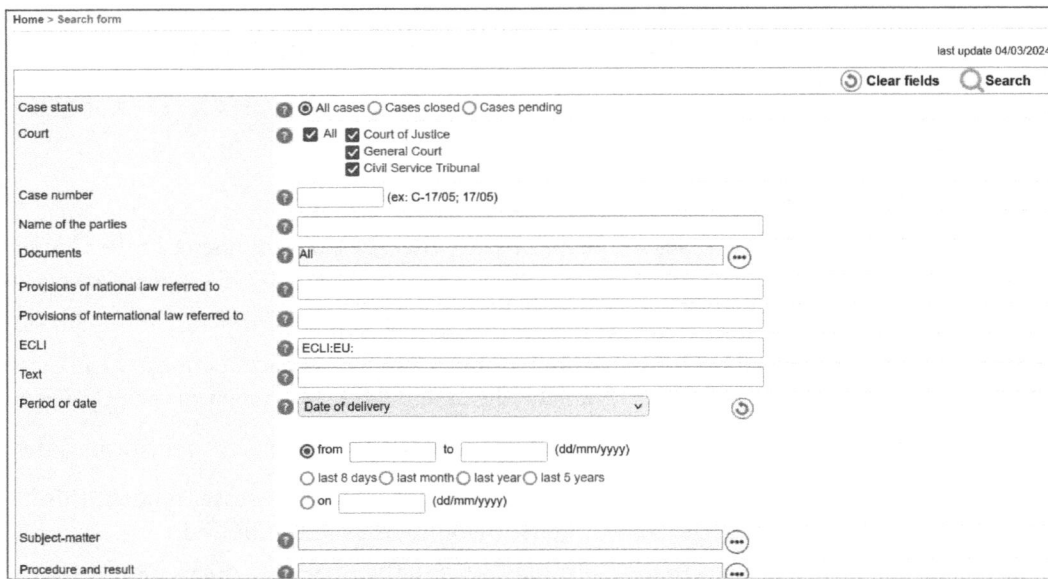

© European Union

After some delay, judgments are translated into all EU languages and then published in the *European Court Reports*.

The paper version of the *European Court Reports* is the authoritative source for EU case law. Electronic versions are available via EUR-Lex. From the home page, select *Case law*. If you know the year and number of the case, search using these details. Alternatively, if you do not know these, use the *Search in case law* link or browse the *Directory of case law* to find cases on the subject.

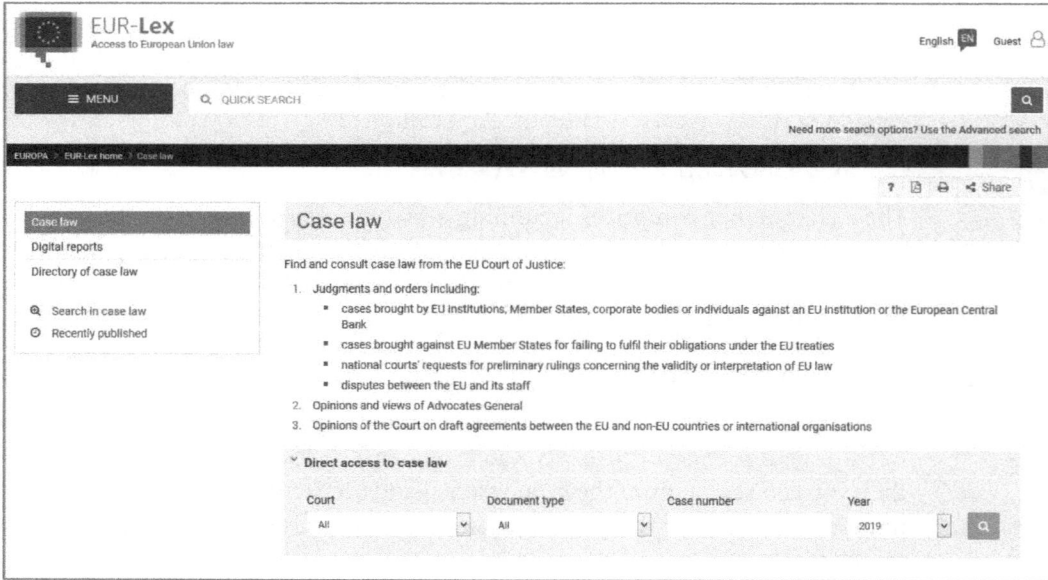

© European Union

Alternatively, from the EUR-Lex home page, select the *Advanced search* option, choose *Case law* as the collection and fill in the search form with what details you have (date, court, subject or party names should be typed in the *text search* boxes).

Researching European Union Law 105

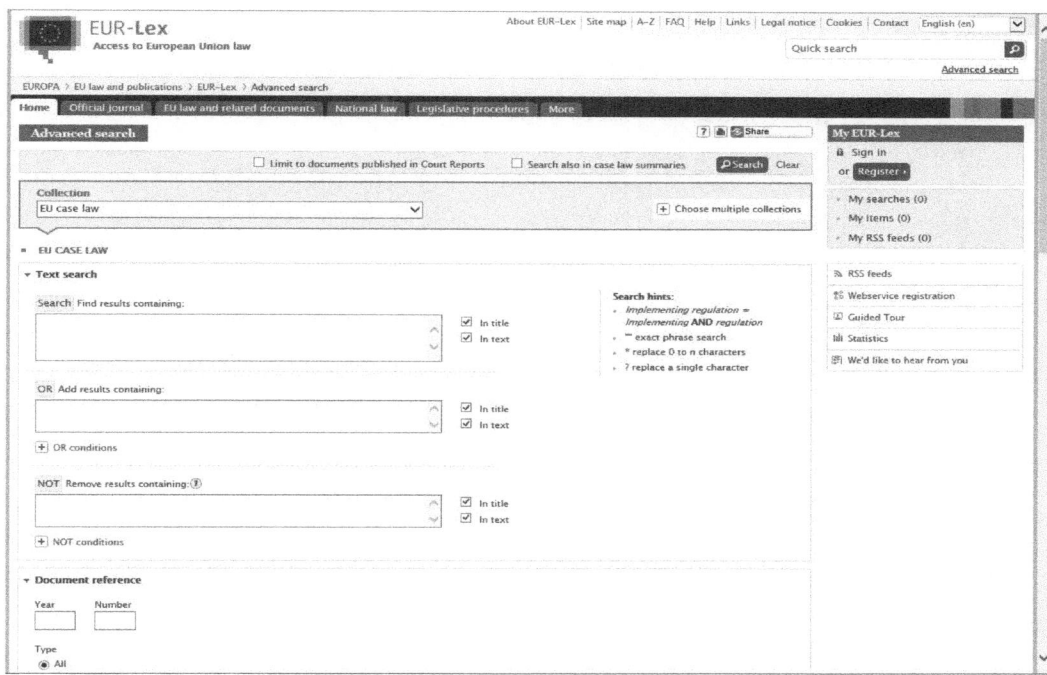

© European Union

Westlaw and *Lexis+ Legal Research* also feature the full text of the *European Court Reports*, and you may find the search engines on these databases easier to use than the *Curia* or *EUR-Lex* websites. From the *Lexis+ Legal Research* home page, select *My Sources*, then *View All Sources*, E, select *EU cases* and then search for your case. From the *Westlaw* home page, click *EU*, tick *filter by Cases* and fill in the search form.

The *Common Market Law Reports* is a more timely (but unofficial) alternative to the *European Court Reports*. All significant EU cases are included, as well as selected decisions of Member State national courts. The full text is available via *Westlaw*. To access them from the *Westlaw* home page, select *Cases* tab, then click *Law reports*, C, scroll down and select *Common Market Law Reports* and you will then be able to search.

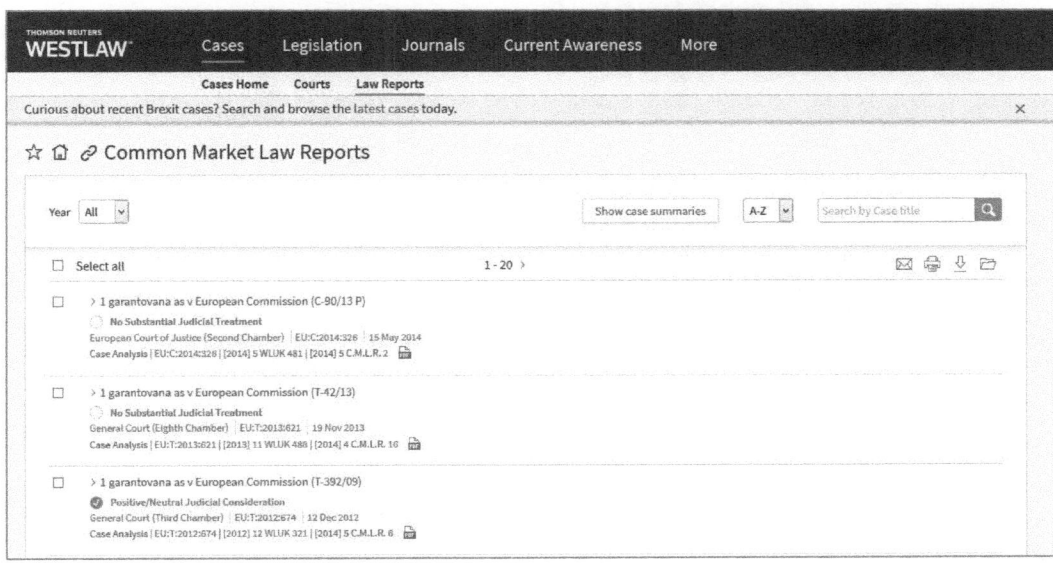

© Reproduced with kind permission of Westlaw UK

CHAPTER 8

RESEARCHING FORMS AND PRECEDENTS

8.1	Introduction	107
8.2	*Atkin's Court Forms*	109
8.3	*Encyclopaedia of Forms and Precedents*	110

> **LEARNING OUTCOMES**
>
> After reading this chapter you will be able to:
> - explain how forms and precedents are used in practice
> - understand how to use *Atkin's Court Forms* and the *Encyclopaedia of Forms and Precedents* in printed and online versions.

8.1 INTRODUCTION

Collections of forms and precedents provide specimens of the documents which lawyers need to draft. They can save much time and effort by avoiding reinventing the wheel, although as we have already learned, they should not be used uncritically (see **1.3.4** above).

Many firms hold their own bank of know-how and precedents for future use in similar transactions. These will often be accessible via the firm's intranet or knowledge management system.

A variety of commercial publications also reproduce versions of prescribed or common documents. Some are limited in scope and aim to assist the specialist practitioner, such as M Waterworth, *Parker's Will Precedents* (10th edn, 2020). Others are more general in scope, such as J Kelly, *Kelly's Legal Precedents* (21st edn, 2014) which gathers into one book the most frequently needed precedents in general practice (and is also available online via *Kelly's Legal Precedents* on *Lexis+ Legal Research*).

Two complementary publications give comprehensive coverage: *Atkin's Court Forms* and the *Encyclopaedia of Forms and Precedents*. Both of these substantial encyclopedias are published by LexisNexis and are available online via *Lexis+ Legal Research*.

In recent years, a variety of online publishers have developed clusters of precedents and other know-how that may be accessed upon payment of a subscription. *Practical Law* is prominent in this field, with know-how services across a wide variety of practice areas. Each service combines a bank of standard documents with commentary and analysis, email updates, and practice notes and checklists. From the *Practical Law* home page, select a practice area, eg Employment, then select a subject, eg unfair dismissal, then choose Standard Documents and Clauses to access a list of precedents in that area.

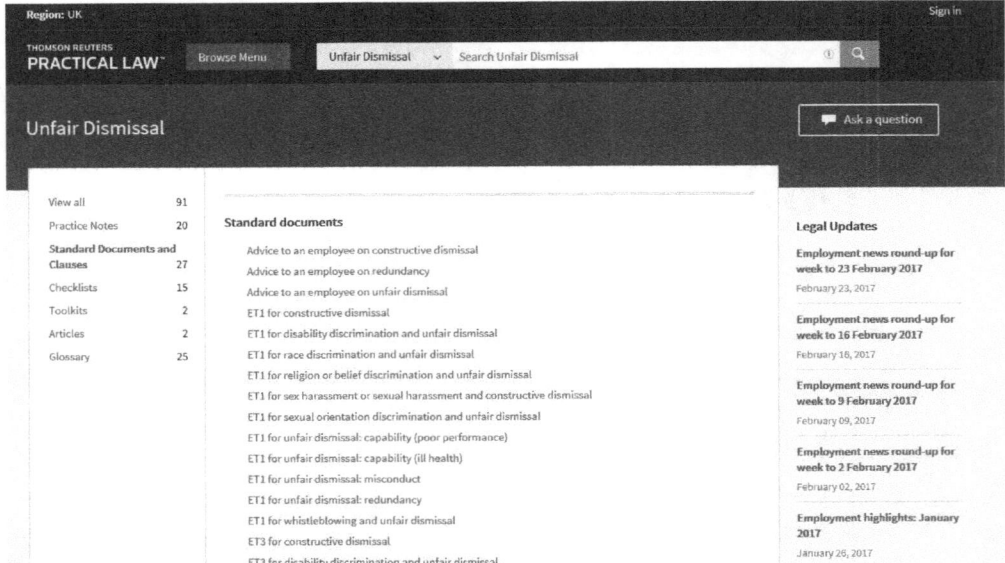

© Thomson Reuters

LexisNexis has also developed another database, *Lexis+ Practical Guidance*. This is intended to be a more pratice-based service, and in each practice area you can access a wide range of useful precedents for legal transactions and procedures. To access these, select the Practice Area tab.

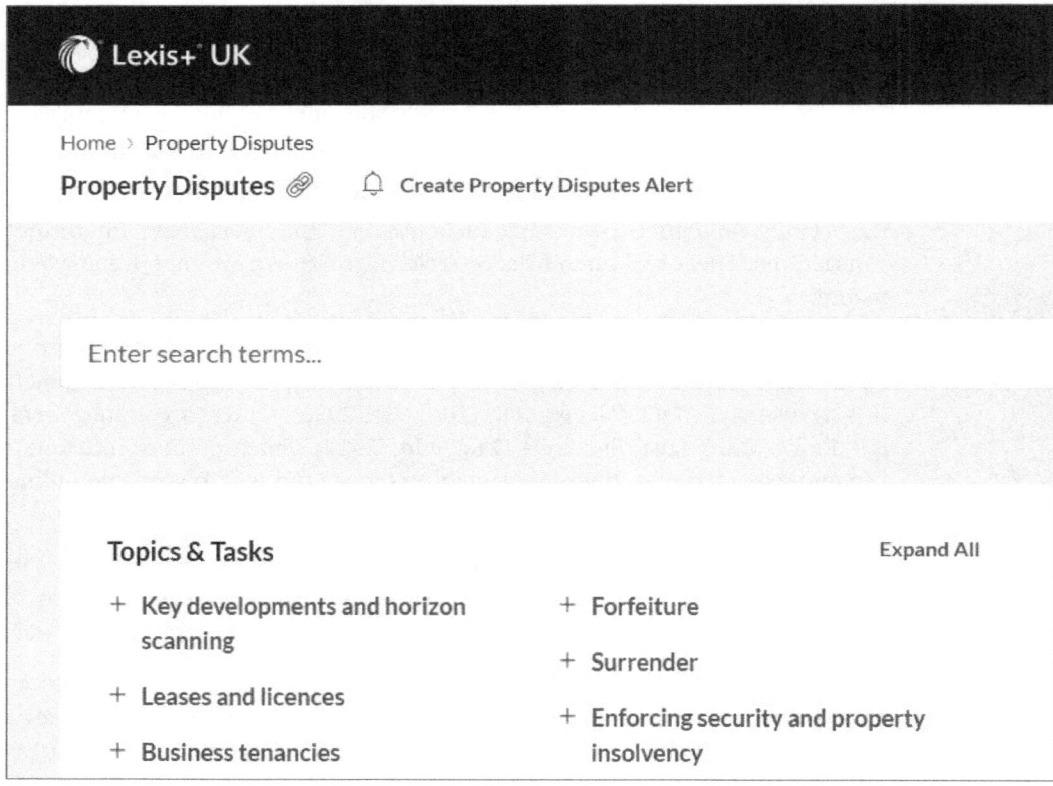

© Reproduced with kind permission of RELX (UK) Limited t/a LexisNexis

Then click on the subject you are interested in under *Topics & Tasks* and then scroll down to find any relevant forms and precedents.

Overview	View All (1)	Practice Notes	View All (12)
Licences, tenancies at will and periodic tenancies for property disputes lawyers—overview		Enforcing a judgment or order for possession of land	
		Property Disputes—new starter guide	
		CPR 55 procedure in relation to commercial property	
		Service occupancy or tenancy?	
		CPR 55 procedure in relation to residential common law tenancies	
Precedents	View All (13)	**Forms**	View All (3)
Vacant possession strategy—schedule		Request for warrant for possession of land (form N325)	
Tenancy at will		Request for warrant of possession of land following a suspended order for possession	
Cover letter to serve second notice without prejudice to the validity of a first notice to determine lease under break option		Claim form for possession of property (form N5)	

© Reproduced with kind permission of RELX (UK) Limited t/a LexisNexis

8.2 ATKIN'S COURT FORMS

Atkin's Court Forms is a comprehensive encyclopedia of forms, precedents and procedural advice connected with civil litigation. It reproduces the main documents required to transact civil proceedings before the courts and judicial tribunals of England and Wales. Arrangement is broadly by subject, or 'title', with each group of forms introduced by commentary on the relevant substantive and procedural law, including step-by-step guidance and checklists. Footnotes refer to useful related information, such as practice directions, case law, legislation and court rules. The value added by commentary and footnotes should not be underestimated: this is more than merely a compendium of forms.

8.2.1 Using the online version of Atkin's Court Forms

To research the online version within *Lexis+ Legal Research*, follow these steps:

- from the home page, under *Content*, click the *Forms and Precedents* link;
- then click *Precedents* and select *Atkin's Court Forms*;
- from here you can carry out a general search across the entire source, or you can select particular volumes and just search those;
- or you can select the *Advanced Search* option to search for forms by title or number.

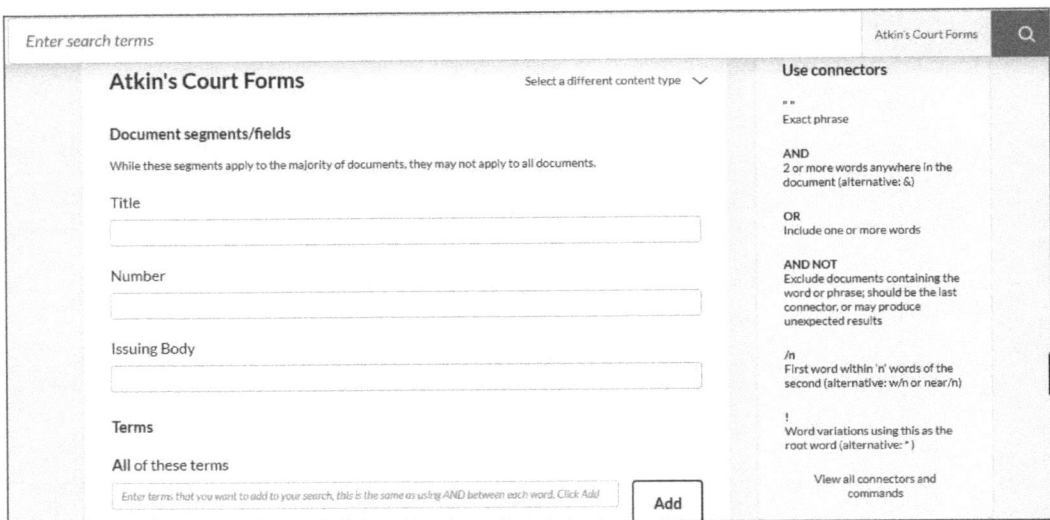

© Reproduced with kind permission of RELX (UK) Limited t/a LexisNexis

Note that it is also possible to search across all forms and precedents content available on *Lexis+ Legal Research*, including but not limited to *Atkin's*. To do so, from the home page, from *Content*, click *Forms and Precedents* and then use the general *Search* option or select *Advanced Search* to provide further search fields.

8.2.2 Using the printed version of Atkin's Court Forms

If you have access and wish to use the printed version of *Atkin's Court Forms*, follow these steps:

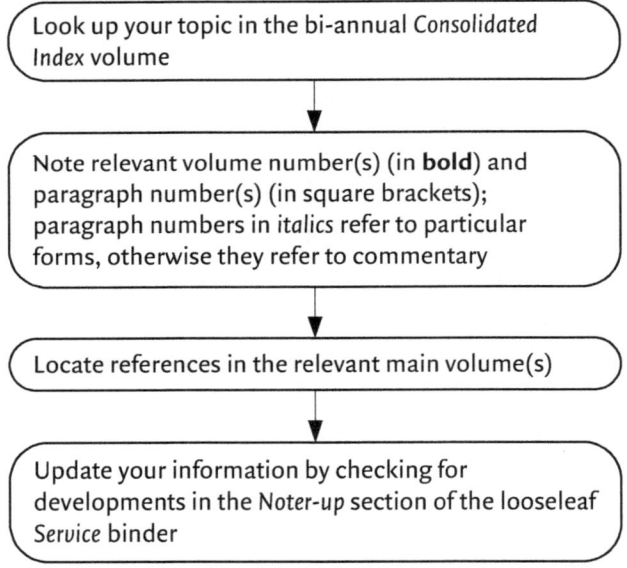

Note that the Civil Procedure Rules and the Family Procedure Rules each have their own separate volume.

8.3 ENCYCLOPAEDIA OF FORMS AND PRECEDENTS

The *Encyclopaedia of Forms and Precedents* (or EFP) is a comprehensive source of precedents for non-contentious civil transactions. It contains around 15,000 complete precedents (including those for sale of land, commercial law, family, wills and trusts). Arrangement is broadly by subject, or 'title', with each group of documents introduced by useful commentary on the relevant law and practice. In addition, annotations to the precedents offer practical drafting guidance and references to other helpful information, such as cases and legislation. As with

Atkin's Court Forms, the value contained in the commentary and footnotes should not be overlooked.

8.3.1 Using the online version of EFP

The online version of *EFP* has two parts, either of which may be searched separately. One component is the full text of the encyclopedia itself. The other is an index that merges the subject approach of the printed *Consolidated Index*, and the *Form Finder* (for locating a specific known precedent). Note that many indivdual forms can be filled in on-screen. A piece of software called 'Hotdocs' may need to be installed in order to edit these documents.

The online version is available via *Lexis+ Legal Research*. It is accessible from *Content, Forms and Precedents*, then *Precedents*, and also via *My Sources* links.

It is usually best to start searching with the *Index* component. This links easily to the full text of documents and is likely to pin down the material you need in the least amount of time. Follow these steps:

- click the *My Sources* tab;
- click *View All Sources*;
- click E in the alphabetical list that appears;
- click on *Encyclopaedia of Forms and Precedents Index*;
- enter *Search terms* where indicated, eg "paternity pay";
- from the results list, you can use filters;
- if you get a large number of results, you can also select the sort by relevance option;
- click any volume and paragraph reference to access the full text of the appropriate precedent.

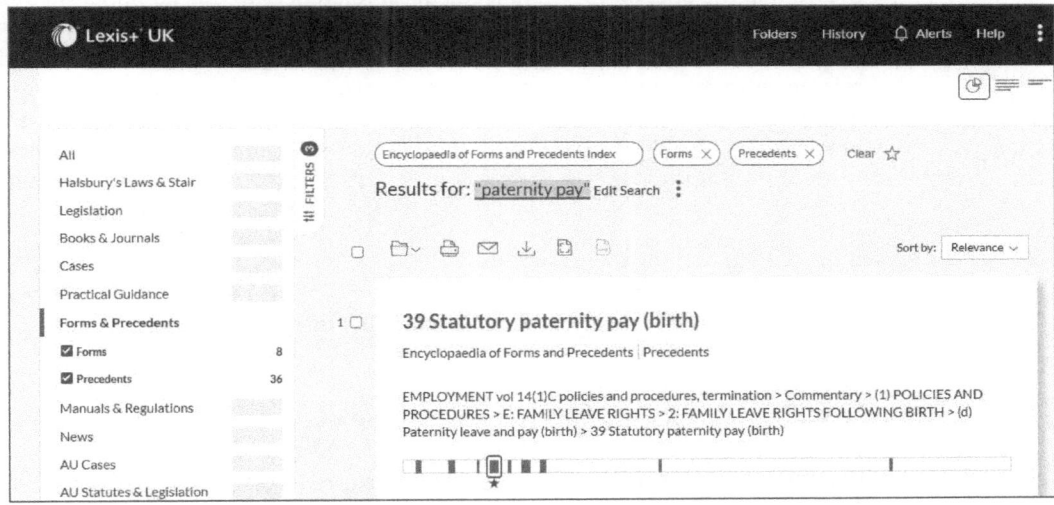

© Reproduced with kind permission of RELX (UK) Limited t/a LexisNexis

As previously mentioned in relation to *Atkin's*, note that it is also possible to search across all forms and precedents content available on *Lexis+ Legal Research*, including but not limited to the *Encyclopaedia of Forms and Precedents*. As a reminder, access this wide pool of material by clicking the *Content* tab, then select *Forms & Precedents*. You can then carry out a general or advanced search across all content, or you can select just to search *Clauses*, *Forms* or *Precedents* (so if you know you are looking for a particular form, select the *Forms* option). Finally, you can search for content on a particular practice area or subject, eg *Pensions*, and then you can add a search term to find relevant forms or precedents.

© Reproduced with kind permission of RELX (UK) Limited t/a LexisNexis

8.3.2 Using the printed version of EEP

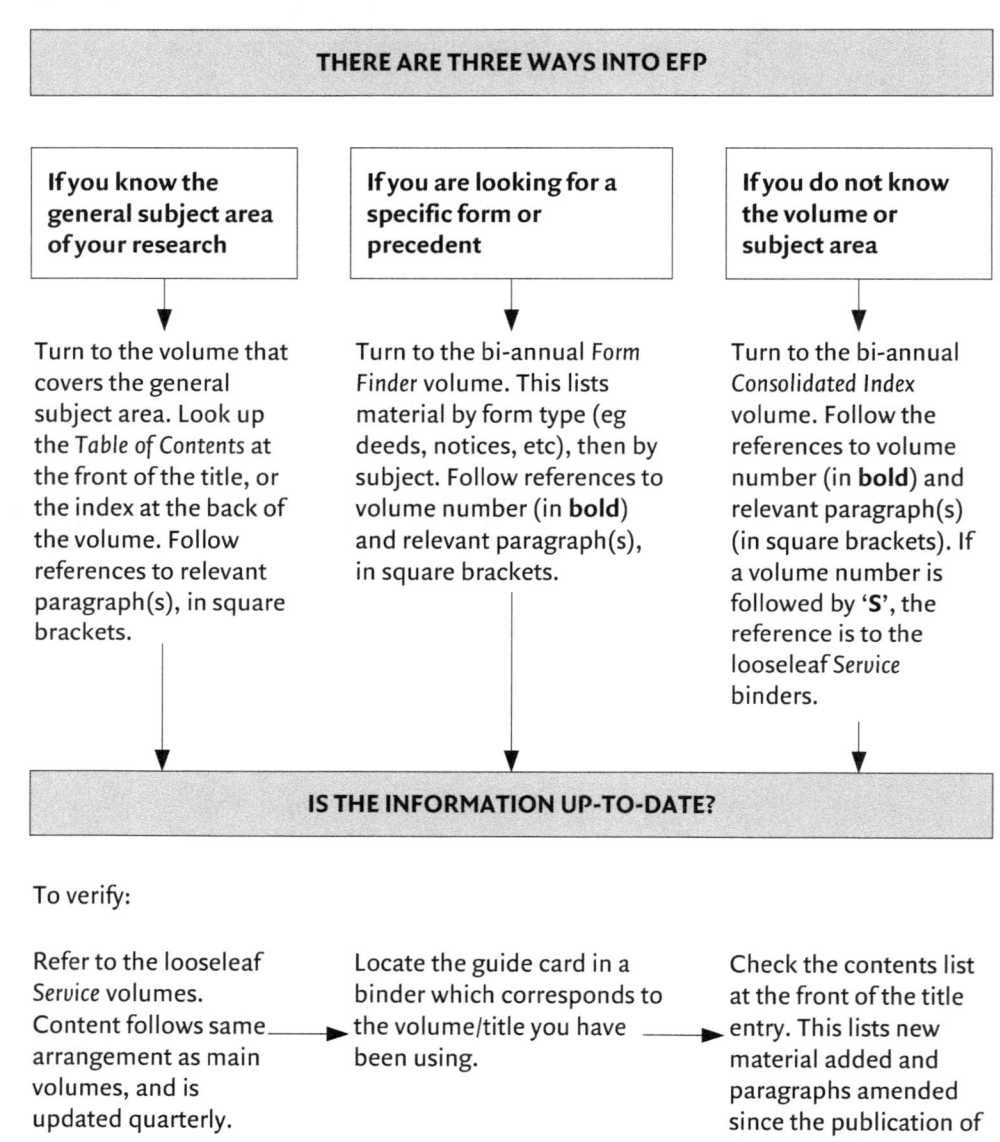

CHAPTER 9

The Result of Legal Research

9.1	Recording research	113
9.2	Reporting research	114
9.3	Cite it right	114

> **LEARNING OUTCOMES**
>
> After reading this chapter you will be able to:
> - explain the importance of recording your research
> - understand how to report your research effectively.

9.1 RECORDING RESEARCH

It may be tempting to jump straight into researching your problem and rely on memory rather than stopping to make notes at each stage. However, this is not an efficient approach. It may be only at the end of a research trail that the value of a particular piece of information becomes clear: accurate references will then save time. And what if your supervisor questions the answer? Or if they ask you to check back on something, or enquire about the steps you took to reach your answer?

At each stage of your research, as well as recording the information you discover, make a note of what you do and when you do it. Your record should include:

(a) the date your research was carried out (especially important with Internet sources, where content may change daily);

(b) full citations for legislation, case law and other primary sources consulted;

(c) for books: the author, title, edition, year and publisher;

(d) for journal articles: the title of the journal, title of the article, author, year and volume number;

(e) for databases: the name of the database, and the name of the section of the database (for example, *UK Parliament Acts* on *Lexis+ Legal Research*);

(f) keywords used during searches;

(g) page references or website addresses for key pieces of information;

(h) dates of publication (including the date of the latest release for a looseleaf source);

(i) any dates to which the law as stated is claimed to be up-to-date by the publisher.

Here is an example of a good research trail for a simple research query:

Topic	What are the penalties for importing cocaine into the UK?
Date of research	4 March 2025
Source used	*Halsbury's Laws of England* (via *Lexis+ Legal Research*)
Keywords used	"Controlled drug" – importation – penalties

Result	Directed to paragraph 561 of volume 75 (5th edition) for a summary of the law, and footnote 3 sets out that for offences concerned with Class A drugs a person is liable on conviction ... on indictment to a penalty ... of any amount or to imprisonment for life or both
How updated	Online database which is updated regularly – no updates to relevant paragraphs on date of research.

9.2 REPORTING RESEARCH

If your research is carried out at the request of your supervisor, it is important that you communicate the results clearly. In any event, it is as well to make a clear record of the legal basis for advice.

During your academic studies, follow the format set out by your institution for any legal research assessment. Reports in practice will take different forms, depending on the purpose and importance of the research, and whether the researcher understands the client's position fully. As a trainee, you are likely to begin with relatively simple tasks, so that a relatively simple form of report will suffice. Suggestions for the content of more elaborate forms of reports, together with useful advice on style and layout, can be found in **Chapter 1**.

The following general points should be borne in mind:

(a) The main aims of the report are to answer the question clearly, including enough detail of the research for sources to be traced and for conclusions to be checked easily.

(b) Begin by restating the objective; if you have a different view of the issue from your supervisor, you are unlikely to produce a satisfactory answer.

(c) Include a brief summary of your conclusions near the beginning of the report, separate from any reasoning or source references, so that the main message is quickly apparent.

(d) If your problem is complex, involving several linked issues, list the issues and report on each one separately.

(e) Consider the recipient of the research in making choices about style and layout. Is it appropriate to report results in note form? Is it reasonable to assume knowledge of the legal background? Will technical language be easily understood?

(f) If the factual context is known, the results should be applied to the facts, and brief notes should be made of obvious practical implications.

(g) Give full source references: include the title and citation of primary sources and the page/paragraph numbers of the publications where they were found.

(h) Consider attaching links, photocopies or print-outs of the most relevant sources.

(i) State what steps were taken to update: give the date of the latest sources used, and also give (where possible) the date to which the law as stated is claimed to be up to date by the publisher.

(j) State the date that the research was carried out. Record the time spent on research. Your supervisor will need this information for billing purposes.

(k) State the date that the report was compiled.

9.3 CITE IT RIGHT

Various guides exist to set standards for the form of citation of legal authorities. It is good practice to follow a standard approach to citation when recording and reporting a piece of research, for the sake of consistency and to avoid ambiguity. However, unfortunately, different organisations have developed different sets of standards. For example, most legal publishers will follow their own in-house rules of citation. There are also differences in approach between countries (which may be significant for solicitors working in the UK offices of US firms, for example).

Again, for any assessment carried out as part of your studies, you should check the assessment regulation for details of any referencing style you are required to follow. In law, one set of rules is now widely used in academia in the UK, and also serves as a reliable and comprehensive style guide for researchers in practice. It is OSCOLA (*The Oxford Standard for Citation of Legal Authorities*, 4th edn, 2012). The text of OSCOLA is available for free online: www.law.ox.ac.uk/sites/default/files/migrated/oscola_4th_edn_hart_2012.pdf. Detailed guidance and examples cover references to a wide range of UK and European primary sources, and commentary. A quick reference guide is available via www.law.ox.ac.uk/sites/default/files/migrated/oscola_4th_edn_hart_2012quickreferenceguide.pdf. A separate guide is also available covering references to international law: www.law.ox.ac.uk/sites/default/files/migrated/oscola_2006_citing_international_law.pdf. At the time of writing, a 5th edition of OSCOLA is planned for publication in 2025 but is not yet available.

During your academic studies, you should check what referencing style is required by your institution. You will usually find guidance and support on referencing available via the Library. Usually, in practice, you will not need to follow a strict referencing style, but as previously mentioned you should ensure that you set out clearly the resources you have used as part of your research.

PART III

ORAL COMMUNICATION SKILLS

CHAPTER 10

INTRODUCTION TO ORAL COMMUNICATION SKILLS

10.1	The importance of oral communication skills	119
10.2	Listening	122
10.3	Questioning	123
10.4	Non-verbal communication	123
10.5	Conclusion	123

> **LEARNING OUTCOMES**
>
> After reading this chapter you will be able to:
>
> - appreciate the importance of good communication skills in practice
> - demonstrate passive and active listening skills
> - explain the difference between open and closed questions
> - recognise the impact of 'body language' on effective communication.

10.1 THE IMPORTANCE OF ORAL COMMUNICATION SKILLS

> One-third of what is said is not heard
> One-third is heard but not understood
> One-third is understood – but may not be accepted
> (adapted from a passage in *The Skills of Negotiating* by Bill Scott)

All solicitors need to possess good oral communication skills in order to defeat the 'one-third rule', quoted above, and to become effective interviewers, negotiators or advocates.

During the working day a solicitor will communicate with a wide variety of individuals. The most obvious occasions when oral communication skills are important are when interviewing clients or presenting a case to a court, but a solicitor will also need to communicate with other professionals, such as accountants, surveyors, estate agents and police officers, and with members of the public, such as witnesses, and, of course, with colleagues in the solicitor's own office.

Solicitors spend a significant amount of time interviewing clients, in discussions with other lawyers, negotiating, acting as an advocate, interviewing witnesses and spending time with counsel. All of these activities involve oral communication skills.

> **PERSONAL INJURY CASE STUDY**
>
> Consider the facts of this case study. If you are acting for Hina Patel, how many different people would you expect to communicate with as you prepare to launch her claim?

> At the very least you will need to discuss the case with the client, witnesses, solicitors acting for the other parties, police officers who attended the scene, the client's GP and any other expert medical witness involved in her ongoing care, and her insurance company and/or its solicitors.

> **TRANSACTION CASE STUDY**
>
> Consider the facts of this case study. If you are acting for the sellers of Toast & Tea, think about the range of people you would expect to be involved in the transaction and with whom you would need to be able to communicate.
>
> Clearly you would need to be able to communicate with your clients, and you may possibly need to obtain information from their employees. You would need to be involved in discussions with the clients' accountants on issues relating to the accounts, valuation of the business and possible taxation advice. Sale of the business may involve the transfer of leasehold and/or freehold premises and therefore contact with surveyors, landlords and/or their agents and banks (if there are mortgages on the properties). There may also be contact with official bodies, such as HM Revenue and Customs in relation to taxation issues and licensing authorities in relation to any licences held by the business which may need assigning to the purchaser.

10.1.1 Communication with clients

> **PROFESSIONAL CONDUCT POINT**
>
> In establishing a range of measures to help solicitors achieve better standards in client care and complaints handling, The Law Society and the Legal Services Complaints Commissioner (4 March 2009) stated that '[e]xcellence in client care, from initial contact through to handling complaints, is an important part of demonstrating your professionalism as a solicitor'.
>
> The Law Society periodically updates its guidance on the management of complaints, the most recent version being the Handling Complaints Practice Note (30 October 2024). Interestingly, in a previous version of this guidance, the Complaints Management Practice Note (1 February 2013), The Law Society observes that '[g]ood communication is essential to ... high quality client care ... Poor communication will result in clients feeling that they have not been understood, taken seriously or valued ... Effective communication can help to resolve disputes quickly and build greater client loyalty.'

Employing appropriate skills when communicating with clients is an inherent part of a solicitor's role.

Proper communication with clients will promote satisfaction with the solicitor's service. There will be fewer complaints relating to the standard of service, which in turn allows the solicitor more time to concentrate on generating more business for the firm. Fewer complaints should also lead to a reduction in the solicitor's professional indemnity premiums.

A happy client will be a loyal client, who will be ready to recommend the solicitor to others. In 'Listen, Inform, Respond: A guide to good complaints handling', the Legal Ombudsman reports that:

> [a] recent survey into the use of legal services found that 82% of consumers would choose a lawyer based on personal experience or recommendations from friends, relatives and work colleagues. Satisfied customers will be loyal ... [and] spread the word; they'll tell other people how much they like your business and value the service you offer.

> **TRANSACTION CASE STUDY**
>
> If, when acting for the purchaser, you provided a good service and kept the client well informed and happy then further instructions are very likely to follow. The client will no doubt have many employees, properties and contracts with suppliers and customers, all of which will, at some point in the future, generate the need for further legal advice.

In its Practice Note of 1 February 2013, The Law Society suggests that a 'satisfied client can recommend up to five new clients, but a dissatisfied client can lose the practice up to 23 new clients'. The impact of better communication in turn leads to a more successful and profitable business for the solicitor with fewer complaints made about the quality of their service.

Looking at it from a wider perspective than just the solicitor's own firm, in the long term The Law Society believes that better communication techniques will lead to an overall improvement in levels of client satisfaction which may reduce the number of complaints and formal claims against solicitors and thereby enhance the public's overall perception of the legal profession.

So, from a personal, professional and business perspective, the solicitor should be very keen to ensure that they establish a good line of communication with their clients.

10.1.2 Communicating with those who are not clients

Solicitors also need to establish and maintain good working relationships with their colleagues in the office (whether professional or administrative); a solicitor who acts in a professional manner and is polite, clear when giving instructions and who is prepared to listen will promote a better atmosphere in the office. People who have a happy and professional working environment are generally more productive and provide a better service.

Consulting or instructing members of other professions, representatives of official bodies (eg, court staff) and interviewing members of the general public are all a regular part of a solicitor's daily workload. Clear, concise, polite and appropriate communications should minimise any delay in getting a response and reduce possible confusion in their interpretation of the solicitor's request, instructions or questions. It is clear to see that using appropriate communication skills will also enhance the solicitor's reputation in the community and amongst the professionals with whom they deal. This will promote more referrals of clients to the solicitor's firm.

Employing appropriate communication skills with people inside and outside the solicitor's own office will improve the service that a client receives and, as explained at **10.1.1**, this has a beneficial impact on the solicitor's reputation and their business.

10.1.3 Developing communication skills

Although oral communication skills are largely based on common sense, people's ability to use them varies enormously. Some people are naturally better than others at communicating, but everyone is capable of improvement. Like any other skill (driving a car, playing a musical instrument, playing a sport), performance can be improved by learning specific skills and techniques, and then practising them.

At first, practising new techniques can feel artificial ('It's just not me'), but after a while the technique usually becomes second nature (like changing gear in a car). However, skills training should not be allowed to suppress natural ability, and it is possible to be a competent interviewer, negotiator or advocate without necessarily having to perform every technique by the book. It is a question of balance; but success comes through practising sound techniques. Brilliant mavericks are rare.

When communicating with anyone, it is important to recognise any difficulties they may have in hearing and understanding the conversation. Individuals may have physical or mental disabilities, or there may be issues relating to culture or language. It is therefore necessary to take these difficulties into account when preparing for such a meeting, for example by employing an interpreter.

This chapter introduces those aspects of oral communication skills which are common to interviewing, negotiation and advocacy. **Chapters 11–13** explain and illustrate with examples how the skills apply to each of these activities.

10.2 LISTENING

In order to advise a client, or to persuade an opponent or the court, solicitors have first to *demonstrate* that they have both heard and understood what the other has said. In its Practice Note of 1 February 2013, The Law Society recommends that you should 'genuinely listen to the client and seek to understand the situation from their point of view'. This will lead to clients feeling 'more confident that they are being taken seriously'.

This involves listening carefully to what is being said. Listening is an underrated skill which requires considerable concentration. Listening as a solicitor is very different from listening in the context of ordinary social discourse, where interchanges are shorter and more fluid and where there is less need to pick up every nuance or recall precisely what was said.

Listening as a solicitor is also different from listening to lectures, where students do not necessarily have to interrelate with the lecturer and may be able to copy up notes from elsewhere later. Nevertheless, students who are good listeners in lectures will find that this skill will help them enormously in practice.

Most authorities on oral communication skills make a distinction between 'passive listening' and 'active listening'.

10.2.1 Passive listening

Passive listening involves using silences and other unobtrusive signals to encourage the speaker to continue. For example, when interviewing, negotiating or conducting advocacy, the solicitor might want to induce the speaker to carry on speaking and thereby perhaps volunteer a crucial piece of information.

Silences can be embarrassing in normal social situations, so many people learn during their upbringing to avoid them. Yet silence is one of the most powerful techniques available to a solicitor. It may require a conscious effort to remain silent for longer than normal in the hope that the speaker will fill the void with more information.

Other non-obtrusive signals a solicitor may give the speaker to encourage them to continue include:

- eye contact;
- posture;
- nodding;
- acknowledgements ('Uh, huh');
- express invitations ('Go on').

10.2.2 Active listening

Active listening, as the phrase suggests, involves more obtrusive techniques which demonstrate to the other person that the solicitor has both heard and understood.

The most common form of active listening is summarising (ie, giving a short, clear precis of what the speaker has just said). Like silence, the technique is not regularly employed in social conversations and so requires a conscious effort.

Summarising is also used by solicitors to check the effectiveness of communication in the reverse direction (ie, that the other person has heard and understood the solicitor).

10.3 QUESTIONING

Questioning skills are well-known tools of the solicitor's trade. Questions may be classified according to the breadth of the response they allow (ie, as open or closed questions).

10.3.1 Open questions

Open questions give maximum freedom to the person being questioned, they encourage expansion and they do not seek to influence the content of the reply:

> 'So what happened next?'
>
> 'What were your reactions to that?'
>
> 'How did you respond to the offer?'
>
> 'Why did you do that?'
>
> 'Tell me about your relationship with the managing director.'
>
> 'Tell me more about ...'

Open questions do not necessarily have to be worded as questions: 'Tell me ...' is a phrase which can be used to invite an open response.

10.3.2 Closed questions

Closed questions invite a narrow answer, from a few words or a sentence to a 'Yes'/'No' reply (sometimes called 'Yes/No questions'):

> 'Were you also carrying a knife?'
>
> 'Did you accept the offer?'

One particular form of closed question is the leading question. For example, the questioner might deliberately seek to influence the content of the reply by asking a question which encourages a particular answer: 'So you must have been drunk, mustn't you?'

10.4 NON-VERBAL COMMUNICATION

Non-verbal communication includes eye contact, posture and gestures, and is often called 'body language'.

Careful observation of the body language of other people can provide clues as to how they are feeling, or how they are responding to advice or to an argument, and may therefore be influential in deciding how to proceed. However, tread cautiously, because the clue might not be conclusive: the interpretation of body language is controversial, and is subject to cultural variations. Avoiding eye contact may be regarded as an indication of evasiveness and even a lack of truthfulness in some cultures. In others it may be a sign of politeness and sincerity. Be aware of non-verbal communication, but do not allow it to distract you from everything else.

Similarly, awareness of how your own body language affects both yourself and others can help in deciding how to convey your message more effectively. Although it is sometimes said that one cannot (or should not) 'fake' body language, cause and effect are often interrelated. Sitting with your arms tightly folded and your legs crossed, or nervously drumming your fingers or tapping your foot, can affect your own feelings as well as influencing others' perceptions of you. Sitting or standing in a physically relaxed manner can help you feel more relaxed and convey the impression of confidence to an observer.

10.5 CONCLUSION

This chapter introduces the oral communication skills which will serve as useful tools for a solicitor, whether they are conducting an interview or a negotiation or acting as an advocate. Reference should be made to **Chapters 11–13** for further discussion and illustration of how these skills may be employed in each of these three contexts.

CHAPTER 11

INTERVIEWING AND ADVISING

11.1	Why is it important for a solicitor to be a good interviewer?	125
11.2	Objectives of a solicitor/client interview	126
11.3	Common failings	127
11.4	Two ingredients for success – skills and structure	127
11.5	The skills	128
11.6	Client care and costs information	136
11.7	An overview of the structure of the interview	137
11.8	Structure and management of the initial interview	139
11.9	The secret of success – practice	156

LEARNING OUTCOMES

After reading this chapter you will be able to:

- appreciate the importance of interviewing skills in practice
- recognise the range of skills you will need to develop to be a good interviewer
- understand the steps that need to be taken when preparing for a client interview
- plan a structured approach to a client interview
- recognise the purpose of each stage of a structured interview
- identify the skills which are appropriate for each stage of a structured interview
- use appropriate listening and questioning techniques
- integrate relevant aspects of the SRA Code of Conduct for Solicitors 2019 into a client interview.

11.1 WHY IS IT IMPORTANT FOR A SOLICITOR TO BE A GOOD INTERVIEWER?

Chapter 10 explored the general importance of good communication skills to a solicitor's standard of service to their clients, and to their own and the firm's reputation and business interests. This chapter will illustrate how those skills are employed when conducting an initial interview with a client.

So, why is it important for a solicitor to be a good interviewer?

11.1.1 Building good relationships and reputations

A significant proportion of a solicitor's working life is spent interviewing clients and witnesses.

The initial interview is usually the first time the solicitor and client meet. As the old saying goes, you never get a second chance to make a first impression. Making a good first impression is crucial if you want the client to feel comfortable enough and confident enough to instruct you to act for them.

This meeting will therefore be the basis upon which you will start to build a rapport with the client.

The information obtained during the interview will influence the direction that the client's case will follow, so good use of listening, questioning and analytical skills will ensure you establish as full a picture as possible. It is also the time to establish the terms and conditions of your retainer so that each of you understands the work that you will undertake on the client's behalf.

Remember, a happy client is a loyal client who will recommend your firm to others. More importantly, failure to communicate effectively with your client may lead to a dissatisfied client, poor or even negligent advice, and the possibility of complaints, disputes and damage to the firm's reputation.

11.1.2 Law Society guidance

As noted at **10.1.1**, The Law Society believes that good communication skills provide the foundations to building long-term relationships with clients, a good personal reputation and a publicly respected profession. In order to promote excellence in both communication skills and professional attitudes to client care, The Law Society has published a number of practice notes and guides which outline the Society's guidance on good professional practice. Whilst having no legal force, firms with robust practice procedures which follow the spirit of the guidance are less likely to find themselves subject to complaints from their clients and more likely to be able to provide a good account of their actions should any such complaints be brought against them.

The following practice notes and guides provide guidance that is of particular relevance to the skills and practice procedures discussed in this chapter:

- 'Client information requirements', issued 8 September 2021
- 'Use of interpreters in criminal cases', issued 31 January 2023
- 'Meeting the needs of vulnerable clients', issued 29 November 2022

(These practice notes and guides will be referred to in the following form in this chapter: 'Practice Note of 8 September 2021', 'Guide of 29 November 2022', etc.)

11.1.3 The Legal Practice Course

When studying the on the Legal Practice Course, a student must meet the Solicitors Regulation Authority's learning outcomes for Interviewing and Advising. The guidance given in this chapter encompasses those outcomes.

11.1.4 The Legal Ombudsman

The Legal Ombudsman investigates complaints made against solicitors for poor service. In 2019, the Legal Ombudsman updated its previous guidance to lawyers when it published its 2nd edition of 'An ombudsman's view of good costs services'. This guidance includes the Legal Ombudsman's view on costs information to be provided during the initial interview with a client. It will be referred to in the following form in this chapter: 'An ombudsman's view (2nd edn)'.

11.2 OBJECTIVES OF A SOLICITOR/CLIENT INTERVIEW

As mentioned at **11.1**, this chapter concentrates on the skills needed during the first interview with a client.

There are five main objectives:

- to establish good *rapport* between the solicitor and the client;
- to obtain relevant *information* from the client;
- to help the client reach appropriate *decisions*;
- to plan future *action*;
- to deal with client care and costs information issues.

Other legal interviews (eg, with witnesses or other professionals) usually serve more limited purposes.

11.3 COMMON FAILINGS

There are many reasons why a solicitor may fail to achieve the above objectives.

For example, the solicitor may:

- fail to listen properly;
- talk too much;
- make a premature diagnosis;
- restrict the areas in which the client feels free to talk;
- be over-directive in suggesting what further action is necessary;
- be over-technical when giving advice.

The skills referred to later in this chapter will reduce the likelihood of any of these failings occurring.

11.4 TWO INGREDIENTS FOR SUCCESS – SKILLS AND STRUCTURE

11.4.1 Skills

In order to achieve the objectives referred to at **11.2**, you need to make effective use of a wide range of skills.

The principal skills involved are:

- listening;
- questioning;
- analysing;
- explaining;
- note-taking.

These will be considered in more detail at **11.5**.

11.4.2 Structure

The objectives at **11.2** are easier to achieve if you prepare for and conduct the interview in a logical and coherent manner.

Structure and management involve:

- creating a *suitable environment* for the interview;
- preparing *adequately* for the interview;
- using an *appropriate 'model'* for the interview itself.

A 'model' is merely a predetermined structure, under which the interview is divided into a logical sequence of stages. Each stage involves the performance of essential tasks and requires the use of different combinations of the skills referred to above.

The model used in this book is:

	GREETING
(1)	PRELIMINARIES
(2)	OBTAINING THE FACTS
(3)	FILLING IN THE DETAIL
(4)	ADVISING
(5)	CLOSING
	PARTING

The model is easy to follow and may be used in any legal context, although the length of time spent on each stage will usually vary depending on whether the interview is litigation or transaction based.

A detailed explanation of these stages will be given at **11.8**, but a brief overview of the three central stages will help your understanding of what follows at **11.5** about the relevant skills.

11.4.2.1 Obtaining the facts

This involves the client giving an account of the matter with as little interruption from the solicitor as possible. It is therefore characterised by the client talking and the solicitor *listening*, observing the client's body language and encouraging the client to continue.

11.4.2.2 Filling in the detail

This involves a more active role by the solicitor to ensure that a complete and accurate picture is obtained and recorded. This stage is therefore characterised by the solicitor *questioning* the client and *taking notes* of what the client says.

11.4.2.3 Advising

This involves supplying the information which the client needs in order to make necessary decisions and to give the solicitor instructions for any further action. This stage therefore usually takes the form of the solicitor *analysing* and *explaining* the client's position, explaining the range of options open to the client and then *engaging in a dialogue* to make necessary decisions and to agree a plan of action.

11.5 THE SKILLS

11.5.1 Listening – an undervalued skill

Encouraging a client to explain why they have come to see you is generally a more effective way of gathering information than attempting to do so by a series of closed questions (see **10.3.2**). You should therefore avoid asking closed questions until you have a reasonably full version of the case.

If the client is verbose, you may need to adopt a more forceful braking role, but this should occur only when absolutely necessary.

Listening is an undervalued skill which involves a range of techniques to sustain information giving.

11.5.1.1 Silence

In everyday conversation, periods of silence can sometimes seem awkward and even cause embarrassment.

In an interview, these periods give the client time to recall facts and to organise their thoughts so that they are better able to tell the story as they remember it and to express the feelings it creates.

You must therefore learn to control the natural urge to fill silences.

11.5.1.2 Body language

Consider how your body language may help or hinder building good rapport with the client. For example:

- eye contact: a friendly, but not prolonged stare;
- posture: leaning slightly towards the client;
- head-nodding: but not too much;

- avoiding irritating/distracting mannerisms, eg, pen-tapping, foot-drumming, reading while the client is speaking, looking at your watch, etc.

11.5.1.3 Acknowledgements

These are brief indications (without interrupting) showing attention, interest, and understanding, such as:

'Yes, I see'

'... in Brussels?'

'Mhmmmm'.

11.5.1.4 Invitations to continue/elaborate

Examples are:

'Go on'

'What happened?'

'Tell me more about that'.

11.5.1.5 Reflecting feeling

This involves making it clear that you understand how the client feels, for example, 'I can quite see why you feel so angry about this' or (in relation to bereavement) 'I'm sorry to hear that'.

It involves expressing empathy with the client's feelings; not being judgmental about them.

The technique is useful in building rapport and is particularly important where the client's emotions will be a major factor in the case, for example in matrimonial cases or where the client has recently been bereaved.

However, reflecting feeling may also be appropriate in interviews which may appear to be less personal, for example when a commercial client has anxieties about losing face within the company if a transaction fails to reach a satisfactory conclusion.

You can gain valuable insights into the client's feelings by observing and correctly interpreting the client's body language, not merely from listening to the client's words and tone of voice.

11.5.2 Questioning

In an initial interview, a solicitor needs to obtain information on:

- the nature of the client's problem or proposed transaction;
- the relevant background facts;
- the client's feelings and objectives.

Whilst much of this may be obtained through use of the listening techniques discussed above, it will usually be necessary to clarify and probe further by questioning.

For an initial interview, particularly in the early stages, open questions usually have more advantages than closed questions and failure to recognise this leads many interviews into an interviewer-dominated style. It is important to avoid asking more than one question at a time.

11.5.2.1 Open questions

The advantages of open questions are that they:

(a) allow the client to select the subject matter;

(b) allow the client to select the information the client believes to be relevant;

(c) allow the client to start with information about which the client feels comfortable;

(d) enable the client to get things 'off their chest';

(e) give the client freedom to reflect and to feel more actively involved in the interview;

(f) encourage memory by association, which may produce information which would be overlooked if the client were asked only closed questions.

> **TRANSACTION CASE STUDY**
>
> Assume you are acting for the sellers. What aspects of the transaction will you encourage the clients to discuss to help you get an overview of the deal through the use of open questions? The clients are most likely to start their explanation with a description of the deal. You would probably need to use open questions to build a picture of the following topics:
>
> (a) the stage that negotiations have reached;
>
> (b) the nature of the business;
>
> (c) who the owners are and the value attributed to the business (some idea of the assets and liabilities);
>
> (d) the plans for employees;
>
> (e) the clients' proposed time frame for the deal and any deadlines that you would be expected to meet (for example the deal must be completed before the end of the current tax year).

The use of open questions should allow a solicitor to get a great deal of information relatively quickly and so form an overview of the situation. However, on their own, open questions are unlikely to be sufficient due to the following disadvantages:

(a) they may initially produce insufficient information;

(b) they may encourage the client to verbosity and/or irrelevance;

(c) they may inhibit a reticent client.

11.5.2.2 Closed questions

Once you have an overview of the case, you can then start to focus on the aspects where you need more detail. The advantages of closed questions are that they:

(a) are a good method of obtaining precise details;

(b) may guide a client less stressfully through a sensitive area;

(c) may give confidence to an initially reticent or anxious client;

(d) may help to prompt memory;

(e) help to clarify and probe areas of ambiguity or uncertainty;

(f) may quieten a verbose client.

The disadvantages are that they:

(a) may lead to an over-clinical or 'processing' style of interview;

(b) may deprive the client of the opportunity to state the case in their own words;

(c) may inhibit rapport;

(d) reduce the opportunity to listen to and observe the client, and to understand their needs;

(e) may lead the solicitor to miss important areas of information because the client is not allowed to associate ideas freely;

(f) may even result in the solicitor directing the interview down a totally irrelevant path;

(g) if overused, may result in the client feeling interrogated.

11.5.2.3 The 'T-funnel'

As noted at **11.5.2.1** and **11.5.2.2**, the use of just open questions or just closed questions does not elicit the range of information that the solicitor needs. By combining the two techniques, the solicitor can achieve a thorough exploration of the information.

The use of open questions followed by closed questions is sometimes known as the T-funnel sequence of questioning:

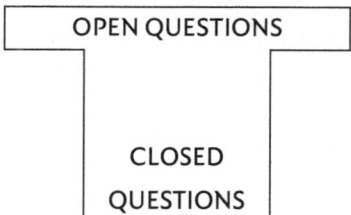

The solicitor introduces a particular topic with a series of open questions. Only after the open questions cease to be productive are they narrowed into closed questions.

Premature use of closed questions may distort the response or lead to important details being omitted.

> **PERSONAL INJURY CASE STUDY**
>
> Assume you are acting for Hina Patel. What general areas would you need to encourage the client to explain by using open questions?
>
> You will need to know:
>
> (a) when, where and how the accident happened;
>
> (b) a description of the personal injury, damage to property and any financial loss the client has suffered;
>
> (c) the consequences of the accident on her personal and working life;
>
> (d) insurance details of the client and the other parties.
>
> The client is likely to be very ready to explain what happened from her point of view, to give her view as to who was at fault, to mention if the emergency services attended and if the police plan to take any action. She is unlikely to have described the scene in sufficient detail for you to be able to give advice. You need to be sure that she has covered the following details:
>
> (a) the direction in which she was travelling;
>
> (b) the speed at which she was travelling;
>
> (c) the weather conditions;
>
> (d) the time of day;
>
> (e) a precise description of the junction (for example if there were traffic lights, road markings, road works);
>
> (f) whether she had any passengers;
>
> (g) whether there were any independent witnesses;
>
> (h) exactly what happened after the collision and what was said by whom to whom;
>
> (i) contact details for all parties and for any police officer who attended;
>
> (j) details of her insurance, including any excess.
>
> In using the T-funnel approach, you can use open questions to establish an overview of the accident based on the client's immediate memory. You can then review what the client has told you, if necessary imposing a logical structure to the order of events as you clarify your understanding. The use of closed questions at this stage should enable you to get all relevant facts before you move on to giving advice.

> **(Open questions)**
>
> Solicitor   'What happened after the collision?'
> Client   'I was really shaken and it took me a few minutes to compose myself. I turned off my radio because the noise was getting to me.'
> Solicitor   'What happened next?'
> Client   'I got out of my car.'
> Solicitor   'Yes ...?'
> Client   'Well, I went over to where he'd parked his car and spoke to him.'
>
> **(Closed questions)**
>
> Solicitor   'Could you tell me exactly where you were both standing?'
> Client   'Yes, he was standing by the offside front wing of his car and as I approached him I am afraid I told him what I thought of him.'
> Solicitor   'Can you remember the words you actually used?'
> Client   'I said "You fool, why the hell didn't you indicate?"'
> Solicitor   'Did he reply?'
> Client   'Yes, he said "I'm sorry – I didn't realise they'd changed the lane markings".'
> Solicitor   'Anything else?'
> Client   'No.'
> Solicitor   'Was anyone else present?'
> Client   'Yes – his work mate was standing right next to him.'

11.5.2.4 Further clarification and probing

It will often be necessary to probe further:

- to resolve remaining areas of ambiguity;
- to jog the client's memory;
- to clarify the client's needs and reaction to the consequences of the action;
- to discover how the client will respond to the legal process (in litigation) or to a counter-argument or proposal (negotiating a transaction).

The following are some techniques to achieve these objectives.

Going back one stage

This involves taking the client back one stage in the narrative and inviting them to relive the sequence of events in order to jog the memory:

> 'Take me through that again but starting from before you were approaching the road junction.'

This technique is useful, as it encourages the client to fill in any gaps in the narrative.

Leading questions

Leading questions may be a useful way of helping clients to convey something which they may have difficulty articulating in their own words:

> 'So you've had disagreements with the managing director before?'
>
> 'So sexual intercourse did take place on that occasion?'

Prefacing a question with an explanation

This can counteract the client perceiving your question as irrelevant, or allay the client's anxiety in a sensitive area. For example:

> 'I know you're very confident of being acquitted, but if you are convicted, the magistrates will sentence you immediately. For that reason I now need to ask you some questions about your financial circumstances.'

There is, however, a danger that the explanation may influence (and therefore distort) the client's reply.

Cross-checking

This is often necessary where the information given by the client reveals gaps or contradictions which require explanation. For example:

> 'Are you quite sure about that because according to the police report you said you'd drunk three pints?'

Devil's advocate

To play devil's advocate is to suggest to the client a different and adverse interpretation of their story. For example:

> 'If you're so sure that the accident wasn't your fault, why did you say to the other motorist: "I'm sorry – I just didn't see you coming"?'

It is generally advisable to explain why you are doing this because, otherwise, your apparent hostility is likely to damage rapport. For example:

> 'I'm sorry to ask you so bluntly but it's a question you are bound to be asked in court if this gets to trial.'

11.5.2.5 Summarising

This is an extremely important and useful technique.

Its purpose is to double-check that your understanding of the facts and of your client's feelings and concerns is correct.

A summary of the key facts should be given at the end of the filling in the detail stage and before moving into the advising stage:

> 'Now before we talk about what needs to be done let me just check with you that I have got a correct and complete list of all your relevant assets.'

Apart from giving the client an opportunity to correct errors and supply additional facts, summarising reassures the client that you have heard and understood what you have been told. It also gives you a useful breathing space to think about the matter and the advice that needs to be given. It may also identify some areas on which further questioning is needed before you can safely advise.

Remember that summarising your understanding of the client's feelings and objectives is just as important as summarising factual information:

> 'So let me see whether I've correctly understood what you are hoping to achieve out of all this ...'

> 'So would it be fair to say that you would only be prepared to go to court if Janice's name could be kept out of it?'

Summarising helps you to identify if further questions need to be asked and to formulate the advice to give.

11.5.3 Analysing

As the facts and the client's goals are being identified, the solicitor must (at least mentally) analyse which facts and legal principles are relevant, how the law applies to those facts and so reach a conclusion about the client's position and the range of available courses of action.

This process is familiar even to an inexperienced solicitor because it involves essentially the same techniques needed to answer traditional problem-solving questions in law examinations.

One obvious difference is that in real life the solicitor has to elicit the relevant information rather than having it spoon-fed in the form of a given scenario. Another difference is that the solicitor has little or no time for quiet reflection before being expected to offer at least a tentative view of the position.

What tends to happen in most interviews is that, at quite an early stage, the solicitor starts to form a provisional theory about the likely end position.

> **PERSONAL INJURY CASE STUDY**
>
> Consider what legal principles spring to mind if, whilst interviewing Hina Patel, she discloses the following information:
>
> 'The van driver was not wearing a seat belt.'
>
> 'The fog was really heavy; why did the van driver not have his lights on?'
>
> 'I was using my mobile phone at the time of the crash.'
>
> 'As a result of the injuries I was unable to go on a pre-booked holiday. I did not have any holiday insurance.'
>
> With each piece of information you will be analysing it and starting to frame advice. Thoughts of contributory negligence, criminal offences and remoteness of damage will begin to take shape. These initial thoughts will help you identify further questions you need to ask, and these ideas will inevitably have to be reviewed and modified as additional information emerges. You must be careful to avoid reaching a conclusion until all the facts have been obtained.

Like all skills, this process becomes easier with experience, practice and greater familiarity with the law in question.

Listening, questioning, note-taking and trying to formulate advice cannot be tackled simultaneously – just one reason why it is helpful to build in periods of 'thinking time' as discussed at **11.5.2.5** above.

11.5.4 Explaining

Once you have analysed the client's position, a number of matters will usually have to be explained before the client can be expected to make decisions and give instructions.

When advising a client, you should ensure that the client understands their legal position and the legal process that will be necessary to achieve the desired outcome.

11.5.4.1 Explaining the legal position

Explaining the relevant law frequently involves explaining concepts which will be second nature to you and which you would normally express in legal terminology (such as 'consideration' or 'implied conditions/warranties', etc).

It is therefore easy to overlook the simple fact that concepts and terminology which seem quite straightforward and normal to you can be totally bewildering and meaningless to a lay client.

Clarity is vital, and legal jargon should therefore be avoided at all costs. You must bear in mind that *accurate and faultlessly reasoned advice is utterly useless to a client who cannot understand it.*

> **TRANSACTION CASE STUDY**
>
> Assume that you have informed the clients that they face a significant capital gains tax bill on the sale of their business. The clients had hoped to reinvest the money in a new business venture and wish to know if there is any way of mitigating their liability to capital gains tax. Consider the clients' reaction to the following explanation:
>
>> 'If the consideration which a person carrying on a trade obtains for the disposal of his interest in qualifying business assets used for the purposes of the trade throughout the entire period of ownership is applied by him, within a specified period, in acquiring other qualifying business assets which are taken into use in a trade then, that person on making a claim, may be treated for the purposes of CGT as if the consideration for the disposal was such that it creates neither a gain nor a loss.'
>
> Whilst wholly correct in law, it is highly unlikely that even a quite sophisticated business client will follow and understand this long sentence, or appreciate the practical consequences of the statement. The use of such complex language will not only inhibit the clients' understanding, but it will also impact on rapport as the clients may well be intimidated, become irritated or even angry at the prospect of paying for advice that they do not understand.
>
> The advice should be couched in clear, simple English with short sentences to facilitate understanding. The following advice covers the same legal point in a much more accessible way:
>
>> 'There is a possibility of claiming a tax relief. This relief applies if you use the money you receive from the sale of Toast & Tea to purchase things such as land and buildings for use in your new venture. The benefit of the relief is that you will not have to pay the tax bill when you sell Toast & Tea. The tax will be deferred. You will still have to pay tax on the profit but not until you come to sell your new business assets in the future.'
>
> With advice given in these terms, the clients will be better able to understand it and be in a position to discuss the implications with you.

It is true to say that, with practice and experience, you will learn your own way of expressing legal concepts in ways that clients will understand.

11.5.4.2 Outlining the relevant procedure

The client's understanding of their legal position is one thing, but appreciating the legal procedures which must be followed is quite another. The client should be made aware of the steps that need to be followed to achieve their desired outcome. It is also wise to flag up the possibility of potential problems, which may mean that the process takes longer than expected or may lead to you having to follow a different course.

Managing your client's expectations in this way should ensure that the client feels more closely involved with the matter, and less likely to believe that things are going wrong or that you have made a mistake in your handling of the case.

You should also bear in mind that, even when you have explained matters clearly, it is often unrealistic to expect the client to remember everything once the interview is over. For this reason, it is desirable in most cases to send a follow-up letter to the client summarising the advice which you have given (see **11.8.10**).

It is often helpful to ask the client whether what you have said has been understood and to offer to repeat the advice. If overdone, this technique may appear patronising. If used appropriately, even the most self-confident client will appreciate your concern, and a more timid client, who may be reluctant to ask directly, will welcome a genuine offer of clarification.

11.5.5 Note-taking

Note-taking is an important and difficult skill.

No solicitor can memorise every piece of information on all their files, and there may be occasions when some other member of the firm will need to take over the file permanently or temporarily.

The file must therefore contain a complete, accurate and legible record of the interview. You must make sure your attendance note records the relevant facts, the advice given, the decisions made by the client and any follow-up steps which you and/or the client will be taking.

This is best achieved by taking manuscript notes during the interview itself and, if necessary, by having a fuller and/or clearer version typed afterwards.

Failing to take notes during the interview, intending to dictate everything immediately after the interview, is fraught with danger because you may unavoidably become involved in other distractions and be unable to do this before memory has faded. The longhand notes must, at minimum, be sufficient to operate as an *aide memoire* of the vital facts, names, dates, assets, etc from which a fuller record can later be prepared.

Difficulties can arise if you try to take detailed notes too early in the interview, while the client is trying to explain why they have come to see you. If you write while the client is actually talking, this can damage rapport for two reasons. First, it is very difficult to follow the meaning of what the client is saying if you are frantically trying to translate it into a written note. Secondly, it is impossible to write at length without losing eye contact with the client. Few things are more off-putting for a client than trying to relate a story to the top of someone's head. On the other hand, it can be equally off-putting if you interrupt the flow of the client's narrative by requesting time to write everything down.

The solution is simple: *do not attempt to take notes during the obtaining the facts stage*; instead, concentrate on listening to the client's version of events and defer taking notes until the 'filling in the detail' stage. This may mean that you have to ask the client to repeat some matters, but this is likely to be less time consuming in the long run. Alternatively, restrict note-taking to very brief jottings which do not destroy eye contact but which will serve at a later stage as a reminder of topics which need to be expanded.

Even when fuller note-taking starts, try to develop a concise style and be selective about what you write down. Headings can be used effectively to give a structure to your notes. Ensure that key names, addresses, figures, dates and verbatim accounts of conversations are accurately worded. Never be embarrassed to ask the client for the correct spellings if names are unfamiliar.

11.6 CLIENT CARE AND COSTS INFORMATION

> **PROFESSIONAL CONDUCT POINT**
>
> You must deal with the client professionally throughout the interview. This means you must comply with your professional and ethical obligations.
>
> The SRA Code of Conduct for Solicitors 2019 sets out the general requirements a solicitor must comply with in relation to client care and the provision of information as to costs. The question here is how many of these matters need to be dealt with during the first interview.

> In its Practice Note of 8 September 2021, The Law Society issued guidance which made it clear that, as a matter of client care and good practice, it is generally appropriate for some matters to be dealt with expressly during the interview, whilst other matters can properly be left to a client care information sheet (see **11.8.1.2**) or a follow-up client care/costs information letter.
>
> The rest of this chapter describes the structure and content of an initial interview with a client. Where relevant, the following chapters incorporate The Law Society's guidance on client care matters to be addressed during the first interview with a new client.
>
> As to costs information, para 8.7 of the SRA Code of Conduct for Solicitors 2019 requires that:
>
>> 'clients receive the best possible information about how their matter will be priced and, both at the time of engagement and when appropriate as their matter progresses, about the likely overall cost of the matter and any costs incurred.'
>
> In *An ombudsman's view* (2nd edn), the Legal Ombudsman reports that 'costs and costs information frequently feature in the complaints' it receives.
>
> The information on costs must be given in plain English and be accurate and not misleading.
>
> It is sensible to give a 'simple overview' of the costs during the interview and, following the interview, if you are retained by the client, to give full information in writing to the client.
>
> There are three separate occasions during the interview which present logical opportunities to discuss different aspects of the costs:
>
> (a) during the preliminary stage of the interview when it is essential to discuss at least the cost of the interview;
>
> (b) during the advising stage of the interview, when discussing the possible options it will be necessary to discuss the potential costs of each option and whether the possible benefit justifies the associated risks (including, where relevant, any risk of the client becoming liable for an opponent's costs);
>
> (c) during the closing stage when, having a complete picture of the client's current situation and the proposed course of action, it is possible to explain the likely overall costs of the matter.

11.7 AN OVERVIEW OF THE STRUCTURE OF THE INTERVIEW

Now that you have an overview of the various skills that will be needed during the initial interview with a client, the next step is to consider the structure of the interview and those skills that will be employed at each stage of the interview.

Having a clear idea of how you plan to structure and manage the interview is the key to retaining control and ensuring that all necessary matters are properly addressed. The following checklist provides you with a handy overview of the stages of the interview. It is a useful guide to keep in front of you to help you maintain your structure. A detailed explanation of each stage of the interview is given at **11.8**.

1. **Plan for the interview**
   (a) Organise an appropriate room for the interview
   (b) Carry out a conflict check
   (c) Ensure the client has been warned to bring proof of identity for an identity check
   (d) Research and prepare a checklist (if appropriate)
   (e) Consider if there is any need for an interpreter
   (f) Prepare two copies of the client care information sheet
   (g) Ensure no interruptions

2. **Greeting**
   Meet, greet and seat the client appropriately, confirm your status within the firm and establish good rapport

3. **Preliminaries**
   (a) Check the reason for the client's visit by way of a closed question
   (b) Discuss any time constraints and the proposed structure of interview
   (c) Explain the cost of the interview, reassure the client that you will deal with costs more fully later in the interview and check that the client accepts the charges outlined

4. **Obtain facts**
   Let the client explain the reason for their visit; use open questions and listening techniques (and avoid note-taking)

5. **Fill in detail**
   (a) Clarify and fill gaps in the facts using the T-funnel approach
   (b) Identify and explore the client's concerns
   (c) Summarise (a) and (b)

6. **Advising**
   (a) Outline relevant law and procedure clearly, accurately and comprehensively, taking into account all relevant factual, practical and legal issues
   (b) Explain available options, both legal and non-legal
   (c) Discuss with the client the advantages/disadvantages of the options (including a discussion on the associated risks/benefits) to assist the client in reaching a decision
   (d) Outline further steps to be taken to implement any proposed course of action

7. **Closing**
   (a) Ask client whether there is anything else they wish to discuss
   (b) Confirm the follow-up tasks of both solicitor and client
   (c) Give the name of an alternative contact within firm
   (d) Estimate the time frame for the *matter*
   (e) Give the best information possible relating to the costs of the *matter*
   (f) Discuss next contact including whether a further meeting is necessary and, if one is needed, when is it likely to be and who is responsible for arranging it

8. **Parting**

9. **General matters**
   (a) Maintain rapport throughout, seeking to establish a professional relationship
   (b) Structure the interview appropriately
   (c) Take appropriate notes
   (d) Manage the client's expectations in terms of your service and the likely outcomes

11.8 STRUCTURE AND MANAGEMENT OF THE INITIAL INTERVIEW

11.8.1 Before the interview

11.8.1.1 The environment

It is important that the interview takes place in an environment which will help rather than hinder effective communication. The aim should be to create an atmosphere in which the client will feel calm and relaxed, and which will give a favourable impression of you and your firm.

> **PROFESSIONAL CONDUCT POINT**
>
> Principle 6 of the SRA Principles 2019 requires you to conduct business in a manner that 'encourages equality, diversity and inclusion'. The environment in which the interview takes place should take into account any specific needs of the client, for example the need for wheelchair access or difficulties arising from being hard of hearing.

You should therefore ensure:

(a) that the client will be physically comfortable;

(b) that the interview will be free from unnecessary interruptions (with a minimum of background noise if the client is hard of hearing);

(c) that the office surroundings convey a sense of well-organised professionalism without being austere and/or impersonal.

Seating arrangements may also help or hinder effective communication. Views on this topic differ, and an arrangement which seems friendly and welcoming to one client may strike another as over-familiar or even invasive.

However, as far as possible, the arrangement should be one in which:

(a) the solicitor and client can see and hear each other clearly (this is especially important in the case of clients who are deaf/hard of hearing and may be reliant on lip reading or sign language);

(b) the client does not feel kept at a distance at one extreme or invaded at the other;

(c) the solicitor and (if necessary) the client can make written notes in comfort.

The traditional arrangement in which the solicitor and client face each other from opposite sides of the solicitor's desk will usually satisfy the above criteria, provided the desk is not piled high with files and papers. It is also the arrangement which most clients will be expecting.

However, depending on the personality of the client and the nature of the matter, you may decide that a less formal arrangement, perhaps without the intervening desk, would be more relaxing for the client and therefore more conducive to communication.

Furthermore, there may be occasions (eg, where the client needs to explain a plan, diagram or map to the solicitor) when sitting alongside the client is the only effective arrangement.

You should therefore consider the possibility of other arrangements and adopt them whenever appropriate.

The above comments presuppose that the interview will take place in an environment over which you have some degree of control, but the interview may, for a variety of reasons, take place in surroundings (eg, hospital ward, prison cell, crowded court corridor, etc) over which you will have little or no control.

11.8.1.2 Preparing for the interview

There are a number of matters to address in advance of your first interview with a client. In its Practice Note of 8 September 2021, The Law Society recommends that, before the initial interview, 'you should obtain information to enable you to carry out necessary background and regulatory checks'.

Conflict check

> **PROFESSIONAL CONDUCT POINT**
>
> Paragraph 6 of the SRA Code of Conduct for Solicitors 2019 says that, generally, a solicitor must not act for a client if there is a conflict of interest, or a significant risk of a conflict of interest, with a current client.
>
> No matter who in the office makes an appointment for a new client to see a solicitor, it is important that they know that they must obtain some basic information from the client. The client should be asked for the following information:
>
> (a) their name, address and telephone number;
> (b) basic information about the subject matter they wish to discuss (for example, a personal injury claim resulting from a car accident or the sale of a business);
> (c) the name of any other person involved in the case.
>
> This information will enable the firm to do a conflict check to ensure that there will be no risk of a conflict of interest arising if the firm accepts instructions from this client.
>
> If the client does not book an appointment in advance then this information should still be obtained and a conflict check carried out before the interview proceeds.

> **PERSONAL INJURY CASE STUDY**
>
> When Hina Patel rings to make an appointment to discuss her position following a car accident, she will be asked for the names of the other parties involved in the accident. She will, of course, give the names of Adam Worcik and Linford Chester. This information will allow the firm to carry out a check in the firm's client database. If the firm already acts for Mr Worcik or Mr Chester then it must not act for Hina Patel. The arranged interview would have to be cancelled.

> **TRANSACTION CASE STUDY**
>
> This case study has an additional complication. The conflict check still needs to be carried out to ensure that, for example, your firm does not already act for Robert Grove Ltd, the proposed purchaser of Toast & Tea. In addition, consideration must be given as to whether you can properly act for all three sellers. It is usually the case that, as long as they are all in agreement as to the general terms of the sale, their interests in selling the business do not conflict and that you are safe to take initial instructions from all three of them, although of course this must be checked at the start of the interview. However, care must be taken to ensure that, even if this is the case at the start, it continues to be so throughout the transaction as further complexities arise. It may well be that, in relation to certain aspects of the sale and purchase agreement, you will need to recommend that they each take independent advice later on. This may happen, for example, if the partners plan to work for Robert Grove Ltd after the sale. They will each need to negotiate their own employment contracts and so will need to take independent advice on this aspect of the deal.

Identity checks

You must identify the person for whom you act. This is generally clear, but confusion can arise, for example, if your initial meeting is with a director of a company (is your client the director or the company?).

In cases where the Money Laundering, Terrorist Financing and Transfer of Funds (Information on the Payer) Regulations 2017 apply, a new client should be warned when booking the appointment that the firm will need evidence of their identity. The client should be asked to bring proof of their identity to the interview. Generally speaking, a solicitor must not accept instructions from a new client involved in regulated activities until the solicitor has confirmation of the client's identity.

Research

In the case of a client who has instructed the firm before, it will facilitate good rapport and promote the efficient use of both your and the client's time if, as far as possible, you familiarise yourself with the client. Research the client's case history and talk to colleagues who have dealt with the client before.

In the case of a new client, where possible obtain background information on the client (and, where relevant, the client's business).

Where relevant and possible, you may decide it would be useful to request documents in advance from the client.

From the information provided by the client you may have some idea as to the law that is likely to be relevant to the case. You may wish to carry out some legal research on that area of law in advance of the interview.

> **PERSONAL INJURY CASE STUDY**
>
> Assume you have been instructed by Adam Worcik. He mentioned to your secretary when booking the appointment that the car driver would not have been so badly hurt if she had been wearing a seat belt at the time of the accident. You may therefore need to check the up-to-date position on the details of the relevant criminal offence and remind yourself of the principles of contributory negligence.

However, in anticipating what may be relevant, be careful not to pre-judge the issues or 'pigeon-hole' the client.

Checklists

Some interviews lend themselves to the use of checklists. As discussed in the previous paragraph, once you know why a client is coming to see you, it is possible to anticipate the topics that may be relevant to their case. Therefore, through careful planning you could draw up a checklist to use during the interview as an *aide memoire*.

Used appropriately, a checklist has the obvious advantage that essential information is unlikely to be overlooked. A checklist also provides you with a concise and convenient source of information for speedy future reference.

However, interviewing a client simply by running through a checklist, particularly at the beginning of the interview, may inhibit effective communication. You may appear to be merely 'processing a case' rather than listening to the client's unique personal problem.

Using a checklist in such a manner may damage rapport. The client may get a feeling of not being listened to if your questions jump from one topic to another rather than follow up on the client's current train of thought. Indeed, premature use of a checklist (ie, before a correct diagnosis of the problem has been made) can waste valuable time while a mass of irrelevant information is accumulated. In other words, make quite sure that your chosen checklist is appropriate before using it.

Vulnerability

In its Guide of 29 November 2022, the Law Society says, 'Solicitors need to adapt their practices to identify and meet the needs of clients who may be vulnerable, due to their personal circumstances and barriers put in place by society.' The term 'vulnerable' is a broad one. According to the Law Society, it extends to anyone who is at a disadvantage because of factors which affect their access to, and use of, legal services. In some instances, the link between the client's circumstances and their ability to use legal services is obvious, for example where the client is a child or has a mental impairment. In others less so, for example a client may have difficulty in using legal services as a result of a low income, limited literacy skills or a recent bereavement.

In preparing for, and conducting, the first interview, a solicitor must be alert to circumstances which are likely to place the client in a vulnerable situation. For example, if the client has limited literacy skills, the solicitor will need to adjust their methods of communication to meet that client's needs; similarly, if the client has learning difficulties, the solicitor will need to take particular care in the language they use to frame their advice.

Interpreters

Give some thought to the use of a language or sign language interpreter, for example if the client does not speak the same language as you or if they have a hearing impairment. In its Guide of 29 November 2022, The Law Society recommends that in preparing for a meeting with a client, it is essential to establish whether they have any specific needs relating to their ability to communicate. If, for example, an interpreter is needed, it is possible the client will bring a member of their family or a friend along to the interview to provide such support. If not, or in cases where it is preferable to have an independent professional interpreter, you will need to organise for this support to be provided. If possible, you should try to brief the interpreter before the interview as to their role and the confidential nature of the interview.

> **PROFESSIONAL CONDUCT POINT**
>
> If you are involved in criminal proceedings, you should refer to the Practice Note of 31 January 2023. This Practice Note explains the importance of the role of an interpreter and gives guidance on identifying the need for an interpreter. There is also guidance on the allocation of responsibility for arranging for and paying interpreters for defendants, prosecution witnesses and defence witnesses. The Practice Note includes useful information as to how to contact and select an appropriate interpreter and the role of the interpreter in the proceedings.
>
> Further, in this Practice Note, The Law Society sets out its guidance relating to ensuring that an accurate record is kept of interviews at police stations involving sign language interpreters. If the interviewee requires use of a sign language interpreter then a solicitor should insist that a video record of both the interpreter and the interviewee be made.

Client care information sheet

> **PROFESSIONAL CONDUCT POINT**
>
> Some information has to be given to a client 'at the time of engagement'.
> - The firm must make clear how it is regulated and ensure that the client understands the regulatory protections available to them (SRA Code of Conduct for Solicitors 2019, paras 8.10 and 8.11).
> - The firm must inform clients of their right to complain and how to complain (paras 8.3 and 8.4) and of their right to complain to the Legal Ombudsman, the time frame for doing so, and full details of how to contact the Legal Ombudsman.

> - Paragraph 8.7 requires the client to receive the best possible information on costs (see **11.6**).
>
> Therefore, during or before the first interview, The Law Society recommends that the firm should give the client an information sheet which the solicitor can explain to the client during the interview. The information would include:
>
> (a) information on the costs of the interview;
>
> (b) details of the client's right to complain and of how to complain;
>
> (c) details of the right to complain to the Legal Ombudsman and how to make contact;
>
> (d) information confirming how your services are regulated.

Once the information sheet has been explained to the client during the initial interview, the client should be asked to sign and date it. A copy of the signed document should be kept by the firm.

> **PROFESSIONAL CONDUCT POINT**
>
> This information should still be supplied in writing, if possible, when conducting an interview over the telephone. Use should be made of e-mail and fax facilities, where available. Alternatively, the information should be covered orally during the interview, and the solicitor should be careful to note that it was discussed.

Ensure no interruptions

You should ensure that the interview will be free from interruptions, so ensure your telephone is put on silent or, more preferably, that it will divert calls.

11.8.2 The interview – a model

```
            GREETING
(1) PRELIMINARIES
(2) OBTAINING THE FACTS
(3) FILLING IN THE DETAIL
(4) ADVISING
(5) CLOSING
            PARTING
```

What now follows is a step-by-step account of each successive stage in the model (see **11.4.2**), indicating the purpose of each stage and which skills need to be employed. The checklist at **11.7** provides a useful overview of this structure.

11.8.3 Greeting

The importance of a warm and friendly greeting cannot be over-emphasised.

When you are ready to see the client, either go yourself to the reception area and escort the client to where the interview will take place, or make sure that some other member of staff does so. A client who is left to find their own way to your office through a bewildering maze of corridors is unlikely to arrive feeling welcome.

The client will form an impression of you as soon as you meet. You should therefore do everything possible to ensure that this impression is favourable and that the client is made to feel welcome, comfortable and relaxed.

Greet the client by making eye contact and addressing the client by name. You should also introduce yourself by name and explain your status within the firm (eg, trainee solicitor, solicitor, partner, etc).

> **PERSONAL INJURY CASE STUDY**
>
> Imagine you are instructed by Linford Chester and are meeting him for the first time. How will you greet him?
>
> > 'Good morning Mr Chester. My name is Alex Ireland and I am a trainee solicitor with the firm. Please take a seat.'

In most cases the greeting will also involve *shaking hands*. This may not always be appropriate, for example if the client is a child.

Be aware of any cultural differences which may make eye contact or shaking hands inappropriate. If relevant, consider telling the client that you are not familiar with their culture and do not wish to cause offence.

Remember, many clients do not regularly consult solicitors. When they do have cause to visit your office, it is likely to be at a time when they are experiencing very difficult situations. The prospect of visiting your office and meeting you may be quite daunting and add to their already stressful state of mind. Friendly conversation about such things as the weather, the client's journey or difficulties in parking their car may help put the client at ease.

Virtual client meetings are becoming more common. It is, therefore, likely that you may be involved in conducting client interviews using video links. Much of the good practice outlined above will still apply when you greet your client in a virtual meeting. You still need to create a first impression that establishes rapport with the client and appears professional and confident. Greeting the client by name, introducing yourself, establishing good eye contact and initiating conversation designed to put the client at ease are, if anything, even more important when you are not meeting in person in your office. Being well prepared and confident will ensure that the interview does not start with awkward pauses.

The above points are simply common courtesy and may seem obvious, but they are extremely important.

After greeting, it is a matter of judgement how quickly you proceed to the business at hand, but most clients will have been rehearsing what they wish to say and will be ready to begin at once.

11.8.4 Preliminaries

As mentioned at **11.8.1.2**, the client will have given some indication of the general nature of the problem and the reason for seeking advice when arranging the appointment for the interview.

Nevertheless, ambiguities may still arise. 'I want to see a solicitor about a will' may not necessarily mean that the client wishes to make a will; they may want to challenge the validity of a will. It is therefore sensible to *ask the client to confirm your understanding of the reason for the visit before encouraging the client to launch into a lengthy account of the facts*. This should be a quick check by way of a closed question to avoid the client thinking they are being invited to fully explain the reason for their visit.

Once this confirmation has been obtained, there are two matters which should be dealt with before the interview proceeds further.

11.8.4.1 How will the interview be conducted?

It makes sense to start by letting the client know how long you have available for the interview *and to find out whether the client is under any time constraints*. If you are using an interpreter during the interview, allow twice as long as normal because everything will need to be repeated.

It is also helpful to say a little about how you propose to conduct the interview:

First, I'll ask you to explain why you have come to see me. Then I will need to ask you some questions and make some notes. Finally, when I have got the complete picture, I shall explain what your legal position is and what options I think are open to you. Between us, we can then try to decide which course of action would best suit your needs.

11.8.4.2 The cost of the interview

> **PROFESSIONAL CONDUCT POINT**
>
> Paragraph 8.7 of the SRA Code of Conduct for Solicitors 2019 requires that clients are given the best information possible, both at the time of engagement and as the matter progresses, about the likely overall cost of their matter.

Clients naturally tend to be concerned about the cost of the interview and, indeed, of the whole matter. Until the complete picture has been obtained, it is usually difficult to say anything meaningful about the latter, and this must therefore be postponed until later stages of the interview (see **11.8.8.2**).

However, now is a good time to ascertain whether the client will be paying the costs or if there is an external source of funding. If the client is a company, its parent company, directors or shareholders may be providing support towards the costs. An employee may be supported by a trade union. It is crucial to establish from the start if the client is eligible for Legal Aid, or if they have the benefit of any legal expenses insurance (if not you should consider whether to advise the client to seek 'after the event insurance').

You must provide full information about the costs to the client even if they are not going to be paying for the charges themselves. If you have any fee-sharing arrangements with relevant third parties then you must make this clear to the client.

Whilst a full discussion of the costs of the matter will need to be delayed until later in the interview, now is a good stage to clarify the cost of the interview. In referring the client to the client care information sheet (see **11.8.1.2**), you should explain to the client what your charging rate is or, if such be the case, that the firm's policy is to charge a fixed fee, for example for an initial half-hour interview. If the firm's policy is to provide the initial interview free of charge, then it will be reassuring for the client if this is confirmed by the solicitor early on in the interview. In *An ombudsman's view* (2nd edn), the Legal Ombudsman says that when quoting a fee and explaining that VAT will be added to that fee, it is helpful to also state the total, VAT inclusive, figure. Once the initial costs have been explained clearly to the client, *you should check whether the client is genuinely content to accept this arrangement*. You may like to mention that you will return to the matter of costs at the end of the interview when you have a better idea of the client's situation.

> **TRANSACTION CASE STUDY**
>
> Imagine you are instructed by the sellers. How will you explain the cost of the interview based on the fact your charge-out rate is £150 per hour plus VAT? In addition, how will you manage your client's expectations as to how long the interview will last? You anticipate that this is going to be a complex interview; you have not arranged any further appointments this afternoon.
>
> Solicitor: 'I realise that there is a lot for us to get through this afternoon. I have no other commitments this afternoon, do you need to leave at any particular time?'
>
> Client: 'No, I really want to sort out as much as possible today so that we can get the deal moving.'

> Solicitor: 'Well, now is probably a good time to mention my firm's charges for this interview. You will see from the information sheet that I have prepared for you that the firm charges my time out at £150 per hour plus VAT. Are you happy to proceed on this basis?'
>
> Client: 'Yes.'
>
> Solicitor: 'Good. I will, of course, return to the matter of costs at the end of the interview when I have a better idea of the work that is likely to be involved in dealing with the sale of your business.'

11.8.4.3 Keeping control

If during the preliminaries stage you need to ask questions, it is important to use only closed questions (see **10.3.2**). In order to keep control of the interview, the client should not perceive any question as an invitation to launch into their reason for making the appointment until you are ready for them to do so.

11.8.4.4 Skills summary

(1) Explaining.
(2) Closed questions.

11.8.5 Obtaining the facts

The objective is to obtain the client's account of the facts or of the proposed transaction. Remember that in some cultures it is not usual to discuss personal matters with strangers, even for professional reasons. You may need to allow time for trust to build, perhaps even over several meetings. It may help to explain why you need the information and what it is to be used for. Such clients may find it easier to talk to someone else in your presence, rather than directly to you.

Encourage the client to give an account of the matter in their own words. This should be with as little interruption from you as possible. In order to provide relevant advice and options to your client, you need to fully understand their situation and needs.

Consider the impact on the client of the following choice of words and expressions:

'So, where shall we start?' (Does not inspire confidence)

'What's the problem, then?' (There may not be a 'problem')

'Thank you for sending me the documentation ... It seems to me ...' (Over-directional – premature diagnosis)

'Things don't look too good, do they?' (Prematurely pessimistic – provokes anxiety)

'Don't worry, we'll sort this out for you.' (Prematurely optimistic – raises expectations)

'Funny, this is the sixth one we've had in like this in the last month.' (Treating client as a 'case' to be processed – not a human being)

'This is the one, I think. Now then, where are we? ... Let me see ... dah dah dah dah ... Oh yes that's right, this is a GBH case, isn't it?' (Disorganised – unprepared – confusing use of jargon)

Clearly, therefore, you must give very careful thought to the form of words which you use to invite the client to begin this process.

If you are interviewing a client about a road accident it may be perfectly sensible to say, 'Perhaps you could start by telling me exactly what happened on the day of the accident'.

On the other hand, if the client wishes to make a will, saying 'Could you now give me some general background information?' or 'Just tell me the story in your own words' is too vague to indicate what sort of information you require. A more focused form of words would be, 'It's a good idea to make a will. Is there any particular reason that has prompted you to do so now?', or 'Perhaps you could start by explaining what you would like your will to deal with'.

Whatever form of opening words you decide upon, it can also be helpful if, during this part of the interview, you also ask questions along the lines of, 'It would be helpful if you could let me know any particular concerns which you have' and 'Do you foresee any problems?' *Remember to avoid asking more than one question at once.*

You should concentrate on using the various listening techniques discussed at **10.2** and **11.4.1** and confine questions to open questions which will encourage the client to continue the narrative.

As the client begins to build up a picture of the reason why they have come to see you, it is important that your questions try to follow the client's train of thought. Your open questions should encourage the client to expand on a particular topic or, as appropriate, to move on to a different aspect. You should avoid jumping around topics and asking questions as they occur to you, irrespective of the particular train of thought that a client is focussing on. You should also avoid just following a random list of questions you prepared earlier. Jumping around topics will hinder your ability to build up a clear picture and is more likely to cause the client to omit facts from their explanation. A good questioning technique should be logical and should facilitate the client's recall and thought processes.

There will be ample opportunity in the next stage of the interview ('Filling in the detail') to clarify matters. You should therefore resist any temptation to do so at this stage, because a series of closed questions can easily destroy the client's concentration.

For the same reason, making written notes should, if possible, be restricted to what can be written without interrupting the client's narrative flow (see **11.5.5**).

This comparatively passive role can be a difficult one to master if you are a naturally talkative person. It does, however, enable you to maintain eye contact with the client and to observe the client's general demeanour and manner of delivery. This is very helpful in building rapport with the client and in picking up body language signals about the client's feelings.

If you employ an interpreter during the interview, it is important to remember that the client is the focus for your attention. The solicitor/client relationship is still central to the interview and there should be no independent discussion of the interpreter's views. This becomes more difficult if the interpreter is a friend or relation of the client. There is more chance that side conversations will take place. You should always ask for a translation of any such discussions. In addition, you should be wary of any sign that the interpreter is adding their own view to the translation.

11.8.5.1 Skills summary

(1) Listening.
(2) Open questions.
(3) Brief (if any) note-taking.

11.8.6 Filling in the detail

The objective is to ensure that you obtain a full and accurate understanding and record of the relevant facts and of the client's wishes and objectives.

You will not usually be able to give the client effective advice immediately after the client has completed their account of the matter in the 'Obtaining the facts' stage.

In most cases, it will be necessary to ask the client to fill gaps or explain discrepancies in the narrative or to supply information which the client had not considered to be relevant.

You will also need to take written notes (see **11.5.5**) and check that you have correctly understood what the client has said.

It may also be necessary to examine documents. You should not try reading a document at the same time as the client is speaking. Not only might this hinder rapport, but it is very difficult to read and listen at the same time. Explain to the client that you need a few moments to read the document so that there is a 'comfortable' silence while you are reading.

This is the stage of the interview during which you assume a more active and directive role.

Questioning skills become more important although, even at this stage, it is generally best to use the T-funnel approach (discussed at **11.5.2.3**). In other words, see what information can be elicited in response to open questions before pinning down the client with more specific closed questions.

It may be necessary to use some of the clarifying and probing techniques (see **11.5.2.4**) to jog the client's memory or to explore discrepancies or weaknesses in the client's version of events.

Before completing this stage of the interview and moving on to give advice, *it is important to summarise what the client has said* in order to double-check that you have correctly understood the position (see **11.5.2.5**).

11.8.6.1 Skills summary

(1) Questioning – the T-funnel approach.
(2) Note-taking.
(3) Clarifying and probing.
(4) Examining documents.
(5) Summarising.

11.8.7 Advising

> **PROFESSIONAL CONDUCT POINT**
>
> Paragraph 8.6 of the SRA Code of Conduct for Solicitors 2019 requires that clients should be in a position to make informed decisions about the services they need, how their matter will be handled and the options available to them.
>
> You will want to provide a clear explanation of the issues involved and the options available to the client. You should explain:
>
> (a) the relevant issues, the different ways in which the matter could progress and any likely complications;
> (b) the available options;
> (c) whether the possible outcomes merit the risk and expense;
> (d) your role and responsibilities and the services your firm can or cannot provide.

In essence you will usually need to:

(a) explain the current legal position of the client;
(b) discuss with the client the main options (both legal and non-legal) if their legal position is not to their liking;
(c) help the client to reach a decision/give instructions;
(d) agree a plan of action.

11.8.7.1 Explaining the client's legal position

> **PROFESSIONAL CONDUCT POINT**
>
> Principle 7 of the SRA Principles 2019 requires those regulated by the SRA to act in the best interests of each client. In addition, it is essential to observe the rules governing solicitors who are conducting financial services activities and to avoid such work unless authorised to conduct it.

This is the first interview. Therefore, if:

(a) the matter is not routine; or

(b) you do not have experience in the particular area of law; or

(c) the client does not insist on preliminary 'off the cuff' advice; or

(d) the matter is not urgent,

it is quite proper to postpone advising until you have had an opportunity to carry out research, or, if a trainee solicitor, to take advice from your supervising solicitor.

Clients do not always need or expect to be given immediate advice. If you are in a position to give advice then it is essential to package it in a way that allows the client to follow your line of reasoning and understand it. The client's legal position should be explained in simple and comprehensible language. You should therefore avoid jargon. Furthermore, you should be aware that the amount of information which a client can absorb is limited (see **11.5.4**).

Every time you are preparing to conduct an interview, you should give conscious thought to the best way of explaining the likely relevant issues to a lay client, for example the fiduciary duties of directors or the dissolution of a partnership at will under the Partnership Act 1890. You should try to work out a jargon free way of explaining, for example, the difference between an off-the-shelf company and a tailor-made company or the difference between the roles of shareholders and directors. There is no need to use statute names, section numbers or case names; in fact such details are undesirable because, rather than impressing a client, they will only serve to confuse or overload a client with unnecessary details.

Clarity of advice also involves trying to structure your advice so that it is given to the client in an order that is easy to follow. For example, in a criminal case it would probably make more sense to explain first what the prosecution has to establish before moving on to explain the availability of particular defences.

In its Practice Note of 8 September 2021, The Law Society recommends that, when advising, 'you should include information on: likely complications which commonly arise ... [and] the different ways a particular matter could progress'. The aim is to ensure that the client appreciates that their case involves a complex matter, and it reduces the risk that, at a later date, the client concludes that 'you did not handle the matter properly'.

11.8.7.2 Discussing the main options

Whilst needing to understand the current legal position, the client is generally less interested in being given a detailed resumé of the law than in being told what courses of action are available. However, some explanation of the law is necessary in order to set the available options in context.

Clients need to be given a clear explanation of what realistic options are open to them in order to achieve their desired objectives. Managing the client's expectations now can reduce the risk of dissatisfaction and complaint later on in your relationship. This explanation must be supported by thorough discussion with the client of the relative merits of each option. Remember, there may be differing potential costs implications for each option.

Clearly, the strength of the legal aspects of the case will influence this discussion, but you must also remember that there are other factors which will have an impact on the client's decision. In particular, the client's decision as to which option to pursue may be influenced by the possible timeframe involved, the level of costs, the commercial risks and personal factors such as emotion, health, family relationships, professional embarrassment, employee relations and possible adverse publicity.

> **PROFESSIONAL CONDUCT POINT**
>
> Principle 7 of the SRA Principles 2019 requires that you act in the best interests of your client. You should discuss with the client whether the potential outcomes justify the expense or risk and, in particular, any risk that the client may have to cover their opponent's costs. It is sensible to make a record of the risk assessment and the risk should be kept under review, with the client being updated as to any changes, as the matter progresses.
>
> In *An ombudsman's view* (2nd edn), the Legal Ombudsman confirms that clients can only make informed decisions if they understand the cost implications of their options. 'This information should be provided before any work starts and it should be updated, when appropriate, as the case progresses.'

> **TRANSACTION CASE STUDY**
>
> Assume that you are acting for the purchaser who tells you that, for tax reasons, this deal must take place within the next 10 days. Your advice may well have been that the purchaser should carry out a very extensive investigation into the assets and liabilities of Toast & Tea (so-called 'due diligence'). This process should discover any problems that exist, for example with the physical state and legal title of the properties or the contractual relationships with suppliers. However, such a process will be time-consuming and expensive. If time is short then due diligence should perhaps focus on the property or contractual relationships which are of greatest interest to the client. If due diligence is to be limited, the client will need to weigh up the risk of buying assets with 'hidden problems', which may give rise to expense in the future, against the risk of losing the deal or losing the tax advantage by not completing in the next 10 days.

The discussion should take account of these non-legal factors. For example, litigation is not only emotionally stressful, costly and time consuming, it can be severely disruptive to a business if employees, partners or directors have to spend days at court waiting to give evidence. It may make commercial sense for a client to do nothing about a particular issue because, despite any injustice, it is not economically worthwhile. It may be that cash flow will prevent the taking or defending of an action. Equally, it may be commercially necessary to defend an action, despite the costs, to preserve a good name, trade mark, goodwill or a position in the market.

You should try to involve the client in the discussion so that you can jointly weigh the advantages and disadvantages of each option. Clients cannot be expected to choose between available options unless the solicitor has clearly explained the pros and cons of each option and the action required to implement each option. This will help the client to reach a decision, as will *entering into a dialogue* with the client to ensure that the client is making the right decision for the right reasons. Even a client who comes to the interview with a clear idea of how they want the matter to progress will be interested in the options. At least then the client's decision is an informed one.

11.8.7.3 Helping the client to reach a decision

All major decisions concerning the case or transaction are for the client to make. It is the client's case, not the solicitor's. However, opinion is divided on how far the solicitor may recommend a course of action for the client.

There are two schools of thought.

(a) The non-directive school suggests that a solicitor should only present the options and leave it entirely to the client to decide which to follow. The advice is characterised by the preamble, 'On the one hand X, but on the other hand Y. However, it is for you to decide'.

This approach may avoid a charge of negligence if the route followed by the client proves to be the wrong option. However, it is not particularly helpful to the client. Given the status, experience and cost of solicitors, clients often expect a recommendation.

(b) The directive school involves the solicitor in taking greater control of the decision-making process.

A combination of each approach is appropriate in most cases. It is important to explain the realistic options to the client and to explore the positive and negative consequences of each. Provided the client actively participates in this explorative discussion and you actively seek the client's views and preferences, the decision will often be clear.

Furthermore, if the matter is non-urgent, difficult or complex, the client may need time to reach a considered decision.

11.8.7.4 Agreeing a future plan of action

Once key decisions have been taken, it will usually be necessary to agree a more detailed plan of campaign, ie, to decide what is the best way of carrying out the course of action which has been agreed. This presents a useful opportunity for you to explain your role and the services your firm can offer.

For example, if your client has decided to try to settle a matter by agreement rather than go to court, you will still need to decide:

(a) whether to approach the other side immediately or await their next move;
(b) whether any first approach should be made by you or the client, and if so:
 (i) whether it should be by letter, telephone or in person;
 (ii) what (if any) opening offer should be made and how far the client is prepared to go in order to settle.

As before, you should explain clearly the range of options and try to engage the client as fully as possible in the decision-making process.

In bringing this discussion to a close, you should ensure that everything has been discussed to the client's satisfaction. A form of wording could be as follows: 'Can I just check whether you clearly understand your position or if there is anything you would like me to clarify.'

11.8.7.5 Skills summary

(1) Summarising.
(2) Explaining.
(3) Listening.
(4) Note-taking.

11.8.8 Closing

Once the issues have been discussed with the client, and the client has decided what needs to be done or has decided to go away and consider their options more carefully, there are still a number of matters to deal with before you conclude the interview.

11.8.8.1 Client care and costs information

> **PROFESSIONAL CONDUCT POINT**
>
> At the closing stage you should ensure that the client has as clear a picture as possible of what will happen next and the costs that they are likely to incur.
>
> The outstanding client care issues to be covered and costs information to be imparted are as follows:

> (a) explaining the possible time frame for completion of the matter;
> (b) giving the best information possible as to the costs of the matter, including any disbursements;
> (c) establishing when your next contact with the client will occur;
> (d) confirming the advice given in the interview in a follow-up letter and maintaining a proper record of the interview.

A guide to the issues to be dealt with during the closing stages is set out at **11.8.8.2**. This guidance encompasses these outstanding matters and includes further recommendations which, as a matter of good practice, should be considered at this stage of the interview.

11.8.8.2 A professional closing

There are a number of matters to be addressed in closing the interview and in ensuring that both you and your client are clear as to what will happen next, how quickly the matter will be resolved and what it will all cost. Whilst most of these matters can be dealt with in any convenient order, it is recommended that asking if the client has anything further to discuss should be dealt with first.

Is there anything else?

You should always make sure that the client has had an opportunity to discuss all matters and concerns.

Make a specific point of asking the client if there is anything else they want to discuss. This forms a bridge between the advising stage and the performance of the other closing tasks. Its purpose is to ensure that there are no other matters which the client wishes to discuss before the solicitor starts to close the interview. This should not be treated as a meaningless ritual, and the client should be made to feel free to respond affirmatively.

This may be characterised as follows, 'Before I start to round off this meeting, can I just check that there is nothing else that you want to bring up or ask me about?'. Two further points need to be emphasised:

(a) This should sound to the client like a sincere and genuine enquiry, not a formality, as in the familiar, 'well if there is nothing else then...'.

(b) The question, 'Is there anything else?' can perform the function described above, but it should not be repeatedly posed throughout the interview as a substitute for asking sensible questions to elicit information.

This question should be asked before dealing with all the other closing tasks. If it is left until the end of the closing then, if the client does have something else to talk about, the closing tasks may change. This means the interview will have to be closed again, possibly with different follow-up tasks, different cost implications and a different time frame. Asking, 'Is there anything else?' at an appropriate stage allows the solicitor to keep better control of the structure at the end of the interview. It avoids any misunderstanding or confusion that could arise from effectively closing the interview twice.

Next steps/follow-up tasks by solicitor

During the interview, it is essential to establish exactly what, if anything, the client is instructing you to do (see **11.8.7.4**). If you are dealing with a new client, especially one who is not used to consulting solicitors, you should explain your role and the services your firm provides. You may already have covered these matters when discussing a plan of action with the client (see **11.8.7.4**)

In the closing stages of the interview, it is helpful to summarise what steps you have agreed to take and when you will take them. The steps will vary from case to case but might involve taking a statement from a witness, obtaining a police or medical report, writing a letter before action, carrying out a company search, preparing a draft will or partnership agreement, or drafting a divorce petition.

In most cases, it will be appropriate to write a follow-up letter (see **11.8.10**) to the client summarising what has been discussed and agreed. Telling the client that you intend to do this is obviously reassuring.

If you have not already done so, now is a good time to discuss the best form of communicating with the client, be it by email, letter or phone call. It is essential to check that you have an accurate note of the client's address, telephone number and email address. Remember to confirm to which address the client wishes correspondence to be sent. This may be relevant if, for example, the matter involves a partnership dispute when the client may prefer correspondence to be sent to their home address rather than business address. Equally, in a divorce case, the client may prefer correspondence to be sent to them care of a friend or family member.

Next steps/follow-up tasks by client

You should also remind the client of any action that they have agreed to take. This might include supplying information or documents which were not available during the interview or thinking about the advice or discussing their options with others and contacting you once a decision has been reached. If there is nothing you need the client to do at this stage, it is useful to state this clearly.

Alternative contact

Giving your name and status in the firm is something which should have been explained when you introduced yourself as part of the greeting or preliminaries stages of the interview.

When closing the interview, it may be useful to remind the client of your name and status. It will not always be necessary to give the name of the person with overall supervision of the matter during the interview itself; this can be left to the follow-up letter or client information sheet. However, in some cases this may be appropriate. For example, if you have introduced yourself as a trainee solicitor, it can be reassuring to the client to be told that your work is supervised.

In all cases you should provide the client with an alternative point of contact in the firm. This is the name of a person they can speak to if, when the client contacts the office, you are not available, or if the client has any complaint. Reference can also be made here to the client care information sheet you prepared in advance (see **11.8.1.2**).

A form of wording which covers all these aspects could be as follows:

> 'As I mentioned at the start of the interview, my name is Joseph Adkin and I am a trainee solicitor with the firm. My work is supervised by Alice White who will be familiar with your case. If, when you contact the office, I am not available, please feel free to speak to Mrs White. Mrs White's contact details are on the information sheet I gave you at the start of the interview.'

Time frame for the matter

The client should be given some indication of how long the matter will take to complete, remembering to take into account any deadlines to which the client needs you to work (for example, the matter must be completed by the end of the tax year). This should help manage the client's expectations and minimise the risk of complaints about delays in situations where the outcome is likely to take some time to attain. Sometimes an estimate is quite easy to give:

> 'As the agreed terms are quite straightforward, I shall be able to send you and Simon a draft of the partnership agreement by the end of the week. Then, if you're both happy with it, it should be possible to sign the final document sometime during next week.'

In other cases, particularly where court proceedings are a possibility, it may be impossible to do more than give a very broad estimate because future developments will to a large extent be unpredictable and outside your control. Even in these situations, you should try to give some indication of time frame, even if it is only to indicate that the matter could potentially take years rather than months.

Estimating the costs of the matter/method of charging

Costs will already have been discussed during the course of the interview. As stated at **11.8.4.2**, it will usually be possible to explain early in the interview how the interview itself is to be paid for, but it is seldom possible at that stage to discuss the likely cost of the matter itself. When discussing the client's options (see **11.8.7.2**) there should have been an analysis of whether the benefits of any proposed course of action outweigh potential risks as to costs, and you may have considered the possibility of offering the client a conditional fee arrangement.

In closing the interview, a summary of the position as to costs ensures the client understands clearly the potential cost implications they are facing. In *An ombudsman's view* (2nd edn), the Legal Ombudsman expresses the view that a client 'should never be surprised by the bill'. The guidance goes on to say that it is expected that the lawyer explains how the firm's charging structure works 'and what is does and does not include. It must be crystal clear.' Information on costs, together with details of possible disbursements (charges or fees that will be incurred by the solicitor in carrying out the legal work which are not included in the firm's charging rate, such as the charge for a company search or payment of stamp duty land tax), should be summarised as part of the closing stage of the interview.

Costs should be discussed in a business-like way. You are providing a service to the client, and you should not therefore appear to be embarrassed at having to discuss money.

> **PROFESSIONAL CONDUCT POINT**
>
> Paragraph 8.7 of the SRA Code of Conduct for Solicitors 2019 requires you to give your client the best possible information on the likely overall costs of the matter.
>
> The Law Society's guidance recommends that you outline your standard billing arrangements and discuss any requirements for receiving funds on account.

Deciding just what information you can reliably give the client will involve consideration of a range of possible ways of handling this particularly tricky aspect of client care.

An agreed fee

In some cases, commonly domestic conveyancing and simple will drafting, the firm may agree a fixed fee for handling the client's matter. The agreed fee should have been mentioned at the opening stage of the interview (see **11.8.4.2**). During the closing stage of the interview, having received detailed instructions and not having found any unforeseen complications, it is appropriate to confirm the agreed fee. You should also confirm the work the agreed fee will cover, when the agreed fee is to be paid and whether there are any disbursements (including how much they are likely to be and when they will need to be paid).

Estimating the likely costs

As most firms calculate their bill by using an hourly charging rate, the likely costs of the matter will involve the solicitor estimating how much time will be involved in handling the matter. While, as a bare minimum, the client should be told the firm's hourly charging rate (and, if relevant, whether the rate may change during the retainer), this information is not in itself helpful if the client has no idea of how many hours' work will be involved. The rate should be coupled with a realistic estimate of the time to be charged.

In non-contentious matters, such as setting up a simple company or drafting a partnership agreement, an estimate of the overall cost is usually possible. For example, in a matter where you are instructed to draft a partnership agreement where the individuals have already agreed the terms that they wish the contract to cover, you may be happy to advise the client as follows:

> 'As I mentioned at the start of the interview, my firm charges my time at £100 plus VAT per hour. In my experience, drafting the sort of partnership agreement which you and your partners will need is likely to cost in the region of £400–£500 plus VAT.'

However, in many cases, it will be necessary to make it clear to the client that a precise figure for the total cost cannot be given because of the uncertainty as to how much work may need to be undertaken and the time it may take. For example, if you are advising an individual who is involved in negotiating the terms of a partnership agreement which have not yet been agreed, you will be less certain as to the amount of time you will be involved in completing the transaction:

> 'As I mentioned at the start of the interview, my firm charges my time at £100 plus VAT per hour. It is difficult to estimate how much of my time will be taken up during the negotiations, and so it is impossible to give you a precise estimate of the overall costs. It may well amount to over £1,000 but I will report to you regularly about the costs as the matter progresses.'

The Legal Ombudsman's view is it is important to manage a client's expectations about the possible cost range. When investigating following a compliant, the Legal Ombudsman will always ask if an estimate of costs was provided to the client. There are many situations, particularly those involving potential litigation, where it may not be possible to give a realistic overall cost of the matter. In such situations, the possible range of costs should be discussed, explaining how different facts could impact the final bill. In such cases, you should also give the best information possible about the cost of the next stage of the matter. For example, in a case where the client has decided that they would like to defend legal action taken against them, you might advise the client as follows:

> 'As I mentioned at the start of the interview, my firm charges my time at £200 plus VAT per hour. Clearly, the cost will depend on how much time is involved and this in turn depends on whether the case can be settled. It is impossible, at this stage, for me to give a precise estimate of the costs involved in taking this matter to full trial if it does not settle. However, a realistic estimate may be £20,000. However, this could be significantly less if a settlement is agreed. We have agreed that the next step will be for me to instruct a barrister to provide an opinion on the likelihood of your defence succeeding in court. In my experience, the cost of my time in preparing the instructions to the barrister and the barrister's fees in providing such an opinion is likely to be in the region of £2,000 plus VAT. Before instructing the barrister, I will need you to provide me with £1,000 which I will hold pending payment of the costs I incur on your account. Once we have the opinion, we can meet again to discuss whether you wish to proceed with your defence and I will, at that time, be in a better position to advise you further as to the likely costs.'

In all cases when you are giving an estimate, you should consider whether either of the following assurances should be offered to the client: reassurance that you will keep them informed regularly as to how the costs are mounting during the matter; or perhaps agreeing a ceiling figure for costs, with the client's agreement being needed before costs beyond this figure are incurred.

If you anticipate the client having to pay disbursements then you must mention this and explain how much they are likely to amount to and when the client will be expected to pay for them.

The client should be reassured that detailed information relating to costs will be confirmed in the follow-up letter (see **11.8.10**).

Next contact

Make it clear which of you is to make the next contact. Does your client expect to hear from you or vice versa?

At the same time, tell your client whether you think that another face-to-face meeting will be necessary and (if so) why and who will organise it.

For example:

> 'So we've agreed that I shall do nothing until you let me know how much you want to offer to Mr Jones. I shall then write to his solicitors offering that sum in full and final settlement.
>
> Obviously, if they confirm in writing that he accepts, that will broadly be an end of the matter.
>
> On the other hand, if he rejects the offer and continues with the court action, I shall need to arrange another meeting with you to give more detailed consideration to the strength of the evidence in support of your defence.'

11.8.8.3 Skills summary

(1) Summarising.
(2) Explaining.

11.8.9 Parting

When the interview is over, you should accompany the client back to the reception area. In the case of a virtual interview you should professionally end the meeting, perhaps by thanking the client for their time and, if appropriate, wishing them a good day.

The parting should be friendly, courteous and (as far as possible) reassuring.

11.8.10 After the interview

After the interview, the notes you have taken during the interview should be used to produce a full written record of the interview as soon as possible, whilst your memory is still fresh. Clients find it frustrating when they are later asked to repeat information previously discussed during your interview with them. A comprehensive file note will ensure that both you and any of your colleagues who are working on the client's matter have access to all relevant details.

In most cases, you will have promised to send the client a follow-up letter. This letter should be drafted and sent in good time after the interview. The letter is effectively confirming your understanding of the instructions you have received. It should confirm the advice you gave and the follow-up action that both you and the client agreed to take. It should contain the detailed costs information that you promised the client during the interview, provide a convenient opportunity to deal in writing with client care issues and may include a copy of your firm's terms of business. Further advice on drafting letters can be found in **Chapter 1**.

In *An ombudsman's view* (2nd edn), it is noted that '[k]eeping a good record of what has been agreed often resolves disputes [between solicitor and client] before they become a major disagreement'. The notes taken during the interview, together with your full attendance note, the follow-up letter, copies of the client's proof of identity papers and the client care information sheet signed by the client during the interview should all be placed on the client's file.

11.9 THE SECRET OF SUCCESS – PRACTICE

The principles set out in this chapter seek to provide something for everyone.

If you have never interviewed a client then the structure and skills that are outlined here will provide a firm foundation for you to prepare for your first interview. By reviewing how that interview went, you will begin to hone your skills and gradually, with further practice, develop a manner and technique with which you feel comfortable, safe in the knowledge that it is based on sound principles.

If you are already used to interviewing clients then reading this chapter may have made you evaluate the skills and techniques that you employ with a view to improving your personal style.

CHAPTER 12

NEGOTIATION AND ALTERNATIVE DISPUTE RESOLUTION

12.1	Introduction	157
12.2	The ethics of negotiation	158
12.3	Negotiating styles	158
12.4	Preparation for a negotiation	162
12.5	The forum for the negotiation	169
12.6	Other considerations before a meeting	170
12.7	Overview of a negotiation	172
12.8	The opening	172
12.9	The middle phase: discussion and bargaining	173
12.10	The end: closing a negotiation	175
12.11	'Dirty tricks'	176
12.12	Alternative dispute resolution	177

> **LEARNING OUTCOMES**
>
> After reading this chapter you will be able to:
> - identify your predominant negotiation style
> - understand the pros and cons of different negotiation styles
> - set out the core preparation you would undertake prior to negotiating
> - identify the key stages in a negotiation
> - select the most appropriate forum for a negotiation
> - explain the different types of ADR available
> - understand basic negotiation strategy and tactics.

12.1 INTRODUCTION

It is essential that lawyers add value in negotiation if they are to serve their clients well. Adding value requires an understanding of the principles of good negotiation and regular practice in implementing the techniques and tools involved. Much recent research has been done into how we make decisions and how we persuade others. This research now informs our understanding of how best to negotiate. In the rest of this chapter we consider some of the basic principles. There are also examples and exercises.

Negotiation is a process by which two or more parties attempt to come to agreement and can include commercial transactions as well as legal disputes. It is a complex skill which requires expert understanding of process, thorough preparation, and skilful use of psychological tools and techniques. Using principled interest-based negotiating techniques, it is often possible for all sides to achieve a solution which satisfies their needs and delivers much of what they want, ie an authentic solution which is acceptable to all the parties. Such solutions are the most likely to endure and add value.

Set out below is a summary of some of the essentials of good negotiating practice which will be explored in more detail in this chapter:

(a) Effective preparation, including mastery of the relevant facts and law, and identification of your best alternative to a negotiated agreement ('BATNA' – see **12.4.4** below).

(b) Use of objective standards of reference, eg industry codes of practice, expert reports, audited accounts etc.

(c) Adoption of an interest-based approach whereby you seek to identify the interests of the other side and better understand their needs and wants.

(d) Identification of omissions in your information or understanding, good questioning technique to assist in eliciting information and strong listening skills.

(e) The ability to develop trust with the other party or parties to encourage information sharing and seek creative solutions.

(f) Maintaining high ethical standards.

(g) The ability to manage your emotions and to be flexible in your choice of negotiating style.

12.2 THE ETHICS OF NEGOTIATION

To practise effectively, it is essential not only to understand the professional and ethical rules which apply but to uphold them. To be an effective negotiator, you must be an ethical negotiator, not simply because you are bound to do so by a professional code of ethics and behaviour, but also because any failure to uphold the highest ethical standards will diminish your effectiveness as a negotiator. You will lose the trust of your client and of the other side if you breach ethical standards. Negotiation is based on establishing trust between the parties. Once lost it is extremely hard to rebuild. Familiarise yourself with all the relevant Code of Conduct provisions and try to anticipate possible areas of difficulty.

You must never lie or exceed your client's instructions. However, you have no duty to volunteer information which is adverse to your client's position. If asked a direct question on such a point you cannot lie, but you can refuse to answer, offer no comment or attempt to deflect the question (eg by offering a partial answer or by parrying with a counter-question). However, it is likely in such circumstances that the other negotiator will guess what the true position is, and it may have been tactically wiser to have made an admission.

12.3 NEGOTIATING STYLES

12.3.1 Categories

Some writers group negotiators into two general styles with labels such as hard/soft or aggressive/co-operative.

However, such categorisation may be a misleading division of a myriad of different styles. **Figure 1** demonstrates this by charting two characteristics of the negotiator which are not necessarily mutually exclusive but which can be integrated with each other to widely varying degrees.

Figure 1

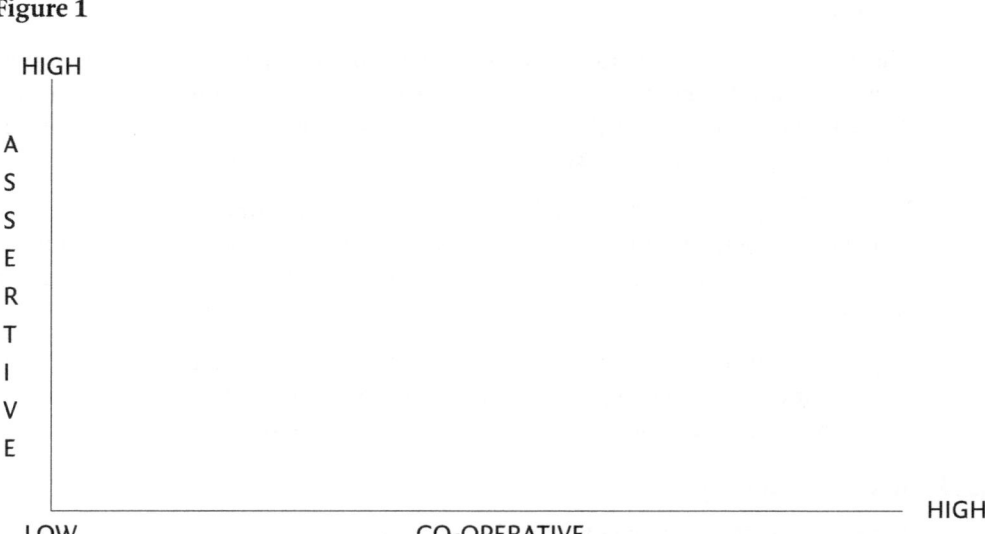

How assertive are you? Mark your point on the vertical axis. How co-operative are you? Mark your point on the horizontal axis. Mark on the graph where your two points meet.

This analysis recognises that everybody's style is different: there are hundreds of points on the graph. However, although it gives a general indication of a person's predominant style, the analysis has inherent drawbacks. First, self-analysis is not always accurate. Secondly, it fails to recognise that you can and should vary your style according to the needs of a particular negotiation. Effective negotiators are highly flexible and will vary their style according to the merits of the case they are pursuing and the style adopted by the other negotiator.

Figure 2

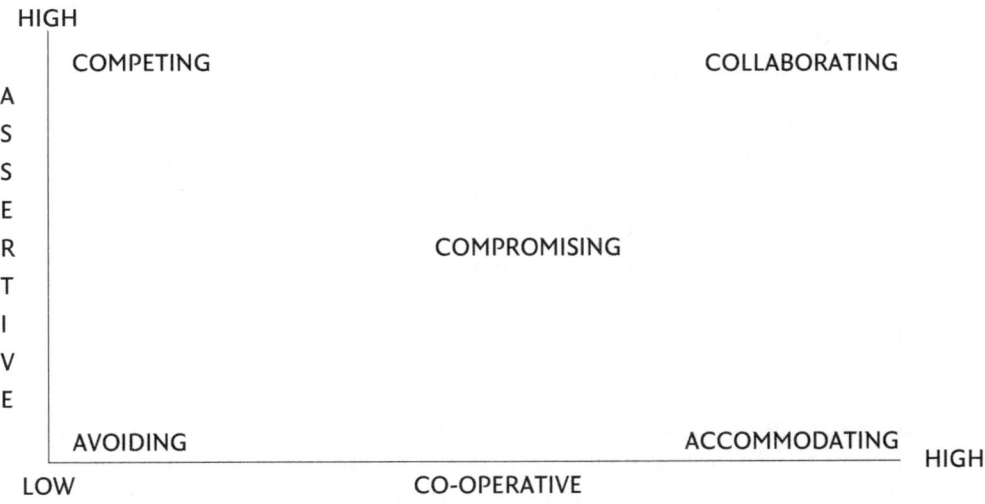

Figure 2 shows the same chart divided into five broad styles, any one of which may be used according to the circumstances.

It is important to:
(a) know the potential strengths and weaknesses of your own predominant style;
(b) learn to vary your own style; and
(c) be able to identify, and react appropriately, to the style of the other negotiator.

12.3.2 Avoiding

The avoiding style is low both on assertiveness and co-operativeness. It is sometimes used by those who are facing actual or potential legal action, or a proposed term in a transaction, against which they have little or no argument. They hope that, if they ignore the problem, it will either go away or circumstances will change in their favour.

It is also an approach that might be adopted by the solicitor on one side if they know the other side has a deadline to meet. They will be trying to put off the real negotiations until the other side is under severe time pressure, knowing that this will then put them into a strong position.

Appropriate responses to an opponent who adopts an avoiding style include adhering to an agreed timetable, imposing time limits or pursuing alternative courses of action which force engagement, for example by issuing and serving proceedings.

12.3.3 Accommodating

A person adopting an accommodating style is keen to accept the other side's proposals and reach agreement.

It may be an unconscious personality preference or may be consciously adopted if the other side has misjudged the parties' positions. If the latter, it might, in some cases, be wiser not to take advantage of the other side's error particularly when the parties will have an ongoing relationship.

12.3.4 Compromising

It is vital that negotiators have the capacity to compromise; otherwise, deals would never be made and disputes would never be settled. The important question for a negotiator is how and when to compromise. Factors which frequently motivate compromise include avoiding:

(a) the uncertainties of trial (on liability or quantum, eg, when a witness 'fails to come up to proof');
(b) the possible publicity arising out of litigation;
(c) the delay involved in going to trial;
(d) the emotional stress that continued litigation could involve;
(e) the legal costs of going any further – even if you win in court, you are unlikely to recover all the legal costs from the unsuccessful party;
(f) the further loss of management time for a commercial client;
(g) the transaction falling through; or
(h) souring an ongoing relationship between two commercial parties or between members of a family.

Although compromise is necessary, a compromising style can be characterised as a readiness to 'split the difference' between the two sides' positions, regardless of the objective merits. There may occasionally be good reasons for securing a deal in this way, but they do not include the easy disposal of the matter or speedier payment of your fees. Always evaluate your reasons for compromise and ensure that you are compromising when appropriate and using relevant criteria to calculate the basis on which you offer or accept compromise.

12.3.5 Competing

Competitors are unco-operative and highly assertive. They may or may not also be aggressive.

If you have a strong case and the other side is accommodating, a competing style can be highly effective.

On the other hand, if it is misused, a competing style is likely to create mistrust, distort communication, increase tension and possibly sour long-term relationships. It can provoke retaliation (the other side become aggressive or unreasonable), and settlement can be severely delayed or a proposed deal can fall apart. Given the potential dangers of this style, it should be adopted with caution.

If you are faced with competitive negotiators, try to avoid counter-productive reactions. Ignore personality and concentrate on the objective merits of the arguments. It may be helpful to ask: 'Why are they behaving like this?' There could be a number of possible reasons, each of which should generate a different response from you:

(a) Their behaviour might reflect their personality and normal style. Research/consult with colleagues to see if this is their experience. Try to separate the problem from the person as far as possible.

(b) Consider whether your own reaction or behaviour is in your client's best interests. It may be that they do in fact have a very strong case.

(c) They may have a very weak case and are bluffing or over-compensating. Stay calm. Take care not to react too hastily. Do not be provoked into departing from your strategy.

(d) They may be under-prepared. As a result, they may be worried that they are running the risk of making an error of judgement and conceding too much. They therefore over-compensate and become less co-operative and more assertive (or avoiding) in order to reduce that risk. If you suspect this to be the reason, the best tactic might be to adjourn the negotiation until they are better prepared.

(e) They may have become competitive in response to what they perceive to be your competitiveness.

Ultimately, it should be remembered that in a negotiation there are no rules or procedures which have to be followed (unless you have agreed to them), and there is no obligation to reach a settlement. The other side cannot force you into anything without your consent and vice versa.

12.3.6 Collaborating

Some people call collaboration 'problem solving' or 'principled negotiation'. It encompasses highly assertive and highly co-operative behaviour. It is often the ideal negotiating style because it gives you the best of both worlds. Assertiveness and co-operativeness are not mutually exclusive.

Assertiveness is not the same as aggression. You should aim to be sufficiently assertive to press your own client's case and to avoid being trampled on by an aggressive opponent; at the same time, you should be sufficiently co-operative to search for any possibility of a mutually beneficial solution. This is particularly important where there will be (or the parties would like there to be) a continuing business or personal relationship after the present dispute has been resolved.

Beware, however, of certain risks:

(a) Watch out for wolves in sheep's clothing, ie the pleasant negotiator who smiles a lot, flatters you, appears to be perfectly reasonable (and may pepper their statements with phrases like 'fair and reasonable' and 'sympathetic to your client's case'), but who on objective analysis is being competitive and offering very little. Do not jump to conclusions; try not to allow personality or manner to influence you; concentrate on the objective merits of the case.

(b) If you are trying to adjust your own predominant style, for example to become more assertive or more co-operative, there is a danger that, as one characteristic increases, so the other decreases. Although it is possible to be high on both, it can be difficult to achieve.

12.3.7 Conclusion

Everyone has a different combination of assertive/co-operative behaviour and a different natural negotiating style. The key is to honestly identify your natural predisposition, and to harness your strengths and be aware of your potential weak points. Concentrate on your client's objectives and treat the negotiation as a common problem rather than a battle of wills.

The rest of this chapter generally assumes a collaborative style. However, thorough preparation, self-confidence and perceptiveness are more important than personal style.

12.4 PREPARATION FOR A NEGOTIATION

12.4.1 Importance of preparation

The successful negotiator possesses many skills; these include the abilities to communicate, listen, persuade, analyse and create. These talents must, however, be supported by a bedrock of knowledge.

A thorough knowledge of the facts, the law and the procedure relevant to a particular case is vital. Without that knowledge, you lose any chance of controlling the negotiating process.

It is also essential to establish clearly your client's objectives in entering into the negotiation. What is the minimum they are prepared to accept? Have they reached this position with the benefit of all available information? If they are proceeding under certain misconceptions, it is part of your role to correct them.

Armed with the requisite knowledge (law, facts and procedure) and your client's instructions, a plan based on the following sections (**12.4.2–12.4.7**) should be prepared.

An effective starting point in your preparation is often to identify all the business issues which are likely to be relevant to your client. These should include consideration of money, risk, control, standards and closure. The details will vary according to the facts of each case or transaction. Set out below are examples of the sort of issues you might consider under each heading.

Money

How much will be paid by any of the parties? What will the currency be? How will the money be paid? When will it be paid? Having cash up front may be a benefit to your client that makes it worth taking a lesser amount or vice versa. What about interest and costs?

Risk

What are the potential risks for your client and how can you minimise them? Who should bear the risk and can you protect against it, eg by purchasing insurance? Risks to be considered will depend on the circumstances of each case but might include risk of insolvency/failure to pay, risk of damage to a product or of damage in transit, risk that markets might change, etc.

Control

Who will have control of the product/business? When will control be transferred? How will control be handed over? For example, in selling a business, when/how might management changes be implemented, and what handover will be required?

Standards

Who will have the power to decide whether any standards set have been reached? For example, if goods are to arrive in 'good condition', who will decide whether this has been met or not?

Will you require independent verification and, if so, who will select, appoint and pay for such services, eg if a valuation is required for goods or property?

Closure

How will the settlement/transaction be completed? At what point will liabilities cease? When will ownership pass? What rights do either party have to reject the settlement/transaction? If goods are being handed over, where will the handover take place, who will deliver and when will this take place?

Using this framework will often help you identify additional information or questions you need to ask your clients.

TRANSACTION CASE STUDY

Using the Toast & Tea transaction case (which may be found at p xii), identify what the likely business issues for the sellers might be.

Business issues for consideration if negotiating the Toast & Tea sale include the following:

- The owners of Toast & Tea ideally want £22 million but are prepared to accept £18 million. On what basis are they prepared to drop from their ideal figure?
- The owners of Toast & Tea want the transaction to proceed quickly, and as they have other investment projects presumably they will need the money quickly. You will need to identify how much money they want and what the timeframe is. Is there a deadline date by which the transaction needs to be complete? Is there a minimum amount the owners need to achieve by a particular date?
- How will the money be paid and over what period? Are the owners prepared to accept payment in instalments? How can they be sure that they will be paid the full amount? What happens if the buyer fails to make a payment? When will ownership of Toast & Tea pass? Who will manage the company during any handover period?
- Valuation of property will be important consideration in this case. Who will appoint the valuer? Who will pay the valuer? When will valuation be made? Ideally the owners of Toast & Tea will want to select their own valuer and will want to select a point of valuation when commercial property prices are most likely to be at their highest. Would they accept an average figure if both sides appoint valuers, or would they consider agreeing to the joint instruction of a valuer?
- What happens if the valuer comes back with a figure below that which the owners are prepared to accept?
- Is Florence Lowe prepared to continue in her current role? If she is prepared to stay, how long is she prepared to commit to this role, and what will her salary and notice provisions, etc be?

Identifying some of the business issues relevant to your client will help you prepare for the negotiation and identify possible gaps in the information you have. It should also help generate possible bargaining points.

12.4.2 Interests not positions

The client will inform you of their negotiating position; they want compensation, a fixed-term contract, the removal of a tenant. You must look behind the client's stated position and try to identify their underlying interests. Why does the client want what they are demanding? Ask – or you may end up negotiating on the basis of false assumptions.

Anticipate the other side's interests. Consideration of these will help you avoid being taken by surprise and will allow you to develop a wider range of bargaining points.

In addition, once the underlying interests or unspoken assumptions are identified, it may be that the underlying interests can be satisfied in some other way and at less cost than you initially expected.

> **EXAMPLE**
>
> In negotiating a lease of the major unit in a new shopping mall, the landlord might demand from its major 'anchor' tenant absolute bars on assignment, sub-letting or change of use. The tenant might demand absolute freedom on all three. This presents an apparent impasse. However, the landlord's underlying interest might be to use the anchor tenant to attract 'satellite' tenants to the other, smaller units, while the tenant's interest might be the long-term freedom to move elsewhere. A compromise which might satisfy both parties' underlying interests would be to have a short-term restriction rather than one which lasted for the whole duration of the lease.

Looking for underlying interests is particularly important in transaction-based negotiations or multi-issue claims. It is less likely to be productive in debt collection, personal injury or other single issue, 'money only' claims. However, it should always be investigated. For example, in debt collection it may be that the creditor has an underlying interest in the survival of the debtor's business.

In a personal injury claim there may be an interest in improving future management or training procedures to avoid similar incidents.

12.4.3 Strengths and weaknesses

The logical next step after a consideration of the parties' underlying interests and identification of your BATNA is to assess the factors which support and those which undermine your client's case (ie, once you know what they want, what are the chances of them getting what they want?).

Identify your client's strengths and weaknesses and those of the other side. Perhaps your client has no pressing need to make a deal, but the other side have financial difficulties which make it vital for them to reach an agreement; perhaps your client's case is supported by strong legal precedent.

Once the other side's strengths have been identified, you can plan how to counter them. For example, can you obtain other evidence or reinterpret existing evidence?

What are the weaknesses in the other side's position? For example, will they risk court action if their main concern is to avoid bad publicity?

Expect the other side to have spotted the weaknesses in your client's case and to ask questions which could expose those weaknesses. Anticipate these questions and prepare carefully worded replies which (without lying or misrepresenting the position), as far as possible, protect your client.

You must behave ethically. Any misrepresentation would constitute professional misconduct, as well as rendering voidable any resulting agreement.

What questions could you ask to exploit your client's strengths and which probe for weaknesses in the other side's position? The phrasing of such questions should be carefully considered to make it difficult for the other side to avoid giving a straight (and it is hoped revealing) answer.

Consider whether you should use 'open' or 'closed' questioning techniques or a combination of both depending on the information you require.

To negotiate effectively you must be assertive in advancing your client's case and tenacious in seeking replies to your questions. However, this should be done within the constraints of a professional and detached approach. If the general tone of your questioning (or answers) is aggressive, sarcastic or discourteous, it is likely to sour relationships and prevent you from having productive discussions.

12.4.4 BATNA

One of the best known books on negotiation is Fisher and Ury's *Getting to Yes*. Their acronym, BATNA, stands for Best Alternative To a Negotiated Agreement. In other words, *if the negotiations were to break down and you failed to settle*, what would you be left with? What would be the true cost or value of that alternative?

In transaction cases, your BATNA could be to do a deal with a third party rather than with the other side, or not to do a deal at all. In dispute resolution cases, the BATNA would often be litigation. Exploring the available alternatives in advance can concentrate the mind wonderfully – both your own mind and your client's. Make sure that the perceived BATNA is a realistic alternative and not just a vague possibility.

Fisher and Ury recommend that you identify, evaluate and develop your own BATNA and also try to guess the other side's. Developing your own BATNA might involve, for example, pressing ahead with litigation procedures simultaneously with trying to negotiate an out-of-court settlement.

The aim of the BATNA approach to planning a negotiation is to provide you with a yardstick against which you can assess the value of any offer made in the negotiation. Identifying your BATNA helps you to decide your 'resistance point' in the negotiation (see **12.4.5.3**). It can therefore protect you from being too generous, ie agreeing to give the other side more than the value of your BATNA. It can also protect you from being too obstinate, ie rejecting a final offer which is in fact better than your BATNA.

If your client appears to have an attractive alternative available, this strengthens their negotiating position; it might therefore be a good tactic to make the other side aware of this alternative.

In some instances, the client may have more than one alternative course of action available. If so, you should discuss with your client the feasibility of each alternative and consider whether it is worthwhile trying to develop each alternative or to concentrate on just one.

12.4.5 Issues, priorities and variables

12.4.5.1 Isolation of separate issues

Many negotiations involve the resolution of several issues. It is a good idea in such cases to isolate each issue. One reason for doing this is that it helps to ensure that all relevant matters are covered in the negotiation.

> **EXAMPLE**
> Your client is a retailer who has a contract with a manufacturer for the supply of an exclusive range of golfing accessories. The client has suffered losses owing to the manufacturer failing to meet agreed supply dates. He wants compensation but is aware that the stocking of the contract goods generates a great deal of his custom.
>
> The issues are:
> - the claim for compensation;
> - the continuation of a profitable relationship.

12.4.5.2 Relative importance of each issue

Having identified the issues, you should discuss with your client the relative importance to them of each, to ensure you have a clear view of the client's priorities. In the above example, your client would almost certainly decide that the claim for compensation should not be pressed too hard if it would put at risk the continuation of the relationship.

12.4.5.3 Opening bids and resistance points

On each issue, make an assessment of the most favourable result that you would hope to achieve and the least favourable result that you would be prepared to accept.

Most favourable result ('opening bid')

To begin by making demands which are wildly optimistic and which bear no relation to the parties' positions will result in your losing credibility. You are bound to lose credibility when you are unable to give sound reasons to justify your position.

The bid you make should be the highest justifiable bid, after taking into account the law and facts which support your client's case; ie, try to predict the settlement you would obtain if all the factors which support your case were accepted without any counter-arguments being put forward by the other side.

> **EXAMPLE**
>
> Through no fault of his own, your client has been dismissed by his employer, with two years of a fixed-term contract left to run. His salary (after tax and national insurance deductions) was £35,000 per annum. The most favourable result would be to obtain the total of lost net salary (£70,000) for the remaining two-year period. It is a bid which can be justified on a contractual basis.
>
> You would expect your opponent to put forward arguments which support the reduction of this figure (eg, the former employee has a duty to mitigate his loss by looking for other work), but if your opponent fails to do so you could achieve a very good settlement for your client (although bear in mind that other factors may lead you to decide not to take advantage of the other side's mistakes).

This is one of the possible benefits of aiming high at the start. Another is that, if valid counter-arguments are raised, it allows you to 'come down' and offer concessions. This can be an important way of showing the other side that you have listened to and understood their case and that you are prepared to compromise. Any compromise requires 'give and take'. It allows people to save face; honour is satisfied. If, however, you refuse to move from your opening figure, the other side may perceive you as obstinate and unreasonable, and therefore may refuse to settle even when your opening figure is in fact realistic.

Generally, you should open at your final figure only if:

(a) it is the tradition or culture in that particular field of law; or

(b) you have a case or bargaining position that is obviously strong.

In either case, you should explain clearly to the other side that it is a case of 'take it or leave it'.

Least favourable result that, on current information, you would accept ('resistance point')

The above process also allows you to decide on the poorest deal your client should accept, ie what settlement you would expect to negotiate if the other side put forward all the relevant counter-arguments to your client's case.

The resistance point is not a 'bottom line'; it should not be rigidly adhered to if further information which affects your client's position comes to light in the negotiation. You must be flexible enough to take on board the significance of any new information and adapt your expectations accordingly.

Deciding on the resistance point is complicated by two other factors. First, in cases where your client has an acceptable alternative course of action, the resistance point is the point below which the client is likely to receive less from the negotiation than might be obtained by pursuing the BATNA. For example, you might decide that (even after taking into account the extra costs) your client would receive more than is currently being offered by allowing the court to decide on the level of compensation.

Secondly, your client may have given you instructions not to settle below a certain figure. If you think they are being unrealistic, you should try to persuade them to adopt a more sensible position, but if they will not be moved, you must comply with their instructions.

With multi-issue negotiations, the position becomes even more complicated. You might be prepared to go below your resistance point on one issue if it means you would obtain a favourable result on another. It is important to keep the whole package in mind.

Your client's priorities are the key to the decisions you make in this area. Items which are of no great significance to your client could be conceded altogether in exchange for concessions which are of more importance to them.

12.4.5.4 Variables and unorthodox approaches

Another consideration in assessing the opening bid and resistance point will be the existence of 'variables'. Variables are those factors which allow for some give and take in the negotiation and which could therefore help to achieve a settlement. For example, your client might be prepared to pay a higher amount of compensation if they are allowed to pay by instalments rather than in one lump sum.

Other examples of variables which might be brought into play (depending on the subject matter of the negotiation) are inclusion/exclusion of costs, payment in a different currency, promises of future orders, quantity of goods (eg, buy more, but at a lower price per unit), quality of goods (eg, buy a lower grade at a lower price).

Sometimes, there may be other unconventional ways to resolve problems which have benefits for both sides. Be as creative as possible in seeking a solution.

> **EXAMPLE**
> You are acting for a business which runs a parcel delivery service. One of its business customers is threatening to take action against your client because of its failure to deliver a consignment of goods. The goods have disappeared and the customer is asking for compensation. An orthodox settlement would involve a cash payment to the customer. A different approach would be to offer to make free deliveries for that customer over an agreed period. Such an offer could represent a good deal for the customer but could still be a cheaper solution for your client compared with a cash payment (the deliveries could probably be accommodated within its regular delivery service and so would not add greatly to overall costs). This approach also gives your client a chance to rebuild the customer's confidence in its service, making it less likely that the customer will go elsewhere in the future.

12.4.6 Settlement zones

The aim of much of your preparation and of some of your questioning during a negotiation will be to attempt to identify possible settlement zones (or lack of them). You can add value as a lawyer by getting the maximum possible within a settlement zone for your client or by minimising what is paid, depending on which side you are on.

> **EXAMPLE**
>
> Use the example of the dismissed employee set out at **12.4.5.3** above. The employee's maximum expectation is £70,000. Assume that his solicitor has advised him that the least favourable result he should expect is a payment of £20,000 (taking into account the duty to mitigate loss and the current job market for the employee's skills). The employer, on the other hand, has been advised that a payment of £17,500 is probably the best result it could hope to achieve, but it is prepared to pay up to £35,000 if necessary to avoid any bad publicity. As illustrated by **Figure 3**, the possible settlement zone between the parties is £20,000 to £35,000. Where within that zone you are able to settle is a measure of how effective you have been as a negotiator. Negotiation is harder when the possible settlement zone is very narrow. By working to identify the settlement zone, you can help to speed the negotiation (saving time and costs), and in some cases you may be able to identify that there is no settlement zone and that either something must change or a negotiated settlement will not be possible.

Figure 3

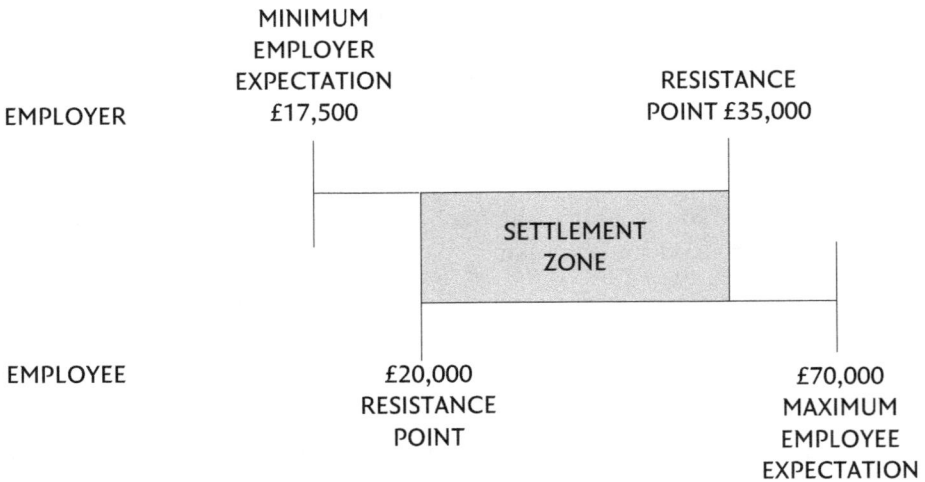

Having completed all your preparation, including as far as possible making an attempt to gauge the possible settlement zone, you should identify your strategy. You should have a clear plan as to how you will conduct the negotiation. Waiting to see how the other party or parties will behave is not a strategy and should be avoided. By waiting to see the other side's approach, you risk losing the initiative. If all the parties 'wait and see', it wastes time and valuable opportunities to build rapport by implementing a clear, interest-based approach to the negotiation. The negotiation should allow for flexibility in response to new information and the attitude of other parties.

Examples of things you might consider in planning your strategy are:

- *Your opening position*

  Will you take an extreme stance and pitch high, or will you start at a reasonable figure which you believe is likely to be conceded by the other side?
- *The order in which you would prefer to deal with issues*

  Is there a key issue which you need to address first? Are there issues you would prefer to keep back?

- *What disclosures to make and when*

    If there is information which may have an effect on the other party or parties, when will you reveal this information and how?

12.4.7 Opening statement

It is usually helpful to begin a negotiation with both parties making a brief opening statement setting out their expectations of the meeting and explaining their clients' status. Having identified your strategy, you are in a position to decide on the content of your opening statement.

There are several points to consider (see **12.8.3**), but a basic consideration at the preparatory stage is to decide upon the information you would want to disclose to the other side at this early point in the talks.

In most cases, the more information you communicate to the other side, the better the chance of reaching an agreement. In particular, there are usually interests which are common to both sides; these should be stressed at the start.

The sharing of information develops trust between the parties and helps to create a climate for successful talks.

There will, however, be some information that you correctly decide not to reveal, either because it is damaging to your client's position (in which case you would hope to avoid disclosing it at any stage) or because you would prefer to introduce it later for tactical reasons (eg, you intend to put it forward as a concession to the other side at the bargaining stage).

12.5 THE FORUM FOR THE NEGOTIATION

The forum for negotiation could be correspondence, telephone, a meeting or any combination of the three.

At the outset, choose the most appropriate medium for your client's case, and then be prepared to change if it proves inappropriate. For example, in many cases you might start by using correspondence, but that could later become unnecessarily rigid and time-consuming. It may be wise to suggest a meeting when you have developed a strong enough case to be able to take advantage of face-to-face contact.

12.5.1 Correspondence

Correspondence has the following features:

(a) It is capable of being orderly and reasoned, and is useful at the outset of complex cases.

(b) It gives parties time to think and therefore to avoid hasty decisions.

(c) There is a risk that certain points in a letter may be left unanswered in the reply.

(d) Some solicitors find it easier to be assertive on paper.

(e) It contains no non-verbal signals ('body language').

(f) It can lead to delay – either as a tactic, or because ambiguities or omissions are not rectified immediately.

(g) It is less fluid and less conducive to information gathering through questions or trading of concessions.

12.5.2 Telephone

Negotiation conducted by telephone has the following features:

(a) It is quick and useful for resolving a single point of issue between parties.

(b) If unplanned there is a risk of under-preparation. It is better to be the person making the call. If you are the receiver, consider scheduling a call back later when you can be fully prepared.

(c) There is no body language, but tones of voice are more noticeable. Silences can be impactful on the telephone and can be used effectively to prompt information sharing or further offers or suggestions.

(d) Some solicitors find it more difficult to be assertive on the telephone than in correspondence, and vice versa.

(e) There is a risk that either of the parties could subsequently 're-interpret' what was said if the call has not been recorded.

12.5.3 Meetings

Meetings have the following features:

(a) They are immediate.

(b) They offer greater commitment to exploring the case thoroughly and/or to settlement.

(c) Body language, tone and silences are readily apparent and can be used to gauge or manipulate the parties.

(d) They are more fluid and have greater potential for developing subtle shifts in position, trading of concessions and making small or nuanced changes which enhance the potential for settlement.

Some solicitors are uncomfortable with face-to-face meetings because of the possibility of making an inadvertent slip or of accidentally agreeing a weakness. If, however, a meeting would objectively be in the client's best interests, you should try to overcome any fears by thorough preparation and practice which will increase your self-confidence.

12.6 OTHER CONSIDERATIONS BEFORE A MEETING

12.6.1 Are you ready to negotiate?

Do not be forced into premature negotiations, which will needlessly increase costs. It is usually advisable to defer talks until you are in possession of all the information you can reasonably expect to collect.

12.6.2 Venue

Decide whether the negotiation should be in person or virtual. Virtual meetings offer potential cost and time savings, but limitations in terms of fluency and rapport building may offset this benefit and make settlement less likely.

In some fields of law, there is a tradition that meetings will take place at the offices of the seller or claimant.

Having the meeting at your own firm's premises may be more convenient and ensures you have full access to papers and to secretarial, catering and other resources. You may prefer to put the other side at ease by meeting at their offices in order to set a collaborative tone. A third possibility is to agree a neutral venue although this will have cost implications.

12.6.3 Agree the time and length of the meeting

As a matter of courtesy to the other side, you should inform them of the time you can devote to the meeting on the agreed date. It is also important for you to determine how long the other side has so that you can manage time when planning and undertaking the negotiation.

12.6.4 Attendance at the meeting

How many people from each side will be attending? Find out their names and roles in advance. If a number of people will be attending, who will chair the meeting – the host, the person who suggested the meeting, or someone else?

Will clients also be present? They are often present at transaction-based negotiations but not as frequently at litigation-based meetings. Clients may sit in separate side-rooms or make themselves available via phone in order to give instructions to their solicitors during the meeting.

It may be a good idea to have clients present at the meeting so that an agreement can be hammered out there and then, particularly if you think:

(a) a lack of communication has been a major problem between the respective clients; or
(b) your client is being unrealistic; or
(c) the other solicitor is exacerbating the problem (eg, not settling a case which their client wants to settle or giving their client overly optimistic advice); and
(d) you can trust your own client (preparation of roles is vital).

Conversely, you might not wish to have clients present where there are personality clashes between the different clients or where you have a difficult client who might hamper progress.

12.6.5 Seating arrangements

Who will sit where? What ambience do you want to try to create? Sitting face to face across a table from each other is more likely to appear adversarial, whereas seating placed at a 90 degree angle is likely to appear more collaborative.

12.6.6 Clarify the purpose of the meeting

Is the meeting to be exploratory only, or is there a possibility of settling? If the latter, check that those attending will have authority to settle on behalf of their respective clients.

12.6.7 The agenda

In a multi-issue case, try to agree the agenda with the other side in advance.

If possible, try to arrange the order of issues on the agenda in a way which will enable you to test their negotiating pattern and their willingness to trade concessions before reaching an item which is of critical importance to your own client.

12.6.8 Which party should make the first bid?

In some fields of law, the issue of which person makes the first bid is determined partly by tradition. For example, in property transactions, the solicitor acting for the landlord or seller draws up the draft lease or contract. In litigation, if the claim is for a liquidated sum (eg, a contractual debt), the opening bid belongs to the claimant. If the claim is for unliquidated damages, in certain cases (eg, personal injury claims) there is an argument that the claimant should simply wait until the defendant makes an acceptable offer.

Where the position is not clear cut, the advantages of going first are that it allows you to exert an immediate and powerful influence and it shows confidence. The disadvantage is that, if you are underprepared, you risk misjudging the bid.

Even if you don't wish to make the first bid, you might still want to make the first opening statement in order to establish the tone of the negotiation.

12.6.9 Final preparation for the meeting

Re-read the file, and refresh your mind on key documents, facts, dates and names.

Make sure that you know your client's position on the issues and on all the possible variables. If no agenda has been agreed, prepare one now.

12.7 OVERVIEW OF A NEGOTIATION

Negotiations should be clearly structured. Decide upon the best process and agree it with the other parties; this is likely to increase the commitment of all sides to the negotiation. Adopting a clear process will help ensure that all parties feel that the negotiation is fair and will facilitate effective structure and tone. You should not start negotiating until you have clearly identified the process. We recommend that you invite all parties to make a preliminary opening statement, then allocate time for discussion of each point on the agenda. It may be necessary to organise separate meetings for different parties to the negotiation. A clear time frame should be adopted and provisional timings set for adjournments. As with interviewing and advising, structure and management skills are closely related to good communication skills.

12.8 THE OPENING

12.8.1 Setting the tone

The opening phase of a negotiation is important for two reasons. First, it creates the climate for the negotiation. Patterns, styles and pecking order establish themselves early and are difficult then to change.

Secondly, energy and concentration are high at the outset of the negotiations but later may deteriorate.

12.8.2 Ground rules

The host should introduce everyone present and confirm the ground rules for the meeting, for example:

(a) the purpose of the meeting;
(b) whether or not it is 'without prejudice' and/or 'subject to contract';
(c) likely duration of the meeting;
(d) the agenda; and
(e) who will make the first opening statement.

12.8.3 Your opening statement

Well prepared opening statements are important because they:

(a) provide structure and order;
(b) clarify the position of the party in relation to areas of dispute and any changes that might have occurred;
(c) provide an opportunity to focus on common interests and encourage creative problem solving and set a constructive tone;
(d) help avoid unintentional false assumptions from hindering the communication process.

Unless you have sound tactical reasons for not following them, there are some general rules relating to opening statements.

12.8.3.1 Do:

(a) say how long your statement will take if it is likely to be more than two or three minutes;
(b) if your opening statement is going to contain a bid, explain your reasoning *before* disclosing the actual bid. This increases the chances of the other side listening properly to your reasons. Otherwise, they will be thinking about the figure and their response rather than your reasons;

(c) present your case concisely and confidently;
(d) use collaborative tone, posture and gestures (unless you have expressly decided to adopt a competitive style);
(e) observe carefully the other side's verbal and non-verbal reactions;
(f) remember the one-third rule (see **10.1**).

12.8.3.2 Don't:
(a) express your assumptions of the other side's interests and priorities, as this could annoy or antagonise them. Allow them to make their own case in their opening statement;
(b) allow them to interrupt or side-track you;
(c) speak for too long.

12.8.4 The other side's opening statement

12.8.4.1 It is important that you:
(a) listen carefully – use all possible listening techniques (see **10.2.1**);
(b) concentrate on identifying their underlying interests;
(c) evaluate their style;
(d) remain non-committal on their proposals and arguments – indicate understanding, if you can, without indicating agreement;
(e) take brief notes (this can be a useful way of concealing your immediate reactions).

12.8.4.2 At the end of their opening statement:
(a) seek clarification if necessary – you must be sure you understand exactly what they are saying. Negotiations can easily break down because of simple miscommunication or misunderstanding;
(b) summarise;
(c) stress areas of agreement;
(d) make sure that they have told you the whole of their 'shopping list' to reduce the risk of being ambushed later by a last-minute demand.

Avoid mentally drafting or rehearsing your own rebuttal, as this will hinder your listening and understanding of their case, and do not interrupt.

12.9 THE MIDDLE PHASE: DISCUSSION AND BARGAINING

Statements generate resistance
Questions generate answers
Silence generates discomfort, answers, new suggestions.
(adapted from a passage in *Getting to Yes* by Fisher and Ury)

I don't go in to do all the talking. Quite the opposite.
I go in to do the listening because that's the best bit.
(insurance company chief claims inspector, quoted in *Hard Bargaining* by Hazel Genn)

12.9.1 Discussion

During the discussion:

(a) Demonstrate that you have heard and understood what the other side has said even if you do not agree with them.
(b) In the middle phase of a negotiation, you should probe the other side's case with a mixture of appropriate open and closed questions. You could question any of the following:

(i) any assumptions you think they might be making;
(ii) their underlying interests or needs ('Why does your client want ... ?');
(iii) whether or not there may be other ways of meeting those interests;
(iv) the criteria or evidence to justify their bid ('What criteria did you use to arrive at ... ?', 'What evidence have you got to support ... ?', 'Where did you get that evidence from?');
(v) their interpretation of the law or of the facts; or
(vi) analogous or comparable circumstances or cases they have had.

(c) Ask one question at a time.
(d) Give them time to answer – do not be tempted to fill a silence too quickly.
(e) Listen and observe carefully when they answer. Was there any hesitation, uncertainty or discomfort?
(f) If necessary, rephrase crucial questions so that all potential evasions or omissions are covered.
(g) Do not allow them to use diversionary tactics such as answering a question with a question, or changing the subject. Be courteous but firm.
(h) Spell out the weaknesses of their position calmly and firmly using objective criteria where available.
(i) Be prepared to answer their questions clearly with answers that protect your client's interests, use silence, counter-questions and deflection when appropriate. Maintain a confident tone of voice and posture.
(j) Review the progress of the discussions at appropriate intervals. If there is an impasse, or one aspect is taking too long, consider the following:
  (i) summarise – this will give you the opportunity to stress the areas on which you have already reached agreement and so reinforce the climate for agreement; it will also give you time to think and, if appropriate, to try to redirect the negotiation;
  (ii) defer further discussion of the particular topic until later in the negotiation;
(k) explore the possibility of settling issues on the basis of objective criteria. For example, you might agree to accept the opinion of an independent expert as a way to resolve the problem. An advantage of this approach is that neither party will feel cheated by the other; another is that you are more likely to achieve a fair result, which can have particular benefits where the parties will have an ongoing relationship.

12.9.2 Bargaining

Generally, you will have agreed to a meeting (other than a purely exploratory meeting) only if both parties are prepared to compromise, ie to bargain.

Although you might bargain item by item or clause by clause in multi-issue cases, try to keep the whole package in mind. It might be sensible not to finalise an agreement on any particular issue until the shape of the whole agreement is clear (including, for example, costs).

Keep searching for variables, for example: references/endorsements; time for payment; payment in a different currency; a promise of future orders or the grant of options; performance-related payments; performance in stages.

Bargaining involves the trading of concessions. Compromise is achieved by both parties moving from their original positions. On the assumption that the other side have aimed high, you should be cautious about accepting their first offer.

A competitive negotiator might refuse to concede anything to you for some time, and then concede only small amounts, slowly and at irregular intervals, and of diminishing amounts. Such a strategy is clearly designed to lower your expectations. However, if in fact there is a significant margin between that negotiator's opening bid and resistance point, the strategy carries the risk of a relatively sudden but very late climb-down (eg, a 'door-of-the-court' settlement). If you suspect that this strategy is being used against you, consider abbreviating the negotiation and press ahead with your BATNA (see **12.4.4**) – for example, by pressing ahead with the litigation if you are representing a claimant or making a Part 36 payment if you are representing a defendant.

When you are offered a concession, it is a question of judgement whether you express appreciation for it, or emphasise the lack of cost to them or both.

When making a concession, emphasise the cost to you of it and give a reason for it. For example, you can often relate it to something the other side have said in the negotiation. Your concession can thus demonstrate that you have taken their point and responded accordingly, rather than appear to be arbitrary.

In order to avoid 'giving away' a concession with nothing in return, or in order to try to move the negotiation forward, always consider offering conditional or hypothetical concessions: 'We could move on X, but only if you could move on Y'; 'I have no authority from my client on this point, but what if X ...?' Although these statements might be interpreted to mean that, if pushed, you would be prepared to concede unreservedly, it is a risk that parties have to take in the dynamics of a negotiation.

Make sure you take appropriate notes and, in particular, keep a record of all concessions or agreements.

12.9.3 Adjournments

Adjournments can be very useful.

The length of an adjournment will depend on its purpose. It could be for as little as 10 minutes, for example in order to have a brief strategy review (on your own, with a colleague, or with your client), or for as long as several weeks or months in order to await the availability of further evidence.

Other reasons for suggesting an adjournment include:

- alertness waning;
- to help resolve an impasse or deadlock;
- to allow a heated atmosphere to cool down; or
- to try to 'close the deal' during the relative informality of a refreshment break.

12.9.4 Resolving deadlocks

In cases of deadlock, the following actions should be considered:

- defer an item on the agenda;
- search for variables;
- adjourn; or
- refer to an alternative dispute resolution ('ADR') process (see **12.12**).

12.10 THE END: CLOSING A NEGOTIATION

12.10.1 When?

The timing of the close of a negotiation will depend on a cost–benefit analysis. How much more do you think you can achieve? Compare the expected achievements against the cost to the client in terms of time, money and stress. Will further negotiation be cost effective? This analysis needs to be conducted at regular intervals. Beware of a variation of Parkinson's Law: 'Negotiating expands to fill the time allotted to it.'

12.10.2 How?

A number of tactics may be used to signal to the other side that you see the end in sight.

(a) 'Last rites' – summarise the position reached, emphasising the concessions you have made and the extent and reasonableness of your movement: 'We have reached our final position.'

(b) Use a refreshment break to suggest informally that the end is near.

(c) Give a deadline or ultimatum.

(d) Make a concession and express it as a final gesture to settle.

(e) If the gap between the parties is small, check your BATNA to see whether you could move further or try to induce the other side to do so. Alternatively seek to find criteria or principles upon which you could agree to divide or accommodate the difference.

(f) If there is one outstanding point, you might be able to agree that the point be adjudicated by an agreed independent third party.

12.10.3 The agreement

Do not allow the euphoria of reaching agreement to distract you from other important and immediate tasks, such as:

- confirming what has been agreed;
- preparing an immediate agreed written summary;
- ensuring that details are clarified in order to avoid later disputes; and
- preparing a list of actions to be taken (if appropriate) by both sides.

12.11 'DIRTY TRICKS'

The phrase 'dirty tricks' is used loosely, and is not necessarily confined to misconduct. You need to be aware of such tricks, not so that you can use them, but in order both to be able to recognise them when they are used against you and, if possible, in order to counter them. They include the following.

12.11.1 Surprise attacks

Surprise attacks can take the form of sudden changes in tactics or demands, intimidation, withdrawal of offers or emotional outbursts. They are often designed to throw you off balance, undermine your confidence, and create anxiety and a desire to placate or settle quickly.

Try to remain unperturbed. Try not to retaliate. If you find it difficult to continue to focus on the merits of the case, consider questioning the other side's tactics openly or calling an adjournment.

12.11.2 'Good person, bad person'

The 'good person, bad person' tactic is sometimes used by a negotiating team of lawyers, or a solicitor who wishes to portray their client as hard and uncompromising.

The aim of the tactic is to capitalise on the relief felt at evading the 'bad person'. Again, you should try to continue to focus on the merits of the case and ignore the personalities of the negotiators as far as possible.

12.11.3 Feinting

Feinting is where the solicitor seems to attach great importance to one particular item. They then concede it in order to 'soften you up' for another item in which they express little interest but which is, in fact, far more important to their client.

Do not take things at face value; always try to ascertain the other side's interests.

12.11.4 False deadlines

False deadlines can sometimes be tested by saying, 'We might be able to offer more, but we will not know until after [the date of the deadline]'.

Question and research any reasoning given for imposing a deadline which you suspect is being used as a tactic.

12.11.5 Limited authority/reneging on 'agreements'

Always make sure at the time of the agreement that it is explicit whether or not the solicitor has the authority to settle and whether the agreement is final, and record the position in writing. If you do not, you may think that a case has been settled only to receive a letter stating, for example: 'I reported on our provisional agreement. My client is fairly happy with it, but there is just one matter …'.

12.11.6 Last minute demands

Make sure you obtain all the other side's demands at the outset.

This will make it less likely that they will surprise you with a sudden new demand.

12.11.7 Environmental controls

If the seating arrangements or environment of the meeting room make you feel uncomfortable, you should immediately and politely ask for them to be changed.

12.11.8 Lying

Try to take accurate notes of key points without being distracted from the negotiation. If you can later prove that the other side lied during the negotiation then the settlement could be rescinded for misrepresentation, and where a solicitor knowingly lied, the matter could be reported to The Law Society as professional misconduct.

12.12 ALTERNATIVE DISPUTE RESOLUTION

12.12.1 What is it?

Alternative dispute resolution (ADR) is not a term of art: it includes any process of dispute resolution other than litigation, arbitration or traditional negotiation between the parties or their solicitors.

The commonest form of ADR is mediation, but other processes – including conciliation, early neutral evaluation and expert determination – also come under the umbrella of ADR.

The object of ADR is to provide a process which efficiently and effectively resolves a dispute. Which particular process or which combination of processes is best, will depend on the circumstances of each case.

The essential ingredients of ADR are:

(a) It is a voluntary, private process. The parties cannot be forced to use ADR; if they do use it, they can control the mechanics and rules of the process; and they can withdraw from it at any time unless and until they make a contractually binding out-of-court settlement or agreement.

(b) There is a third party neutral (often a mediator) who facilitates settlement, often by 'shuttlecock' diplomacy, but who has no power to order or impose a solution on the parties.

In essence ADR is intended to be an efficient and structured form of negotiation involving a third party. It can thus be interposed between traditional negotiating and litigation (or arbitration): if traditional negotiating fails, try an ADR process; if that fails, then either stalemate or litigation (or arbitration) remains.

12.12.2 Types of dispute resolution

12.12.2.1 Conciliation

Conciliation is similar in process to mediation but the third party neutral tends to take a more activist role in putting forward terms of settlement. The Advisory Conciliation and Arbitration Service (ACAS) offers free conciliation for many types of employment dispute.

12.12.2.2 Early neutral evaluation

A preliminary assessment of facts, evidence or legal merits. This form of ADR is often used to help avoid further litigation or serve as a basis for further negotiation.

12.12.2.3 Expert determination

An expert independent third party is appointed to decide the dispute. This process is often similar to neutral fact finding and will frequently be restricted to certain issues.

12.12.2.4 Complaints and grievance procedures

Generally the first port of call for any complainant. It is usually important to exhaust the provisions of any relevant schemes before proceeding further.

Ombudsman schemes (eg, Parliamentary Ombudsman, Estate Agents Ombudsman)

Ombudsmen are independent, impartial adjudicators who consider complaints about maladministration in particular areas (often public services/government departments). Schemes vary but often combine elements of neutral fact finding, mediation and adjudication.

Regulators

Regulators are watchdogs who generally oversee the way complaints are handled (eg, OFWAT, the water regulator). They are generally free but tend to focus on how a complaint or grievance was handled.

12.12.2.5 Mediation

> Mediation, with recognition in the UK under the Civil Procedure Rules since 1999, is a flexible process conducted confidentially where a neutral person actively assists the parties in working towards a negotiated agreement of a dispute, with the parties in ultimate control of the decision to settle and the terms of resolution. (Tony Allen, solicitor and Director of the Centre for Effective Dispute Resolution (CEDR))

Mediators are neutral third parties who facilitate a settlement between the parties in a dispute. They act as brokers or facilitators. Mediators do not advise on the law or the merits of the case. They seek to foster agreement between the parties themselves. At present there are no statutory qualifications required to mediate, but in practice mediators generally require some form of training and accreditation. There are a number of organisations which provide qualifying courses which are recognised by the Legal Services Commission, including CEDR and the School of Psychotherapy and Counselling.

The use of mediation has been actively promoted by the civil courts through a number of important cases.

In the landmark case of *Dunnett v Railtrack plc (in Railway Administration)* [2002] EWCA Civ 303, Railtrack had attempted to protect its costs position by making a modest Part 36 offer to Mrs Dunnett. Despite winning the appeal, Railtrack was not awarded its costs. In his judgment Brooke LJ remarked on the efficacy of mediation and its potential benefits: 'A mediator may be able to provide solutions which are beyond the powers of the court to provide'.

He also highlighted the potential consequences of failing to give adequate consideration to ADR:

> It is hoped that any publicity given to this part of the judgment of the court will draw the attention of lawyers to their duties to further the overriding objective in the way that it is set out in Part 1 of the Rules and to the possibility that, if they turn down out of hand the chance of alternative dispute resolution when suggested by the court, as happened on this occasion, they may have to face uncomfortable costs consequence.

The case of *Halsey v Milton Keynes General NHS Trust* [2004] EWCA Civ 576 established that mediation should be considered whenever appropriate. Whether a refusal to participate in ADR is unreasonable will be determined having regard to all the circumstances of that particular case. Factors which the court considered as likely to be relevant include:

(a) the nature of the dispute;

(b) the merits of the case;

(c) the extent to which other settlement methods have been attempted;

(d) whether the costs of ADR would be disproportionately high;

(e) whether any delay in setting up and attending ADR would have been prejudicial; and

(f) whether ADR had a reasonable prospect of success.

Case law has continued to underline the increasing importance of ADR. In *Burchell v Bullard* [2005] EWCA Civ 358, the comments of Ward LJ confirm its status:

> *Halsey* has made plain not only the high rate of successful outcome being achieved by mediation but also its established importance as a track to a just result running parallel with that of the court system ... The court has given its stamp of approval to mediation and it is now the legal profession which must become fully aware of and acknowledge its value.

The recent case of *Laporte v The Commissioner for the Police of the Metropolis* [2015] EWHC 371 (QB) has again reinforced the *Halsey* principles and pro-ADR stance of the courts.

Although usually used in the litigation field, ADR may also be used in commercial transactions. First, a commercial contract could incorporate an ADR clause, ie, a non-binding (but influential) promise that if any dispute later arises between the parties, they will refer that dispute to an ADR process before resorting to litigation or arbitration. Secondly, if parties are negotiating the terms of a transaction and reach an impasse on one particular term, they could agree to refer that one item to an ADR process.

12.12.3 How and when should you consider ADR?

With civil litigation in particular, consideration of ADR has now become an essential part of case evaluation and strategy. Knowing that it should be considered in most cases, you must carefully decide what might be the most appropriate method of dispute resolution in each particular case.

The following should form part of your analysis:

(a) Is ADR an option?

    (i) Is the other side willing to take part?

    (ii) Can ADR provide your client with the result they seek? (For example, if they want a public hearing or a judgment about who is legally right or wrong, then litigation may be the best option.)

    (iii) Certain types of case are not suited to ADR, eg:

        where a legal, commercial or other precedent needs to be set;

        where summary judgment is available and likely to be granted;

        where one of the parties requires emergency relief, eg an injunction or other form of immediate protection;

180   Skills for Lawyers

> where publicity is actively sought; or
>
> where there is no real interest in settlement.
>
> (iv) ADR is particularly suitable in cases where:
>
> costs are likely to be disproportionate;
>
> the parties are deadlocked in settlement negotiations;
>
> the case is likely to be particularly long/complex;
>
> there are multiple actions involving common parties;
>
> the issues involved are particularly sensitive; or
>
> the parties are anxious to avoid publicity.
>
> (b) What method of ADR is appropriate?
>
> (i) What method is most likely to meet the client's objectives?

> **EXAMPLE**
>
> Your client is pursuing a claim for medical negligence against the local NHS trust. If their prime objective is to bring the problem to the attention of those managing the hospital and to prevent it happening again, then using the Health Service Ombudsman would be an ideal choice. If the prime objective is to obtain maximum compensation, then this option is less suitable.

> (ii) What are the client's resources/how do they want the dispute managed? You need to consider the comparative cost of the available options, the length of time likely to be involved and the impact on your client's business/life.

12.12.4 The advantages

Like traditional negotiating, ADR can be quicker, cheaper and more private, and produce more flexible terms of settlement, than litigation or arbitration.

The third party neutral:

(a) may provide a view that is perceived by both parties as being more objective;

(b) by shuttlecock diplomacy may be able to identify potential solutions that neither party alone could see; and

(c) has a better chance of preserving relationships between the parties.

This last point can be very important in commercial or family disputes, but is less so where neither party has any intention of continuing any future relationship with the other.

12.12.5 The disadvantages

(a) One reason why ADR is relatively quick and cheap is that the evidence is not investigated or examined as thoroughly as in litigation or arbitration: instead, only what are thought to be the key issues and interests are explored. Parties cannot have it both ways, ie, a wide, in-depth investigation which is also quick and cheap. In each case, it is a question of choosing the lesser of two evils.

(b) Because ADR is a voluntary process, it is not appropriate, as we have seen, when one party needs immediate judicial relief.

(c) Likewise, ADR is unlikely to resolve 'non-genuine' disputes, for example where a defendant is clearly stalling for time and refusing to admit liability simply in order to hang on to their money for as long as possible.

12.12.6 A note about arbitration

'Arbitration is the settlement of a matter at issue by one to whom the parties agree to refer their claims in order to obtain an equitable decision' (*Shorter OED*). Arbitration differs from

ADR in that, as with litigation, the parties are passing control of the outcome of the dispute to a third party or parties.

Arbitration has been an alternative to litigation through the courts for centuries. It was used as early as the thirteenth century by English merchants who preferred to have their disputes resolved according to their own customs rather than by public law.

Arbitration is a huge specialist subject and encompasses a wide range of different institutions and procedures. It varies from informal to court-like proceedings. It is used particularly to resolve commercial disputes, often in an international context.

> **SUMMARY**
> - You must prepare fully in order to negotiate effectively.
> - Preparation should include identification of:
>   - your client's BATNA;
>   - your client's objectives;
>   - the optimal process for the negotiation;
>   - any information you would like to obtain;
>   - any independent/objective expertise or information that may be relevant;
>   - what you know about the other side, their needs and likely position;
>   - a clear strategy for the negotiation;
>   - a plan for how to deal with problems or difficult tactics;
>   - a clear agenda and endgame.
> - Be self-aware and learn to adapt your predominant style to best advantage.
> - Develop a clear strategy and implement it, but be flexible in your approach and style.
> - Look behind stated positions and seek mutual gain.
> - Maintain high ethical standards and develop trust for the best long-term results.
> - Understand the different types of ADR, and be prepared to advise your client as to the most appropriate forum for any dispute.

CHAPTER 13

Advocacy

13.1	Introduction	183
13.2	Skills	184
13.3	The basics	186
13.4	Opening the case	190
13.5	Examination-in-chief	191
13.6	Cross-examination	194
13.7	Re-examination	196
13.8	Closing the case	196
13.9	Ethical issues	197
13.10	Criminal cases: bail and mitigation	198
13.11	Civil cases: interim applications	214
13.12	Conclusion	238

LEARNING OUTCOMES

After reading this chapter you will be able to:

- identify the skills required of an advocate
- understand the purpose of opening and closing speeches
- explain the three stages in the questioning of a witness at trial
- identify the advocate's ethical duties
- make appropriate representations in a contested bail application
- prepare and present an effective plea in mitigation
- explain the nature of interim applications and make appropriate submissions.

13.1 INTRODUCTION

In its widest sense advocacy is the art of influencing outcomes. It is about convincing others: the art of persuasion. In this general sense, it is a valued accomplishment in many areas of life. This chapter is, however, concerned with the specialised meaning of the word as used by lawyers; in its legal context, advocacy is the art of presenting cases in court.

There are many reasons why advocacy is a skill worth studying. You may wish to become an advocate and, if you do, you will want to do the best possible job for your client. Also, understanding the task of the advocate in presenting a case for court is central to understanding the litigation process. Without such an understanding, you will struggle to give realistic, cogent and confident advice to clients. Even if you do not appear as an advocate, you may want to instruct one. By understanding advocacy, you will be better able to prepare the case for others to present. You will also be better placed to evaluate the advocates you see and recommend one who is best suited to speak on your client's behalf. Advocacy is not just important in the courtroom. It is often useful, and sometimes vital, in client interviewing, in negotiation and in meetings, presentations to clients and public lectures. Even if later you decide not to practise law, the principles of advocacy will be useful in whatever you do. Advocacy is about persuading people, and you cannot go through life without, on occasions, needing to persuade. Advocacy is a valuable skill to have – a transferable skill, a lifelong skill.

In answer to the question, 'Are good advocates born or made?', most people would say, 'They're born. Advocacy is not one of those things which can be taught'. Many lawyers would probably say the same. Skilled advocates are seen as being eloquent, articulate and able to think on their feet: all qualities which at first sight seem to be innate rather than acquired. Undoubtedly, some advocates are more naturally gifted than others, but many of these so-called gifts can be acquired through hard work and practice. Perhaps the worst mistake is to assume that good advocacy is simply a matter of flair, and little else. The advocate who demolishes an opponent's witness in cross-examination rarely achieves this by jumping to their feet and firing off the first thing that comes into their head: a great deal of thought and preparation will have gone into every aspect of the challenge they make.

This chapter gives a basic introduction to advocacy. For those who wish to practise as advocates, it represents the first stage of a continuous learning process. However, others may never appear before a court as an advocate at any stage of their professional careers. Even so, the skills covered in this chapter will prove useful in any situation where effective oral presentation is required.

13.2 SKILLS

The skills of an advocate divide into oral skills and organisation skills.

13.2.1 Oral skills

Advocates are skilled talkers: this is an obvious point which should never be overlooked. Within the stylised atmosphere of the courtroom, the task of the advocate, subject to the rules of professional conduct, is to talk their way to the best result that can be obtained for their client. The three major oral skills are as follows.

13.2.1.1 Presentation

Every advocate needs to be a good storyteller, especially when they are opening a case on behalf of either the prosecution or the claimant. It is not generally realised that a criminal court, in particular, may know next to nothing about the facts of the case it is about to try or the issues involved; it therefore needs to be put in the picture in a way which will engage its interest.

13.2.1.2 Argument

Every advocate also needs to be a good persuader. Much of an advocate's time will be spent addressing the court with a view to persuading it to find in favour of their client. Argument may be as to the overall issue of guilt or liability, or as to a subsidiary issue such as bail, the grant of an interim order, or a point of law.

13.2.1.3 Questioning witnesses

The questioning of witnesses is the skill which young advocates tend to find the most complex and difficult to master. English trials are characterised not only by their adversarial nature but also by the fact that much evidence is still given orally. The ability to extract the relevant evidence from your own witnesses by means of examination-in-chief (especially important in criminal cases) and to challenge the testimony of an opponent's witnesses in cross-examination is still seen as the most important attribute of the experienced advocate.

In the course of a civil or criminal trial, all three of the above skills will be exercised, but in many other situations advocacy will consist almost exclusively of presentation and argument. This is particularly true of the vast majority of applications in civil cases, because evidence will almost invariably be given by witness statements. Bail applications and pleas in mitigation in criminal cases also involve very little questioning of witnesses.

13.2.2 Organisation skills

In addition to the oral skills, a good advocate also draws upon other back-up skills which are exercised outside the court room. When an experienced advocate is performing in court, it all seems effortless: they have all the facts at their fingertips, nothing seems to throw them off their stride, and witnesses are examined and cross-examined incisively and in a logical sequence. On top of this, the advocate manages to maintain the appearance of being calm and dignified at the most crucial moments, and never loses their temper. At all times, they are courteous to the court, their opponent, and the most recalcitrant witnesses. To the uninitiated, it may look easy, but this level of competence is achieved only by hard work and experience. It is also dependent upon the advocate having thoroughly prepared and organised the case beforehand.

The most important organisation skills are set out below: there is nothing magical about any of them – in fact some of them may appear positively mundane – but no advocate can do without them.

13.2.2.1 Fact gathering and analysis

No advocate can begin to prepare a case until they have thoroughly mastered its facts. Until this is done, it is impossible to analyse its strengths and weaknesses. Ignorance of the facts will also make it far more difficult to perform adequately in court. For example, when cross-examining a witness, it will often be necessary to fire a sequence of rapid questions in order to try and shake their testimony. The task will be made immeasurably easier if the advocate's mastery of the facts is such that there is little or no need to refer to prepared notes before proceeding to the next question. Many readers will have seen US courtroom dramas on television in which advocates never use notes. In real life, they are trained to memorise the whole case file. Although UK courtroom style is very different, advocates should try to rely on notes as little as possible.

13.2.2.2 Knowledge of the relevant law

It is essential to research the relevant substantive law. The advocate must also develop a detailed knowledge of the law of evidence and the relevant procedural law. So far as evidence is concerned, it will always be necessary to study the relevant facts carefully in order to analyse:

(a) what the issues are;
(b) which issues are in dispute;
(c) who has the burden of proof; and
(d) what admissible evidence is available to prove or disprove those issues.

However, that is not enough: you will also need to memorise as much of the law of evidence as you can since an evidential problem may arise unpredictably during the course of a trial. Advocates rarely have time to look the law up in advance of raising an objection.

Similarly, procedural points have a habit of cropping up unexpectedly: an advocate's effectiveness will be greatly enhanced if their level of knowledge is such that these can be identified as soon as they arise.

13.2.2.3 Handling paperwork

In some respects, handling paperwork is the most neglected organisation skill of all, but it is in fact one of the most important, especially in civil cases. Even quite simple cases can end up producing masses of papers, some of which may need to be referred to at some time during a case. It is important therefore not only to devise a system which enables a required document to be located at a moment's notice, but also to know the contents of every document. This is particularly vital in applications in civil proceedings so far as witness statements are concerned. The judge may intervene by suddenly asking a question on a particular issue. The advocate should immediately be able to refer them to the relevant paragraph in the appropriate witness statement.

The ability to handle paperwork is also important in civil trial advocacy with rules requiring pre-trial exchange of witness statements and experts' reports.

13.3 THE BASICS

This section contains a simple checklist to assist in preparation of a case. It also deals with wider aspects of court behaviour and protocol.

13.3.1 Preparation

Good advocacy depends on planning and preparation at every stage. In particular, the order in which you address each task needs to be carefully considered so as to achieve the maximum benefit. The following checklist should always be followed.

13.3.1.1 Master the relevant facts

If the facts are simple, try to commit them to memory. In more complicated cases, prepare a written chronology for reference purposes which should ideally then be memorised as far as possible.

13.3.1.2 Analyse the facts

By applying the appropriate substantive, evidential and procedural law, you should be able to identify the following:

(a) the legal issues in dispute. Consider in this context whether there are any submissions you will need to make, for example as to admissibility;

(b) the factual issues in dispute. Identify what findings of fact the court will have to make if your client's case is to succeed;

(c) develop a 'theory' of the case consistent with your client's instructions. The more plausible the case advanced, the more likely it is to succeed.

Based upon the analysis above, plan objectives for each stage at which you will be called upon to speak or examine witnesses.

13.3.2 Presentation

Although presentation has been categorised as a specific oral skill, every aspect of the advocate's courtroom role in effect involves conducting a presentation, not only of the client's case but also of the advocate themselves. The following list sets out a number of presentational rules which should always be followed:

(a) Maintain eye contact with the person whom you are addressing.
(b) Never read from a prepared text.
(c) Be aware of 'body language'. The way in which an advocate behaves can affect the court's perceptions of their case. Try always to bear the following points in mind:
    (i) Stand still. Advocates who are nervous have a tendency to sway from side to side.
    (ii) Stand up straight when in court. Make sure you know your case well enough to avoid frequent references to your papers.
    (iii) Do not speak with your hands in front of your face. This is another common mannerism when a speaker is nervous. Be especially conscious of this trait in proceedings where advocates remain seated.
    (iv) Keep your hands and arms still (within reason). Although arm and hand gestures can sometimes be an effective means of emphasising a point, they should be used sparingly.

(v) Keep your emotions under control. To be an effective advocate, you will need to be able to hide all kinds of feelings. For example, never appear shocked because a witness says the opposite to what you expect. Learn to sail on unperturbed through the most stormy waters.

(d) Speak slowly in a clear, low tone. If you are anxious, you are likely to speak quickly and in a high voice. In particular, always 'watch the judge's pen'. You are hardly likely to be persuasive if the court cannot keep up with you. The same rule applies when taking the court through documents; it takes time for the court to read them and digest their contents.

(e) Do not be afraid of pauses. What may seem to the advocate to be a long gap in presentation is often not even noticed by the court.

(f) Avoid being long-winded and unnecessarily repetitive. These are both traits which suggest that you have not prepared the case very well.

(g) Know your court. All your planning must be with a view to persuading the court of the strength of your case. It is perhaps obvious but nevertheless important to realise that, for example, a judge will need to be addressed differently from a lay magistrate. Tailor your style to suit your audience.

(h) Be honest and courteous. At all times, bear in mind the need to build and maintain your reputation with the court. The advocate who loses the court's trust is of no use to their client. Always be scrupulously courteous to the court and to your opponent, even if you are disappointed with the way your case has gone.

(i) Dress appropriately. Check whether you need to be robed. In general, robes are not required in the magistrates' court or hearings in the room of a civil judge (known as 'chambers') (*Practice Direction (Court Dress) (No 4)* [2008] 1 WLR 357).

13.3.3 How to address the court

Nothing reveals an advocate's lack of experience more than a failure to adopt the correct mode of address. The following list should therefore be committed to memory:

Court	Mode of address
High Court Judge	'My Lord' or 'My Lady' as appropriate
Circuit Judge	'Your Honour'
Recorder	'Your Honour'
District Judge of the High Court or County Court	Judge
District Judge of the magistrates' court	Judge
Master of the Supreme Court	Judge
Supreme Court Costs Judge	Judge
Magistrates (lay and stipendiary)	'Sir' or 'Madam' as appropriate.

A particular problem is whether it is appropriate to address the court in the second person singular ('You'). In the case of district judges, masters and magistrates, it is perfectly permissible provided 'Judge' is interposed at appropriate intervals. For example, in a plea in mitigation to a district judge, it would be perfectly appropriate to proceed as follows:

> Judge, there are three matters relating to the defendant's involvement in these offences that I should like to draw to your attention. First, Judge, there are two specific aspects of the pre-sentence report which I should like to refer you to ...

High Court and circuit judges pose more of a problem. As a general rule, 'you' should be substituted by 'Your Lordship(s)', 'Your Ladyship(s)' or 'Your Honour(s)' as the case may be. For example, in the Crown Court before a circuit judge, the previous address would begin:

> May it please Your Honour, there are three matters relating to the defendant's involvement in these offences that I should respectfully like to draw to Your Honour's attention. First, Your Honour, if I might be permitted to draw Your Honour's attention to two specific aspects of the pre-sentence report ...

To those who are unfamiliar with courtroom protocol, this version may sound unnecessarily obsequious. Nevertheless, this is the level of courtesy expected and you depart from it at your peril. The odd 'you' or 'your' here and there may be acceptable, but do not take risks until you are experienced and know your court.

13.3.4 How to refer to your opponent

It is equally important to extend all the appropriate courtesies to your opposing advocates. Choose from 'My friend' or 'The prosecution/defence' or 'Mr/Ms/ Mrs/Miss Smith'. The term 'My learned friend' is traditionally reserved for barristers, although this is no longer a hard and fast rule. If you are opening the case, you should always ascertain the name of your opponent, since it is a normal courtesy to introduce them to the court. For example: 'Judge, my name is Mr Jones and I appear to prosecute this case and my friend Ms Smith appears on behalf of the defendant.'

13.3.5 Three golden rules when addressing the court

As well as knowing how to behave in court, an advocate must be able to create an impression of being experienced. Failure to observe the following will tend to reveal precisely the opposite.

13.3.5.1 Do not give evidence yourself

Not only is this improper, it also suggests over-involvement in the client's case. Avoid phrases such as 'My client tells me ...' or 'I happen to know that ...'. However, it will often be necessary to put the client's views to the court, for example in a civil application or a plea in mitigation in a criminal case. In civil applications, the phrases 'I am instructed that' and 'my instructions are' are perfectly acceptable, but in criminal cases they are sometimes interpreted as being coded messages that the advocate does not believe a word the client is saying. Phrases such as 'I have discussed this with my client and they want you to know' or 'My client wishes me to inform you' are more appropriate.

13.3.5.2 Do not give your opinion

Avoid using phrases such as 'In my opinion ...' or 'I think ...'. When an advocate wishes to persuade the court to adopt their view of the case, phrases like 'I submit' or 'I would seek to persuade you' or 'I would urge you' are more appropriate. The important thing to remember is that the only opinion that counts is that of the judge.

13.3.5.3 Object rarely, but quickly

There is an enormous temptation, especially when you have thoroughly researched a case, to object at every opportunity. Indeed, this often impresses the client. However, it will not endear an advocate to the court unless the point is one of substance. Do not object unless the point advances your case or diminishes that of your opponent. Be alert: the decision to raise an objection will often be a split-second one, especially if it involves the issue of whether an inadmissible question has been put to a witness.

13.3.6 Five golden rules when questioning witnesses

Although the examination of a witness is as much an art as a science, the following are basic rules for questioning witnesses whatever the nature of the proceedings.

13.3.6.1 Keep your questions short

Formulate questions so that, ideally, they do not exceed 10 words. If the question is convoluted, there is a risk that neither the witness nor the court will be able to follow it.

Nothing takes the wind out of an advocate's sails more than being asked to repeat or rephrase a question because it is incomprehensible.

13.3.6.2 Ask one question at a time

For reasons similar to those given above, it is essential to refrain from asking multiple questions. The last thing you want is for your opponent to rise to their feet and say, 'Judge, I wonder if my friend would be kind enough to indicate to the witness which question she wants him to answer first'.

This means that a quite simple point may often need to be broken down into several questions before it can effectively be put to a witness. For example, if you are seeking to extract a concession from an identification witness that they were standing 50 feet away, it was dark and it was raining, etc, you may need to ask a whole series of short questions in order to succeed in this objective.

13.3.6.3 Know your objectives in respect of each witness

This applies as much to your own witnesses as to those of your opponent, but is particularly important when planning a cross-examination.

13.3.6.4 Try to avoid asking questions in cross-examination to which you do not know the answer

This rule should not be taken too literally because sometimes one has no choice but to probe. The main thing is to ensure that you are never floored by the unexpected. For example, let us assume that you are cross-examining an identification witness on the issue of where they were standing at the time of the incident. If you were simply to ask 'Where were you standing?', you would have no control over the answer. Contrast:

> Q. You said earlier that you were standing on the corner of Main Street and Underwood Road, didn't you?
>
> A. Yes.
>
> Q. And there's no dispute, is there, that that is about 50 feet from the incident you say you saw?

Even if the witness says 'No', you have much more control over where to proceed from there. Alternatively, if you can easily prove that the witness was standing 50 feet away, you could quite safely ask the question 'Where were you standing?', because you know that if the witness were to reply 'About 6 feet away', you would have plenty of ammunition with which to contradict them.

13.3.6.5 Know when to stop

There is always a danger in going on for too long, but it is particularly important not to fall into the trap of asking one question too many. It is a great temptation to press on when you have a witness 'on the run'. However, that is the time to pause and reflect briefly upon whether, having secured some favourable concession, it might not be wiser to refrain from cross-examining further.

For example, if you have managed to extract from the identification witness referred to above concessions that they were standing 50 feet away, it was dark and it was raining, it is a great temptation to then say with a final flourish, 'So how can you be so sure it was the accused that you saw?'.

This is the one question you (and your client) may live to regret!

13.3.7 Witnesses: court formalities

There are a number of matters of court protocol concerning witnesses of which you need to be aware, especially since it will be your task to explain them to your client and other witnesses before they give evidence.

13.3.7.1 Criminal cases

In a criminal case, witnesses other than the defendant should be asked to stay out of court until called.

If the defendant is to give evidence, they must be called before other defence witnesses unless the court directs otherwise.

Witnesses may refresh their memories from their written statements prior to being called to give evidence. Other parties must be informed if this has taken place.

13.3.7.2 Civil cases

In a civil case, witnesses may sit in court throughout the hearing. If the advocate wishes to exclude witnesses from court, the advocate must apply for an order to that effect.

The claimant and defendant are both usually called first by their advocate.

Witnesses may refresh their memories from their written statements prior to being called to give evidence. Other parties must be informed if this has taken place.

13.4 OPENING THE CASE

This section considers opening speeches in all types of proceedings. Although the length and purpose of such speeches may vary widely, they are all vitally important. They provide the advocate with an opportunity to make the first impression. This may be vital, as the court or tribunal may know little or nothing about the case it is about to try. For example, in a criminal trial before magistrates, the court will probably know nothing about the case other than details of the charges.

13.4.1 Criminal trials in the magistrates' court

The prosecution always have the right to make an opening speech before calling their evidence. In simple trials, this right is sometimes waived. If the prosecutor does open, they will usually:

(a) introduce themselves and their opponent to the court;
(b) take the court briefly through the charges;
(c) outline the facts of the case and the evidence that they intend to adduce in order to prove the charges; and
(d) explain the law, where necessary.

The opening speech requires the advocate to be a good storyteller so that the relevant incidents are brought to life. If there is an item of evidence for which admissibility is in dispute, the prosecutor should make no mention of it when opening, leaving admissibility to be determined at a later stage.

Defence advocates rarely make an opening speech before calling their evidence, because by doing so they lose the right to make a closing speech. Since the prosecutor may make a closing speech, the defence advocate will usually take advantage of having the last word.

Apart from the right to make speeches, either advocate may at any stage make a submission on a point of law. In particular, the defence may submit that there is no case to answer at the close of the prosecution case. In such an event, the opposing advocate always has a right to reply.

13.4.2 Civil trials

The claimant's advocate has the right to open (unless, unusually, the burden of proof of all issues lies on the defendant). As judges have power to dispense with opening speeches, their use has declined, and the practice of providing a written 'skeleton argument' to the judge, often in lieu of an opening speech, has increased. As in criminal cases in the magistrates' court, if the defendant's advocate elects to make an opening speech, they are not entitled to make a closing speech except with leave of the court.

The purposes of the advocate's opening speech in a civil trial will be to:

(a) introduce themselves and their opponent to the court;

(b) indicate the nature of their claim, for example, 'Your Honour, this is a claim for damages for breach of contract';

(c) summarise the areas of dispute between the parties;

(d) outline by reference to the statements of case the alleged facts of the case (nothing which cannot be proved should be asserted), indicating areas of dispute;

(e) introduce the evidence, including any relevant matters contained in the trial bundle;

(f) summarise the legal principles involved, indicating areas where a ruling will have to be made.

13.5 EXAMINATION-IN-CHIEF

Examination-in-chief is in many respects more difficult than cross-examination because an advocate should always be seeking to succeed on the strengths of their own case rather than on the weaknesses of their opponent's. Accordingly, the way your own witnesses give their evidence has a vital bearing on the overall impression that your case creates in the mind of the court.

13.5.1 The characteristics of examination-in-chief

Although, with one exception, advocates have a complete discretion as to the order in which witnesses are called, it is usual in civil cases for the claimant or defendant, as appropriate, to be called first. In criminal cases, the prosecutor will usually call the victim first, but the defence advocate is obliged to call the defendant before other witnesses as to fact unless the court directs otherwise (Police and Criminal Evidence Act 1984, s 79). The advocate calling the witness will, as a matter of courtesy, begin by announcing each witness in turn, for example, 'Your Honour, I now call the claimant, Margaret Brown'.

The principal objectives of examination-in-chief are:

(a) to present the witness's evidence in a logical sequence (usually chronologically or by topic);

(b) to cover all the relevant issues upon which the witness is able to testify; and

(c) to anticipate matters likely to be raised in cross-examination.

The major characteristic of examination-in-chief (and what makes it so difficult for the advocate) is that the witness must, so far as possible, be left to tell their own story with minimal prompting from the advocate. In order to achieve this objective, leading questions are not generally permitted.

Although there is a degree of controversy over what constitutes a leading question, the generally accepted definition is that it is a question which suggests its own answer by seeking to put words into the witness's mouth. For example, if an advocate was seeking to establish that a witness saw the defendant, James Smith, in The Mitre public house at midday on Monday, 21 August (all of which is in dispute), it would not be permissible to ask, 'Did you see James Smith in The Mitre public house at midday on Monday, 21 August?'.

Instead, the advocate would need to proceed by means of a number of non-leading questions as follows:

> Q. Can you remember what you were doing on Monday, 21 August? (This question is arguably leading, but probably not objectionable.)
>
> A. Well, let me see. Oh yes, I went into work in the usual way.

Q. Did you stay there all day? (non-leading)
A. No, I went out for an early lunch.
Q. About what time was that? (non-leading)
A. Oh, about ten to twelve I think.
Q. And where did you go? (non-leading)
A. A pub called The Mitre.
Q. Did you see anyone there you recognised? (non-leading)
A. Yes, I saw James Smith ...

and so on. As can be readily appreciated, this technique requires the advocate to prepare very carefully in advance to ensure that they are able to guide the witness through their evidence without resorting to prompting.

The technique also requires stamina, since it may take time even to elicit a simple set of facts in this way. The only three occasions on which leading questions are permitted by way of exception are:

(a) when the witness's evidence relates to a matter that is not in dispute;

(b) where a denial is invited from the witness; and

(c) on those rare occasions when a witness is declared to be hostile.

An example of exception (a) above would arise if the only dispute was as to the date on which the witness saw James Smith:

Q. Do you recall an occasion when you saw James Smith in The Mitre public house? (leading, but not disputed)
A. Yes.
Q. And can you remember when that was? (non-leading)
A. Yes, it was on Monday, 21 August.

The advocate should always check in advance with their opponent as to what matters can be led to the witness. Matters such as name, address and occupation may always be led, but some advocates prefer to ask witnesses to state these details in their own words to help put them at their ease.

An example of exception (b) would be if Mr Smith's advocate was seeking to extract a denial from his client. It would then be permissible to proceed as follows:

Q. Mr Smith, were you in The Mitre on Monday, 21 August at midday? (leading)
A. No, I was not.

Exception (c), namely the hostile witness, is rarely encountered.

13.5.2 The witness who does not come up to proof

13.5.2.1 Criminal cases

If the witness displays an unwillingness to tell the truth at the instance of the party calling them, the court may declare the witness to be hostile. This allows the advocate who has called the witness to ask leading questions and, with leave, any previous inconsistent statement made by the witness may be put to them (Criminal Procedure Act 1865, s 3). Such a statement may be used not only to discredit the witness's testimony but also to prove the truth of anything contained in the statement (Criminal Justice Act 2003, s 119).

In most cases, however, the witness's failure to say what the advocate is hoping for is the result of forgetfulness, incompetent examination-in-chief or a poorly-taken statement. In such a situation, witnesses cannot be cross-examined. The advocate can only try to repair the damage by calling additional evidence which supports the advocate's case. The problem of the forgetful witness may also be avoided if a note of the witness's earlier evidence is available (see **13.5.4**).

13.5.2.2 Civil cases

The position of the hostile witness in civil cases is broadly similar to that in criminal cases (see Civil Evidence Act 1968, s 3).

If the witness is not declared hostile, the advocate's options are limited in the same way as in criminal cases (but see **13.5.4**).

13.5.3 Exchange of witness statements

The exchange of witness statements in civil proceedings has made a fundamental difference to examination-in-chief. If a party has served a witness statement and wishes to rely at trial on that witness's evidence, the party must call that witness to give oral evidence unless the court orders to the contrary. The witness's statement will stand as their evidence-in-chief unless the court orders otherwise. This means, in cases involving exchange of witness statements, that examination-in-chief has been reduced to:

(a) formally calling the witness and establishing their name and address;

(b) asking the witness to identify their statement; and

(c) asking the witness whether the contents of the statement are true.

13.5.4 Introducing documents and real evidence

Documentary evidence may be introduced for a variety of reasons. The term 'document' includes items such as photographs, tape-recordings, video films and computer data. From an evidential point of view, it is important to remember, not only that a document's authenticity must be established, but also that its contents must be admissible for the purpose for which they are tendered. The rules differ materially in criminal and civil proceedings.

13.5.4.1 Criminal cases

A witness must normally be called to prove the authenticity of any document which is to be adduced in evidence. Although documents cannot be agreed (contrast the position in civil cases), in practice many documents, such as agreed plans of traffic accidents, are routinely admitted. Copies of the documents are generally sufficient (see Criminal Justice Act 1988, s 27). A police officer will normally be called to prove the authenticity of a defendant's written confession. This will be done by asking the officer to identify the defendant's signature and recount the circumstances in which the statement was made. If accepted, the original will be admitted as an exhibit. The police officer will then normally be invited to read the defendant's written confession to the court. Although most interviews with suspects are now audio-recorded, the written summary of the interview will basically be proved in the same way.

The other commonly encountered document is the 'memory refreshing document'. The basic rule is that a witness may refresh their memory in the witness box from any document which was made or verified by them at an earlier time and 'his recollection of the matter is likely to have been significantly better at that time than it is at the time of his oral evidence' (Criminal Justice Act 2003, s 139(1)).

Police officers, in particular, will frequently ask for leave to refresh their memories from notes contained in their pocket books, but other witnesses may also be permitted to refer to their original statements.

Real evidence consisting of other objects, for example a weapon, must likewise be proved by a witness who can show that they are what they purport to be and that they are relevant to the issues. It will also be necessary to prove that an appropriate chain exists which links the object to the defendant.

13.5.4.2 Civil cases

In theory, a witness must be called on to prove the authenticity and originality of each document which is to be adduced in evidence. However, in civil cases, documents are almost invariably agreed. They will usually be put in as one or more agreed bundles by the claimant's advocate in the course of their opening speech. Furthermore, the use of documents is inextricably bound up with the rules as to disclosure, expert evidence and exchange of witness statements, all of which are outside the scope of this chapter.

The rules relating to the use of contemporaneous notes to refresh the memory and the court's discretion to allow the witness to leave the witness box to read their statement are the same as in criminal cases. These rules have effectively been overridden in cases where there are exchanged witness statements.

13.6 CROSS-EXAMINATION

Effective cross-examination is generally regarded as representing the highest level of advocacy. The skilled advocate, by harrying their opponent's witnesses with probing questions, can effectively demolish the other side's case. However, it is an art hedged with misconceptions, most of which derive from watching too many fictional courtroom dramas. The aggressive language and sarcastic manner that are characteristic of the television soap opera are usually inappropriate in the real world.

13.6.1 Defining objectives

Advocates should always give careful thought to what they hope to achieve by cross-examination. In order to do this effectively, it will be necessary to develop a 'theory' of the client's case. This theory should be a plausible version of the events, consistent with the available evidence and the client's instructions which, if accepted, will result in the court finding in the client's favour. Once the advocate has developed this theory, they will find it easier to work out their tactics.

Another point to be borne in mind is that, whatever tactics are to be adopted, the cross-examining advocate must always 'put their case' to their opponent's witnesses. In other words, the advocate must confront their opponent's witnesses with all aspects of the client's case which conflict with the witnesses' evidence. This need not be done directly. One often hears advocates saying, 'I put it to you that ...', as if it were an essential ritualistic device. However, it is possible to be more subtle than this. For example, using the illustration at **13.5.1**, if Mr Smith's advocate needed to put to the witness that it was in fact on 22 August that they saw Mr Smith in The Mitre, it would be permissible, but inadvisable, simply to state, 'I put it to you that you are mistaken; it was on 22 not 21 August that you saw Mr Smith in The Mitre, wasn't it?'.

If the answer were to be, 'No', that would be the end of the matter.

Suppose, however, that the cross-examining advocate knew that the witness regularly went to The Mitre at that time: the client's case could be expressed more effectively in the following way:

Q. It's true, isn't it, that you regularly go to The Mitre for lunch?
A. Yes.
Q. At about the same time each day?
A. Yes.
Q. Around midday?
A. Yes.

The cross-examiner could continue by trying to establish that there was nothing special about 21 August, before suggesting to the witness that they had in fact got the day wrong and that they had seen the defendant on a different day.

In other respects, the cross-examiner has considerable freedom of manoeuvre in deciding how to structure their cross-examination. There are four main questions to consider.

13.6.1.1 Should I cross-examine at all?

It may well be that, unless the advocate needs to put the client's case, it is better to ask no questions at all. This is especially so if a witness has not directly damaged the case. Cross-examination may increase the risk of eliciting unfavourable material that would otherwise not come out.

13.6.1.2 Are there any favourable matters that I can extract?

It is far better for an advocate to get a witness on their side, rather than to confront them. For example, in a case involving disputed identification, try gently to elicit concessions from the witness that it was, for example, dark and raining at the time, rather than suggest aggressively that their evidence is worthless.

13.6.1.3 Is there any way in which I can discredit the witness's evidence?

Witnesses can, and often do, make mistakes or erroneous assumptions that may be exposed by cross-examination. Very few witnesses deliberately give false evidence. This always needs to be borne in mind when probing for weaknesses. Again, an indirect rather than a confrontational approach is likely to yield better results. Exposing inconsistencies by reference to a previous inconsistent statement is a particularly effective method. It is governed by special legal rules which are outside the scope of this chapter.

13.6.1.4 Is there any way in which I can discredit the witness themselves?

It is rare for the advocate to find themselves in a position to insinuate, for example, that the witness is biased. It is a particularly risky tactic when done on behalf of a defendant in a criminal trial because of the dangers of falling foul of s 101(1)(g) of the Criminal Justice Act 2003. In any case, the tactic should never be adopted unless there is independent evidence available to substantiate the allegations.

The above four questions are not mutually exclusive: a cross-examining advocate may wish to adopt those parts of a witness's testimony which favour their client whilst challenging other parts which do not. This is a highly skilled and complex operation.

13.6.2 The technique of cross-examination

The major difference between examination-in-chief and cross-examination is that the advocate cross-examining is permitted to ask leading questions. This is a particularly valuable right since it enables the advocate to retain tighter control of the witness than is the case with non-leading questions. However, leading questions should not be used to excess since this may give the impression that the witness is being brow-beaten. The tactic can, however, be particularly effective when an advocate wishes to expose inconsistencies or illogicalities. The trap can be set by asking the witness a series of non-leading questions on peripheral matters as a preliminary to confronting them with weaknesses or inconsistencies in their testimony by means of a series of tightly controlled leading questions. This is a highly skilled exercise.

Two general examples will suffice. Suppose that you were trying to discredit the testimony of an identification witness. There would no doubt be a number of matters which you had thoroughly researched beforehand, such as where they were standing, how far away they were from the incident, the time of day, the weather conditions, etc. You would no doubt wish to keep tight control of this part of your cross-examination by means of leading questions. However, it might also be appropriate to probe into what the witness had been doing beforehand by means of non-leading questions. For example, you might ask, 'Now Mr Smith, you say you were on your way home when you witnessed this incident; where were you coming from?'. The answer might be, 'I'd been down The Mitre for a drink'.

Not all cross-examinations will yield such promising results, but it can be seen that much useful information can be gleaned from peripheral matters by means of non-leading questions without running any risk to your case.

A second example might be in the case of a witness whom an advocate wished to confront with a previous inconsistent statement. It might be appropriate to begin by inducing the witness by means of non-leading questions to embellish their story still further before confronting them with the inconsistencies. This is a particularly effective technique where the allegation is that the witness is biased.

13.7 RE-EXAMINATION

Once cross-examination is completed, the advocate who called the witness has the right to re-examine. That right is limited in that: first, the advocate may deal only with matters raised in cross-examination; and, secondly, leading questions are not permitted. Very few advocates are skilled re-examiners. It is a sophisticated art. As a general rule, it is most unwise to re-examine unless you are absolutely certain as to your objectives. Its principal function is to repair any damage done in cross-examination by giving the witness an opportunity to explain or qualify their previous answers. It is useful where, for example:

(a) cross-examination has confused the witness;
(b) the cross-examiner has attempted to impeach the witness's credit;
(c) the cross-examiner has elicited only partial details of an incident which appears to favour the opponent's case.

13.8 CLOSING THE CASE

Closing a case can be more difficult than opening, because a greater degree of improvisation is required. An opening speech can be worked out in detail beforehand: by the time an advocate rises to make a closing address, all the evidence will be before the court and the case may look very different by then. However, it is rare that the central issues will have changed, only the details. It is absolutely vital, therefore, to have identified the likely issues and evolved a 'theory' of the case in advance. It is only in this way that a closing address can deal with all the outstanding issues in a coherent and persuasive manner. It is important to remember that, just as the advocate who opens the case has the advantage of the first word, so the closing speaker is the last advocate the court will hear before retiring to consider its verdict.

13.8.1 Who closes the case?

13.8.1.1 Criminal cases

In magistrates' court trials, both the prosecution and the defence may make final speeches. The prosecution may make a final speech where the defendant is represented or if the defence introduce evidence other than that of the defendant. The defence will have the final word.

13.8.1.2 Civil cases

Except where the defendant began or where the defendant calls no evidence, the advocate for the claimant has the last word in a civil case. If the judge says that they do not wish to hear a closing speech, the claimant has probably already won.

13.8.2 The purpose of the closing speech

13.8.2.1 Criminal cases

Be brief. Magistrates' courts are very busy places and you will be well advised to confine yourself to the essential points which advance your client's case. However, the experienced advocate will not allow themselves to be rushed. If you need a few moments to compose yourself and go over your notes, do not hesitate to ask for them. You should always cover:

(a) any relevant points of law;
(b) the key issues in dispute;
(c) any part of the evidence which weakens the prosecution case and strengthens that of the defence.

Avoid saying too much about the burden and standard of proof. Magistrates need little reminding of this. It is better to concentrate on those parts of the evidence which genuinely raise a reasonable doubt.

13.8.2.2 Civil cases

The position in civil cases is broadly similar to that in criminal cases, except that an advocate must always be aware that they are addressing a judge, not magistrates. Modify your style accordingly. Since civil trials still take place on the statements of case, a closing speech which follows the issues raised by the statements of case will greatly assist the court. Judges are particularly grateful to advocates who not only summarise the issues that are still outstanding but also emphasise the essential findings of fact which the judge will have to make in order to decide the case.

13.9 ETHICAL ISSUES

An advocate's reputation with the court is their most valuable asset. An advocate who has lost the court's trust through some piece of unethical conduct is a liability. All advocates should be familiar with the SRA Code of Conduct for Solicitors 2023.

13.9.1 Criminal cases

13.9.1.1 Duties of the prosecution advocate

The duties of the prosecution advocate are:

(a) to ensure that all relevant facts and law are before the court;
(b) to make available to the defence any evidence which is inconsistent with the evidence which a prosecution witness gives at the trial.

13.9.1.2 Duties of the defence advocate

The duties of the defence advocate are:

(a) to say on a client's behalf all that the client would properly say for themselves;
(b) to keep confidential all information received about a client and their affairs which the client wishes to keep confidential;
(c) to ensure that the prosecution discharge the onus placed upon them to prove the guilt of the accused. The defence advocate is entitled to put the prosecution to proof even if the defendant has admitted their guilt;
(d) to disclose to the prosecution and to the court all relevant cases and statutory provisions relating to the case, even if unfavourable to the defence. However, unfavourable evidence need not be disclosed;
(e) not to participate in a positive deception of the court. A solicitor may not continue to act for a client who misleads the court (eg, by giving a false name, or giving evidence which the advocate knows to be untrue) unless the client is prepared to reveal the truth;
(f) not to act for two or more clients whose interests are in conflict, even if invited to do so by the court.

13.9.2 Civil cases

Advocates for the claimant and the defendant are bound by the same rules which are:

(a) to ensure that all relevant facts and law are before the court;

(b) to say on a client's behalf all that the client would say properly for themselves;

(c) to keep confidential all information received about a client and their affairs which the client wishes to keep confidential;

(d) where relevant, to ensure that the opponent discharges the onus placed upon them by the burden of proof;

(e) to disclose to the court all relevant cases and statutory provisions relevant to the case, even if not favourable to the client. The advocate may then seek to show that decisions which are against them are erroneous, not binding, per incuriam or distinguishable. As in criminal cases, the theory is that unfavourable evidence need not be disclosed. However, the rules as to disclosure and exchange of witness statements are such that, in practice, both parties may be required to disclose such evidence;

(f) not to participate in a positive deception of the court. A solicitor may not continue to act for a client who misleads the court (eg, by giving evidence which the advocate knows to be untrue) unless the client is now prepared to reveal the truth;

(g) not to act for two or more clients whose interests are in conflict.

13.10 CRIMINAL CASES: BAIL AND MITIGATION

A detailed study of criminal advocacy in bail applications and pleas in mitigation is outside the scope of this chapter. However, a very basic guide to the skills required is set out below. Because most criminal advocates will begin their careers with a simple bail application or plea, it is often erroneously assumed that this is 'easy' advocacy. Nothing could be further from the truth: there is nothing easy about a situation in which the client may face a period in custody if their advocate fails them.

13.10.1 Bail

The skills of the advocate will be required only when the application is opposed. Although bail is always ultimately a matter for the court, it will normally be granted as a matter of course unless the prosecution object. Since defendants have a right to bail prior to conviction, it is customary for the Crown Prosecutor to begin by formally setting out their objections by reference to the prescribed criteria in Sch 1, Pt I to the Bail Act 1976. The objections will almost invariably be based on an assertion that there are substantial grounds for believing that the defendant will either abscond and/or commit further offences while they are on bail. The risk of the defendant interfering with witnesses or otherwise obstructing the course of justice is also sometimes advanced as an objection.

The task of the defence advocate is twofold. First, they should seek to put forward arguments which tend to minimise the risks adverted by the Crown Prosecutor. Thus, for example, if the prosecution claim that there is a substantial risk of the defendant absconding, this might be rebutted by arguing that:

(a) the defendant is pleading not guilty and the evidence against them is weak;

(b) the defendant's record (if they have one) reveals that they have never absconded whilst on bail in the past;

(c) even if they are is convicted, the likelihood of a custodial sentence is remote.

These are very general illustrations: each case must be dealt with on its own facts. Whatever the facts, thorough preparation is always essential.

Secondly, the advocate must neutralise any substantial risks by putting forward a sensible package of conditions, such as a surety combined with a condition of residence, which will be sufficient to persuade the court that it can afford to take a risk and grant bail. Although s 4 of the Bail Act 1976 is supposed to secure a right to bail, in reality if a prosecutor raises substantial grounds for withholding bail, the defence advocate has a difficult task upholding that right. An effective application therefore requires as much advance preparation as the circumstances permit. The Crown Prosecution Service (CPS) should always be approached (in advance if practicable) in order to obtain as much information as possible about both the offence and the defendant.

If possible, you should obtain detailed instructions from the client concerning their personal circumstances and the existence of any potential sureties. It may be that this will avoid a contested application altogether. If you can produce an appropriate package of conditions to the CPS before the hearing, you may be able to persuade it to withdraw its objections. So far as the actual application itself is concerned, an advocate should always bear three things in mind:

(a) Structure the application in such a way that each prosecution objection is countered in a logical sequence, and conclude with any package of conditions you wish to put forward.

(b) Keep the application as short as circumstances permit and remember that courts usually have a long list of cases to hear.

(c) Tailor the application to the individual client. Magistrates are often offered the same platitudes whatever the nature of the application, such as, 'The defendant strenuously denies the charge, has a fixed address and has been offered work on a building site'. The statement may be true, but it is vitally important to interest the court in your client's personal circumstances. It might therefore be more appropriate to explain a little more about why your client's denial is so significant. For example:

> 'Judge, if I might begin by referring you to the case against Mr Smith, I submit that it is tenuous in the extreme. The evidence consists solely of hotly disputed identification evidence ...'

and so on.

PROSECUTION PAPERS – GARETH DAVIES

Charge: Inflicting grievous bodily harm (Offences Against the Person Act 1861, s 20)

The defendant, Gareth Davies, is jointly charged with Stephen Jones. Last night he assaulted Phillip Bennett, outside the Seagull fish and chip shop in High Street, Weyford.

At about 11.15pm Bennett was outside the fish and chip shop waiting for his friends who were inside the shop. He saw Stephen Jones and Gareth Davies walking along High Street from the direction of Market Street. Both Jones and Davies used to be regulars at Cindy's nightclub in the High Street where Bennett works. Some two weeks earlier Bennett banned them because of an incident at the nightclub.

When they saw Bennett they crossed the road and started talking to him, trying to persuade him to lift the ban. At first the conversation was good natured and then things changed. Jones became more and more aggressive and despite Bennett's attempts to calm him down Jones punched Bennett hard in the face. Bennett fought back but he fell over. Whilst on the ground he was hit at least a dozen times on the face and arms. He was also punched and kicked in the chest and stomach. The punches were coming from his left and right and Bennett now saw that Gareth Davies was involved. He could not be sure which of the two men was more responsible but he is sure both were involved. The assault finished when a friend of Bennett's, John Bevan, intervened.

Bevan, who also works at Cindy's, knows both Jones and Davies. He said that he was inside the fish and chip shop heard a commotion outside, rushed out and saw Bennett being attacked by both Jones and Davies. He managed to break it up and then Jones and Davies ran off.

The police were called and both Jones and Davies were arrested about half a mile away. On arrival at the police station both men were found to be under the influence of alcohol. They were unfit to be interviewed and left in the cells to sleep.

Jones denied the offence in interview. He said he was defending himself having been attacked by Bennett. He denied causing all of Bennett's injuries saying that Davies must have caused them.

When interviewed at 9.30am today Davies denied any involvement in the offence saying all he did was to try to pull Jones off Bennett. He said that Jones was the one that was responsible for causing all the injuries to Bennett. When told that Jones had put the blame onto him Davies said 'I'll get him for this. He'll regret saying that. You wait until I catch up with him.'

As a result of the attack Bennett suffered a deep cut above his left eye; cuts and bruises to his face; a bleeding nose; grazes to his hands and knees; bruises to his stomach and arms; a broken nose and a broken left arm. Bennett was treated at Weyford General Hospital and released earlier today.

Jones, who has no previous convictions, was granted unconditional bail. He is due to appear before Weyford Magistrates' Court in seven days time.

Previous convictions:

4 years ago	ABH	Fined £500; Compensation £70
	Absconding	Fined £100
3 years ago	Criminal damage	Community sentence with a supervision requirement
	Absconding	Fined £75
18 months ago	ABH	3 months' imprisonment

Antecedents:

Aged 27, married (separated from his wife), unemployed, previous employment all casual – barman, bouncer etc. Since his marriage break-up some three months ago he has slept on friends' floors and in their spare rooms. He is staying with friends at the moment but has to move out by the end of the week. Previous offences all alcohol related.

The case will be adjourned. Apply for a remand in custody for seven days.

DEFENCE PAPERS

Mr Davies says:

I live with friends at 36 Town Lane, Weyford.

THE OFFENCE

I am charged jointly with Stephen Jones with inflicting grievous bodily harm on Philip Bennett. I will plead not guilty.

Last night I went out for a drink at the Ship public house in the High Street and met Stephen Jones there. I used to go out with him a lot. I thought he was my friend until this happened. We used to go to Cindy's Nightclub but about two weeks ago we both got banned by the bouncer there called Philip Bennett. Stephen got very drunk and started hitting on some girls who didn't like it. The girls complained and Bennett became involved. There was an argument and Stephen threatened him. I wasn't involved but because I was with Stephen I got barred as well.

After having a few pints in the Ship we were walking along the High Street on the way home. Neither of us were drunk. We saw Bennett outside the Seagull fish and chip shop with a group of girls and Stephen said that we should try to persuade Bennett to let us back into Cindy's. I told him that it wasn't a good idea but before I knew it Stephen had crossed the road and was talking to Bennett. I thought that Bennett would tell Stephen to get lost but he seemed quite happy to talk to him. The girls then went into the fish and shop and one of the girls recognised Stephen from the night we'd been banned from Cindy's and said something like 'Not you again, you tosser' and then Stephen lost it. He started to argue with Bennett about how out of order Bennett had been to ban him from Cindy's and then he punched Bennett in the face.

I didn't want to get involved. With my record I didn't want any trouble but I knew that things were getting out of hand. Bennett had fallen to the ground and Stephen was now kicking him. I tried to pull Stephen off Bennett but he just kept laying into him on the ground. Another man, who works with Bennett called John, then came out of the fish and chip shop and managed to get Stephen off Bennett. Stephen then ran off and I chased after him.

The police later arrested us. When I arrived at the police station, I was given some written rules about my rights and asked if I wanted a solicitor, but I didn't see the need, I hadn't done anything wrong. We were both kept in cells until this morning. I wasn't told that was because I was drunk or unfit to be interviewed. I just slept on and off. During my interview, I admit that I was still very fed up with Stephen's behaviour. When they put us into the police van we had had a bit of an argument.

I told the police what had happened. They said Stephen had put all the blame on me. I don't understand why as I thought he was a mate, but I suppose he's afraid of getting a criminal record and decided that the best thing to do was to land me in it. So, I was a bit aggressive about Stephen during the interview. In fact, I think I said that I'd sort him out but I was tired and emotional and didn't mean it. I'll stay away from him now.

We were both charged but I was refused police bail. Stephen was granted police bail.

Personal background

I am aged 27. I left school when I was 16 and have done casual jobs as a bouncer, barman and general labourer. I am currently unemployed. I've lived in the Weyford area for about ten years. I married five years ago but split up from my wife about three months ago when our tenancy came to an end. After we split up I've slept on friends' floors, and in their spare rooms. I'm staying with friends now but they've told me that I have to move out by the end of the week.

My parents live in Scotland and will not put me up even if I wanted them to. The last time I got into trouble I stayed at Weyford Bail Hostel and I'd readily stay there again.

Four years ago my marriage hit a bad patch and I began to drink. Drink is at the root of all my previous offences. I pleaded guilty to them all.

The ABH some four years ago took place in a pub. I'd been drinking and watching the football when this bloke said something I didn't like about my team. I lost my temper and got into a fight with him.

The first absconding offence was a mistake – I got the dates mixed up. I was arrested under a warrant.

The criminal damage offence was when I thought my wife had left me. She went to stay at her mother's. I'd had a few pints at the pub and went round to see her but she wouldn't let me in. I lost my temper and ended up smashing a few of the windows. I didn't attend court on time because I overslept and turned up about three hours late.

I continued to drink and the last offence was also committed whilst drunk. Someone picked on me in a pub. I defended myself but overdid it. It was about that time that I decided I had to pull myself together. I voluntarily went on an alcohol awareness course run by a local charity and my drinking is now under control.

Mr Davies wishes you to apply for bail on his behalf. The Probation Service were consulted this morning and should Mr Davies be granted bail there is a place available for him at the Weyford Bail Hostel.

PROSECUTION SUBMISSIONS

Judge, the prosecution oppose bail because, if released on bail, there are substantial grounds for believing the following: first, that the defendant will fail to surrender to custody; second, that he will interfere with witnesses or otherwise obstruct the course of justice; and, third, that he will commit offences whilst on bail. I shall deal with each of these grounds in turn.

Judge, the first ground of objection is failure to surrender to custody. This was a serious, unprovoked attack on Mr Bennett resulting in grievous bodily harm.

At about 11.15 last night the victim, Mr Bennett, was outside the Seagull fish and chip shop in the High Street, Guildfleet waiting for his friends who were inside the shop. He was approached by Mr Davies and his co-defendant Mr Jones. Both men are known to Mr Bennett as he banned both men from his place of work, Cindy's nightclub, some two weeks ago. Mr Jones tried to persuade Mr Bennett to lift the ban. At first the conversation was good natured but then Mr Jones became more and more aggressive. Mr Bennett tried to calm him down. Then Mr Jones punched Mr Bennett hard in the face. Mr Bennett fought back but he fell over. Whilst on the ground Mr Bennett was hit at least a dozen times on the face and arms. He was also punched and kicked in the chest and stomach. The punches were coming from his left and right and Mr Bennett could see that not only was Mr Jones involved but Mr Davies too. He couldn't be sure which of the two men were more responsible but he is sure that both were involved. The assault finished when a friend of Mr Bennett's, John Bevan, intervened. Both Mr Jones and Mr Davies ran off.

The police were called and both men were arrested. On arrival at the police station both men were too drunk to be interviewed and they were left in the cells to sleep. Earlier this morning, Mr Davies was interviewed and denied any involvement in the offence.

Judge, the strength of the evidence against Mr Davies is strong. Not only does Mr Bennett identify Mr Davies as being involved but Mr Bevan does too. Mr Bevan, who works with Mr Bennett at Cindy's nightclub, also knows Mr Jones and Mr Davies. He said that he heard a commotion outside the fish and chip shop, rushed out and saw Mr Bennett being attacked by both Mr Jones and Mr Davies.

If convicted the defendant is likely to receive a custodial sentence for this offence. As a result of the attack Mr Bennett suffered a deep cut above his left eye; cuts and bruises to his face; a bleeding nose; grazes to his hands and knees; bruises to his stomach and arms; a broken nose and a broken left arm. Mr Bennett was treated at Weyford General Hospital and released earlier today. What makes a custodial sentence even more likely in this case is the defendant's list of previous convictions. He has two previous convictions for offences of violence; an assault occasioning actual bodily harm some five years ago for which he was fined £500 and another assault occasioning actual bodily harm some eighteen months ago for which he received three months' imprisonment.

Judge, as can also be seen from the defendant's list of previous convictions, he already has two previous convictions for failing to surrender to custody five years and four years ago. When seen in the context of the current offence, this must raise substantial doubts that the defendant will surrender to custody.

Another factor which may lead the defendant to fail to surrender is his lack of community ties. He is unemployed and since the breakdown of the defendant's marriage some three months ago he has been sleeping on friends' floors and in their spare rooms. He is staying with friends at the moment but has to move out by the end of the week. The defendant therefore has no permanent address, nor any employment to keep him in the Weyford area.

Judge, the second objection to bail being granted is that the defendant may interfere with witnesses or otherwise obstruct the course of justice. Mr Davies is jointly charged with Mr Jones. In his police interview Mr Jones denied all involvement in this offence. He said that he was defending himself having been attacked by Mr Bennett. He denied causing all of Mr Bennett's injuries saying that Mr Davies must have caused them. When told in his police interview that Mr Jones had put the blame on him Mr Davies said 'I'll get him for this. He'll regret saying that. You wait until I catch up with him.'

Judge, the third objection to bail being granted is that the defendant may commit offences if released on bail. Judge, this is a defendant with a history of violent offending. The defendant has been convicted of two offences of violence in the past five years. All these offences appear to be connected with alcohol. This offence was alcohol related too.

Judge, for the reasons that I have outlined the prosecution oppose bail being granted to the defendant and invite you to remand the defendant in custody for seven days.

DEFENCE SUBMISSIONS

Judge, I wish to apply for conditional bail on behalf of Mr Davies. It is my submission that any concerns that you may have about whether Mr Davies will fail to appear, interfere with witnesses or otherwise obstruct the course of justice, or commit further offences whilst on bail can be more than adequately dealt with by granting Mr Davies bail with conditions.

Judge, I shall deal first with the allegation that Mr Davies will fail to surrender to custody if released on bail. The charge Mr Davies faces is a serious one, this makes it all the more likely that Mr Davies will attend the next court hearing. When interviewed by the police, Mr Davies denied any involvement in the offence saying all he did was try to pull Mr Jones off Mr Bennett. Mr Davies intends to plead not guilty to this offence. He is anxious to clear his name and does not wish to worsen the situation by failing to surrender.

The prosecution evidence is not strong. Mr Bennett claims that both Mr Jones and Mr Davies were involved in this offence. The prosecution allege that Mr Bennett was punched by Mr Jones and then Mr Bennett fought back but he fell over. He was then hit, punched and kicked to the body. Presumably Mr Bennett was protecting his head, as anyone would do, whilst defenceless on the ground. It is unlikely therefore that Mr Bennett would be able to say for certain that he saw Mr Davies hit, punch or kick him. The evidence of Mr Bevan should also be treated with caution. He works with Mr Bennett and is a friend of his. It is only natural that his evidence is favourable to Mr Bennett. The prosecution have no independent evidence to support their version of events.

Judge, if convicted on the prosecution's version of events, then under the sentencing guidelines Mr Davies played a lesser role suggesting category B, Medium culpability. Harm does not appear to be permanent or irreversible and therefore at category 3. That gives a starting point of one year's custody but a range that includes a high level community order. It is correct that 18 months ago he was convicted of ABH and imprisoned for 3 months. However, the court should be aware that he pleaded guilty to this and indeed all his previous offences. Should he be convicted I submit that he may well be dealt with by a high level community penalty.

The prosecution seek to place reliance upon the defendant's previous convictions for failing to surrender to bail. This must be placed in context. Mr Davies has not previously actively absconded. His first failure to surrender was a mistake on his part. He thought that he was due to appear in court at a later date. His second failure to surrender was due to him oversleeping. He attended court about three hours late. Judge, you will see that both offences resulted in the imposition of fines which indicate that these were not the most serious examples of failing to surrender to custody. I would urge you to give little weight to the prosecution's arguments on this point.

Judge, the prosecution also suggest that Mr Davies' lack of community ties mean that he is likely to abscond. Mr Davies has lived in the Weyford area for about ten years. He is currently unemployed but has been employed locally as a bouncer, barman and general labourer. Until some three weeks ago he was living in rented accommodation with his wife. Unfortunately they have now split up and he has been sleeping on friends' floors and in their spare rooms. However, the Probation Service were consulted this morning and should Mr Davies be granted bail there is a place available for him at the Weyford Bail Hostel.

Judge, the second ground raised by the prosecution is that Mr Davies will interfere with witnesses or otherwise obstruct the course of justice by interfering with his co-defendant, Mr Jones. When Mr Davies was told what Mr Jones had to say, Mr Davies was upset. Mr Jones is someone whom Mr Davies regarded as a friend and Mr Davies cannot understand why Mr Jones is implicating him in this offence. Mr Davies was also upset by the police keeping him in the cells overnight when he believed he was fit to be interviewed. He was tired and emotional when he made those comments about Mr Jones. He did not mean them and has no intention of seeking to influence Mr Jones's evidence.

Judge, the third ground of objection raised by the prosecution is that Mr Davies will commit further offences if released on bail. I would submit that this is not the case. Mr Davies intends to plead not guilty to this offence. In addition, Mr Davies does not have a lengthy list of previous convictions. He has two convictions for violence spread over a four-year period. Moreover, whilst the prosecution allege that his offending continues to be alcohol related, I would ask you to take into account that after being released from prison he voluntarily went on an alcohol awareness course run by a local charity and his drinking is now under control. He denies being drunk on this occasion. He was not told that he was being kept in police cells overnight because he was drunk.

Judge, for these reasons I would ask you to grant conditional bail to Mr Davies.

There are a number of conditions that I would invite you to consider imposing to remove any concerns you might have as to Mr Davies' willingness to attend court on the next occasion. He can reside at the Weyford Bail Hostel and report to Weyford Police Station on a regular basis.

Any concerns that Mr Davies would obstruct the course of justice can be met by imposing a condition that he does not contact or associate with Mr Jones.

Finally, Judge, any concerns that Mr Davies will commit further offences if released on bail can be met by a condition that he should not enter any licensed premises or the Weyford town centre other than for the purposes of seeing his solicitor.

Judge, unless I can be of any further assistance, those are my submissions.

13.10.2 Pleas in mitigation

As with bail applications, advance preparation is essential. Courts can sentence only on the basis of information, and although the sentencing court may have a written pre-sentence report (PSR) available (this is mandatory when the court is considering a custodial sentence or certain types of community penalty), there will often be a great deal of further relevant background information which the defence advocate may put before the court. The Sentencing Act 2020 and the Sentencing Code place the seriousness of the offence at the forefront of the matters to which the court must have regard when passing sentence. Nevertheless, the court is not precluded from considering the circumstances of the individual offender by way of mitigation. A useful starting point in the magistrates' court is to consult the sentencing guidelines published by the Sentencing Council, and in particular the Magistrates' Court Sentencing Guidelines.

The following points should always be considered when preparing a plea:

(a) Thoroughly research the realistic sentencing options available, referring, where appropriate, to relevant statutory or judicial guidelines.

(b) Take as full a written statement as possible from the client, dealing with the circumstances both of the offence and of the client. Make sure you cover all factors that may increase or reduce the seriousness of the offence, as well as the client's personal mitigation.

(c) Obtain an up-to-date copy of the client's criminal record, and deal thoroughly with the circumstances of any offences which the court may regard as being aggravating factors.

(d) If a PSR has been ordered, try to contact the Probation Service in advance of the case to see if it will discuss its contents informally.

(e) Discuss your mitigation speech with the client and obtain their approval of your proposed course.

(f) When called upon to address the court, check that they have had the opportunity to read the PSR and any other relevant documentation.

(g) When the court has read the PSR, begin your speech by dealing with matters which affect the seriousness of the offence. Then go on to deal with matters of offender mitigation, referring where appropriate to the PSR. Never read paragraphs of the PSR aloud, because the document is confidential. Instead, invite the court to consider the appropriate paragraph. For example:

'Judge, you will recall that Mr Smith's family history is dealt with at the top of page 2 of the pre-sentence report. I would particularly draw your attention to the matters dealt with in paragraph 3 ...'

and so on.

(h) Conclude by 'showing the court the way home'. In other words, if you can suggest a realistic sentencing option which the court can take, you are not only discharging your duty to the client, but you are also assisting the court. Sentencing an offender is never easy, and anything which helps the court discharge this onerous duty will be gratefully received.

GARETH DAVIES

Following the contested bail application Davies was released on bail with conditions. The prosecution subsequently obtained CCTV footage and witness statements from Philip Bennett, John Bennett and three other witnesses who were in the Seagull fish and chip shop. The prosecution evidence showed that Jones and Davies were both involved in the assault. At the next court appearance both defendants decided to enter guilty pleas and the case was adjourned for the preparation of pre-sentence reports. Jones was granted unconditional bail and Davies bail with conditions.

Gareth Davies says:

I was not telling the truth when I made my earlier statement. I did assault Bennett. My initial reaction was to pull Jones off him but then I decided to give him a good hiding. I decided to get my own back for unfairly banning me from Cindy's by punching and kicking him whilst he was on the ground. I was somewhat drunk at the time. I now realise that it was a foolish thing for me to do and I am sorry for my actions. I accept that I still have an alcohol problem. My wife has been telling me for years that I have a drink problem. I took no notice of her. I have been drinking heavily since I left my wife. I want to get back together with her and I need to address my offending which is associated with my drinking. She is now staying at her mother's house.

Pre-sentence report:

BLANKSHIRE
PROBATION SERVICE   Chief Officer: John Evans

This is a Pre-Sentence Report as defined in Section 158 of the Criminal Justice Act 2003. It has been prepared in accordance with the requirements of the National Standard for Pre-Sentence Reports. This report is a confidential document and has been prepared for these proceedings only. Its value on other occasions and for other purposes will therefore be limited.

PRE-SENTENCE REPORT

COURT	Weyford Magistrates'
NAME	Gareth Davies
AGE	24
ADDRESS	Weyford Bail Hostel 27 Carter Street Weyford Blankshire WE2 1HA
PETTY SESSIONS AREA	Weyford
OFFENCE(S)	GBH (s 20)
OFFICER PREPARING THIS REPORT	Enid Barton
TITLE:	Probation officer
REF CODE:	JW/DF/11224/M4/5/010/N/MEBP/W02
34 Bennetthorpe Weyford WE2 6AD	Tel: (00002) 730099 Fax: (00002) 730220 (General) Fax: (00002) 730720 (Divisional Manager)

PRE-SENTENCE REPORT ON GARETH DAVIES

INTRODUCTION

1. This report is based upon two interviews with Mr Davies; one at Weyford Bail Hostel and one at my office. I have read the prosecution papers and seen a copy of Mr Davies' previous convictions. I have also liased with Mrs Davies, Mr Davies's solicitor and Mr Williams the manager of the Weyford Bail Hostel.

OFFENCE ANALYSIS

2. Mr Davies inflicted grevious boldily harm on another man outside the Seagull fish and chip shop in the High Street, Weyford. Mr Davies' co-defendant punched the victim in the face. There was a fight. The victim then fell over and Mr Davies together with his co-defendant punched and kicked the victim to his head and body whilst the victim was lying on the ground. The assault finished when a friend of the victim intervened. Mr Davies was under the influence of alcohol at the time of the offence and was not fit to be interviewed by the police until the following morning.

3. Mr Davies told me that he knew the victim and disliked him. The victim worked at Cindy's nightclub in Weyford and had, some two weeks before the offence, banned Mr Davies from the nightclub. Mr Davies' co-defendant Stephen Jones was very drunk and made some unwanted advances towards a group of girls in the nightclub. The girls complained to management and the victim became involved in handling the complaint. Mr Jones then had an argument with the victim in which he threatened him. Mr Jones was banned from the nightclub and since Mr Davies was with Mr Jones he was banned too even though he was not involved. Mr Davies felt that his banning from the nightclub was unwarranted.

RELEVANT INFORMATION ABOUT THE OFFENDER

4. Mr Davies has appeared in Court for sentencing purposes on three previous occasions. His offending began four years ago and consists of assaults occasioning actual bodily harm, criminal damage and absconding. The assaults and criminal damage offences were all committed whist he was under the influence of alcohol.

5. Eighteen months ago Mr Davies was sentenced to 3 months' imprisonment. He found the experience of prison a chastening one and he told me that he was determined to keep out of trouble as a result. He believes that his offending is alcohol related. He voluntarily went on an alcohol awareness course run by Addiction, a local charity, and found the course useful. However, from the enquiries I have made the course was not an intensive one and since alcohol abuse appears to be at the root of his offending then such a course is unlikely to prevent him committing offences in the future.

6. Mr Davies is one of five children and he originates from Scotland. He is literate and numerate but tells me that he left school with no qualifications. During his last two years at school he increasingly played truant because, he says, he was bullied. Shortly after leaving school he met a woman who is now his wife, Carolyn Davies. She originated from Weyford and Mr Davies moved to Weyford to be near her. After going out together for about five years they married. Mr Davies tells me that his marriage was a happy one but his wife felt that he had an alcohol problem which he failed to acknowledge. Some three months ago he split up from his wife believing that his wife was having an affair with another man.

7. Since leaving his wife he has been sleeping on friends' floors and in their spare rooms. During these proceedings, Mr Davies has been living at the Weyford Bail Hostel. I understand from the manager of the hostel, Mr Williams, that since his time there Mr Davies has been a model resident.

8. Mr Davies still has feelings towards his wife. He was accompanied by his wife when he attended our second interview. He now believes his wife when she says that she was not having an affair. They intend to get back together and are looking for rented accommodation together locally in Newtown. Mrs Davies is in full-time employment as a waitress.

9. Whilst on remand Mr Davies has been making attempts to obtain work. He has attended three interviews for different types of manual work. He did have a job for a short while in a timber yard but he was sacked because he turned up for work after lunch under the influence of alcohol.

10. It is very unfortunate that Mr Davies has not been able to hold down a steady job since he seems to have great difficulty in structuring his time. He is in good health although he drinks to excess when he has the money to do so and I feel that this has caused many of his problems.

11. Mr Davies accepts that he has an alcohol problem and he is making efforts to control it. He says that he has reduced his alcohol intake and is feeling healthier for it. He realises that his lack of formal qualifications is hindering his search for employment. However, because he did not enjoy school he is reluctant to return to an educational environment. He accepts that he is unlikely to be bullied at his age. He says that he lacks the motivation to study.

12. At the time of the interview Mr Davies was in receipt of income-based job seeker's allowance.

RISK TO THE PUBLIC OF RE-OFFENDING

13. Mr Davies is a gregarious man, although his manner can easily seem aggressive. I believe that many of his problems relate to his alcohol problems. The harm inflicted on the victim was intentional. As the court mentioned when adjourning for sentence, Mr Davies was fortunate that the victim did not sustain more serious injuries as a result of the assault. Since Mr Davies has an alcohol problem and difficulties controlling his temper, which he acknowledges, there is a high risk that Mr Davies will cause further harm in the future.

14. I have no concerns as regards the possibility of deliberate self-harm in the community. Mr Davies presents himself as a fairly confident individual and I suspect that he will cope easily if his offending were to result in a custodial sentence.

CONCLUSION

15. Mr Davies seems genuine when he says that he is determined to address the causes of his offending. I feel that he could benefit from a community sentence with the three following requirements:
    - Supervision requirement
    - An alcohol treatment requirement (Addressing Substance Related Offending – ASRO)
    - An anger management treatment programme requirement

    I have discussed these requirements with Mr Davies and he has agreed to co-operate with the Probation Service. He has been assessed as suitable.

    A supervision requirement would focus on increasing his employability and encourage him to improve his educational qualifications or secure training. The alcohol treatment requirement and anger management programmes would address his alcohol and anger management problems.

16. If the court is of the view that a custodial sentence must be imposed, I am required to identify and comment upon any adverse effects of custody. Since Mr Davies has experience of a custodial setting, is currently looking for accommodation and is jobless, I can identify no major concerns.

Since Mr Davies would benefit from requirements designed to address the causes of his offending the court may consider that a suspended sentence is more appropriate. Such a disposal would also enable Mr Davies to address his alcohol and anger issues. He would also be able to find work, thereby placing him in the position to pay compensation to the victim. Mr Davies has no savings and therefore any compensation ordered by the court would have to be paid by instalments.

Signed: *Jason King*
            Probation Officer

Dated: _ _ 20__

PLEA IN MITIGATION

Judge, I understand that you have had the opportunity to read the pre-sentence report prepared by the Probation Service.

Clearly, Judge, this is a serious matter, and you may be minded to impose an immediate custodial sentence on Mr Davies. I hope to persuade you that a more suitable method of disposing of this case would be for you to impose a community sentence as recommended by Mr King at paragraph 15 of his report.

I shall begin by addressing the circumstances of the offence, I shall then provide you with details of Mr Davies' personal circumstances, before concluding by addressing the requirements of the community order which I hope to persuade you to impose.

Judge, Mr Davies pleaded guilty to this offence and accepts the version of events outlined to you by the prosecution. He expresses remorse for his actions.

Once Mr Davies saw Mr Jones fighting with Mr Bennett he foolishly became involved. His motivation for becoming involved was Mr Bennett banning him from Cindy's nightclub. The banning arose as a result of Mr Jones becoming drunk at the nightclub and Mr Jones making some unwelcome advances to a group of girls. The girls complained to the management and Mr Bennett became involved. Mr Jones began an argument with Mr Bennett and threatened him. Mr Davies played no part in the incident but since he was with Mr Jones he was banned as well. Mr Davies felt aggrieved by the way he had been treated by Mr Bennett. He felt angry and upset. When he saw Mr Jones fighting with Mr Bennett he decided to get his own back and whilst Mr Bennett was on the ground he punched and kicked him several times to the face and body. No weapon was used by Mr Davies. Whilst the banning from the nightclub should not condone Mr Davies' later actions, it does help to explain why Mr Davies acted in the way he did. There was another factor which influenced his behaviour that night: his excessive consumption of alcohol, a factor which I shall return to later.

Judge, Mr Davies is 27 years of age. He has lived in the Weyford area for some ten years. He is currently unemployed though he has been employed for much of that ten year period as a bouncer, barman and general labourer. Whilst on bail for this offence Mr Davies did manage to get a job for a short while in a timber yard. He lost his job because he has been drinking at lunchtime. Mr Davies realises that it was a foolish thing for him to have done. He tells me that he went to a local public house because he was depressed and wanted to drown his sorrows. He is still looking for employment but realises that in the present economic climate jobs are hard to come by and he regrets throwing away what could have become a permanent job at the timber yard.

Judge, Mr Davies does have previous convictions for offences of violence and criminal damage.

His offending began some four years ago when his marriage was in difficulties and he started to drink to excess. He was convicted of an assault occasioning actual bodily harm following an argument in a public house. Mr Davies had been watching some football. A supporter from another team said something derogatory about the team that Mr Davies supported. Mr Davies lost his temper and there was a fight.

The criminal damage occurred at a time when he thought that his wife had left him and his wife went to stay at her mother's house. Following a few pints to drink Mr Davies went round to see his wife. She would not let him into the house because he had been drinking. Mr Davies lost his temper and an angry and drunk Mr Davies picked up some stones, threw them at the windows breaking them.

Mr Davies' last conviction was some eighteen months ago. He was out drinking in a public house. He says that someone attacked him and in defending himself he used excessive force. The court considered the offence serious enough to merit a custodial sentence. Mr Davies coped with prison life but realised that he had an alcohol problem.

On release from prison he decided to address what he considered to be the cause of his offending: his drinking. To his credit Mr Davies sought help and he voluntarily went on an alcohol awareness course run by the local charity Addiction. He reduced his alcohol consumption and things were progressing well. Then he mistakenly thought that his wife was having an affair with another man. He left his wife some three months ago and started to drink heavily again culminating in this offence.

Mr Davies and Mrs Davies are now back together again and are looking for somewhere to live. Until they do so they intend to stay with Mrs Davies' mother.

Judge, there is a theme running throughout Mr Davies' offending. That theme is the misuse of alcohol. All his offences are alcohol related. The pre-sentence report says that unless he addresses his alcohol problem the risk of his re-offending is high.

As you will be aware one of the five purposes of sentencing is the reform and rehabilitation of offenders. The sentence suggested by Mr King in his pre-sentence report is a community order comprising a supervision requirement coupled with alcohol treatment and anger management programme requirements. Such an order would give him the help and support that he needs to overcome his alcohol and anger management problems.

I would submit that the imposition of an immediate custodial sentence, whilst achieving the goal of punishing Mr Davies, would not prevent Mr Davies from re-offending. He was sentenced to a term of imprisonment some eighteen months ago and on release thought that he could address his alcohol problem himself. He managed to keep out of trouble but Mrs Davies has informed me that throughout this period his alcohol consumption was a constant source of tension between them. Mr Davies thought that he had his drinking under control. Mrs Davies thought that he was still drinking to excess; a view that Mr Davies now belatedly accepts. You will be aware Judge that many offenders who receive prison sentences offend again because prison fails to address the root causes of their offending.

Judge, should you feel that a community sentence is inappropriate then I submit that a suspended sentence would be appropriate in Mr Davies' particular circumstances. When imposing such a sentence you can make a supervision order with the alcohol treatment and anger management orders. This would satisfy the need to punish Mr Davies, but also address preventing him from offending in the future. Should Mr Davies re-offend or fail to comply with the terms of the suspended sentence then he knows that a custodial sentence is inevitable.

You will also be aware Judge that another purpose of sentencing is the making of reparation by offenders to those affected by their offences. I would submit that such a purpose could be satisfied in this case by the making of an order that Mr Davies pay compensation to Mr Bennett. Should you order compensation to be paid, or should you order that Mr Davies pay the cost of the prosecution then Mr Davies would ask for time to pay. He has no savings and until he can secure employment he will be in receipt of income-based job seeker's allowance.

Judge, in conclusion, I would urge you to adopt the sentence recommended by Mr King in his report, namely a community sentence incorporating a supervision requirement plus alcohol treatment and anger management programme requirements

Unless, Judge, you have any questions, that concludes my submissions on behalf of Mr Davies.

13.11 CIVIL CASES: INTERIM APPLICATIONS

13.11.1 Key characteristics

It is particularly important to master the skills relevant to interim applications in civil cases because trainee solicitors have full rights of audience. An interim application is any application made to the court before the trial of the claim. In the High Court, those interim applications requiring a hearing will be dealt with by a master (in the central office in London) or a district judge (in the district registry). In the County Court, these will be dealt with by a district judge. All interim applications, whether in the High Court or the County Court, share a number of common features:

(a) There are no 'live' witnesses. With rare exceptions, all the evidence will be in witness statement form (or, for freezing injunctions and search orders, by way of affidavit). Hence, the principal tasks of the advocate are to present their case and to argue for the order sought.

(b) Advocates are seated (except for some applications before a judge in the High Court which are beyond the scope of this book).

(c) The proceedings are heard in public (unless the court otherwise directs).

13.11.2 Preparing for the application

Although the subject-matter of an application may vary considerably from case to case, there are a number of steps which should always be taken:

(a) Try to agree as much as possible with the other side in advance.

(b) Make sure all relevant witness statements are served before the hearing. Although the court may be prepared to accept a late witness statement, it will usually result in your client being penalised in costs.

(c) Make sure that you have mastered the facts of the case and that you are familiar with the contents of the statements of case and witness statements. You may find it useful to prepare a written chronology of the case including the key events and steps in the action from issue of proceedings to date. It is not uncommon for the judge to deal only with those particular points in the case which they consider need arguing. Your grasp of the facts and documentation therefore needs to be such that you can locate them instantly. If the case is a complex one, consider handing to the judge a written chronology which you have agreed with your opponent.

(d) The judge should have a copy of the court file. However, you will need to ensure that you have copies of any relevant documents to hand to the judge, should the court file be incomplete.

(e) Prepare brief notes. Although you should never read out your submissions, it will help you to have a list which sets out the points that you intend to raise. Focus on the main facts to be addressed. You might use a highlighter pen on copy documents (never the originals) for this purpose. Write in the margin of a copy witness statement a brief summary of what each paragraph contains. An example of such a note in a contract case might be, 'Para 3 – Summarises the dispute as to time of delivery'.

(f) Make sure you have read and flagged the relevant passages in the Civil Procedure Rules 1998 and Practice Directions.

(g) Have a very clear idea of the order you want the judge to make. If you are making the application, you should attach to the application notice a draft of the order you propose (except in the most simple applications).

(h) Work out in advance any relevant interest calculation and costs order the judge is likely to make. Also consider whether the judge should make any directions for the future conduct of the claim.

(i) Consider the prospect of an appeal should your application be unsuccessful. An application for permission to appeal may be made to the judge at the end of the hearing.

13.11.3 Conducting the application

Whether the claimant or the defendant is the applicant, the party whose application it is will begin. The order of speaking will be the same whether the proceedings are in the High Court or the county court.

13.11.3.1 The applicant's case

If you are representing the applicant, the procedure is as follows.

(1) Formally introduce yourself, your opponent and the application and identify any relevant document on the court file to which you intend to refer

For example:

> 'Judge, my name is Mr Holtam and I am from ULaw LLP.
>
> I represent the claimant, David Mills. Miss Gibson, from Evans and Co, represents the defendant, Christopher Marlow.
>
> The claimant's application today is for summary judgment in a debt claim arising out of ...'

You should then check that the judge has all the documents you intend to refer to on the court file.

Remember, the judge will not have copies of the correspondence between the parties or their solicitors. You should refer to such correspondence only if it is exhibited to a witness statement.

You should then ask the judge if a brief summary of the facts would assist, and proceed accordingly.

(2) Concisely identify the issues (legal and factual) for the court to decide and, by reference to the documents, highlight the relevant facts

State the issues clearly before taking the judge through the documents. Argue for the order sought on the basis of the issues you have identified from the documents.

Take the judge through the documents at a sufficiently slow pace to enable them to digest their contents. It is not normally necessary to read them out verbatim; you should merely refer to relevant paragraphs and summarise their effect. If the judge has read the papers, your summary can be quite concise. More detail is needed where the papers have not been read. Refer to any exhibits in a way which ties them in with and explains the contents of the relevant witness statement. You do not need to refer to matters that are not in dispute between the parties.

Anticipate and deal with all disputed matters revealed by your opponent's evidence.

(3) Succinctly refer to the relevant law and/or procedure

Apply the relevant law when highlighting the relevant facts. Explain simply which Rule you are relying on and apply it to the facts of the case.

(4) Conclude submissions for the order sought

Emphasise what you consider to be your best points and explain briefly why you are entitled to the order sought. Be prepared to address the court on an alternative or 'second best' order if you think the court is not prepared to grant the order you really want.

Make it clear to the judge that you have finished your application. For example, 'Judge, unless I can help you further, that concludes my application'.

13.11.3.2 The respondent's case

The respondent's case will be structured differently as the court should by now have been taken through most of, if not all, the evidence. Nonetheless, the respondent's case follows a similar model.

(1) So far as necessary, identify any relevant document on the court file to which you intend to refer

The applicant should have introduced you, and therefore there is no need for you to introduce yourself again. If the applicant failed to introduce you, then you should introduce yourself.

You should identify the documents that you will be relying on as a basis for your response, for example, 'Judge, in opposing this application I will be relying on the same documents as my friend but, in addition, the Defence'.

(2) By reference to the documents, concisely identify and deal with issues (legal and factual) for the court to decide, highlight relevant facts and address the applicant's submissions

You should identify what you want the court to do and why.

The applicant should have already taken the judge through the statements of case (if appropriate) and the evidence. Take the judge to the relevant paragraphs in the statements of case and the witness statements which support your arguments. Present a positive case in support of your opposition to the order sought by the applicant. Do not just reply to the points made by the applicant. While making your submissions and presenting your positive case, deal with each of the applicant's points.

(3) Succinctly counter the applicant's arguments on the relevant law and/or procedure

Reply to the legal points raised by the applicant. Distinguish, if possible, the applicant's authorities and introduce any you rely on.

(4) Conclude submissions against the order sought

Briefly emphasise why the order requested by the applicant should not be made (or at least, if it is made, why it should only be in modified form). Stress the effects of making the order on the claim and, if it be the case, that the application is an attempt to blur the real issues and/or to prevent them being properly decided by the court after hearing oral evidence.

Make it clear to the judge that you have finished your opposition. For example, 'Judge, unless I can assist you further, those are the grounds upon which I oppose the order sought'.

13.11.3.3 The applicant's final word

The judge will normally invite the applicant to respond to matters raised by the respondent.

The applicant should deal with the points made against them, preferably in the same order in which they were put. This can be done very briefly if it is a point which has already been dealt with by the applicant earlier. If it is a new point, face it squarely and be quick to point to any evidence or document that supports your assertions. Encapsulate why the court should make the order you seek.

MARKS (TRADING AS MARKS ROOFING) V MASTER BUILDER HOMES LTD

You will find on the following pages:

(1) Chronology
(2) Claim Form
(3) Part 24 Application Notice
(4) Claimant's witness statement in support of the application
(5) Defendant's witness statement opposing the application
(6) Claimant's witness statement in reply

Richard Marks is a roofing contractor and the owner of Marks Roofing. He has carried out work before for Master Builder Homes Limited. He entered into a contract to provide flat roofing for 50 double garages for Master Builder Homes Limited at a total cost of £150,000 plus VAT. Master Builder Homes Limited was attracted by the competitive price and Richard Marks's agreement that the roofing would be completed by November 2023.

The work was completed by the deadline and so far as the Claimant was aware there were no difficulties. Richard Marks has been pressing for payment but Master Builder Homes Limited has refused to pay anything despite several reminders.

A Claim Form endorsed with the Particulars of Claim has been issued out of the Weyford District Registry of the High Court claiming the £150,000 plus VAT and interest. An acknowledgement of service has been filed indicating that Master Builder Homes Limited intends to defend the claim. An application notice pursuant to CPR Part 24 has been issued on behalf of Richard Marks. You have a copy of the supporting witness statement together with Master Builder Homes Limited's witness statement opposing the application. You also have a copy of the Claimant's witness statement in reply.

You may assume that both Claimant and Defendant have served upon each other a statement of costs for the hearing at least 24 hours in advance. They have agreed their respective figures for costs subject to an order being made by the court.

(1) CHRONOLOGY

Marks v Master Builder Homes Limited

2023

7th March	Contract entered into for the construction of 50 garage roofs at agreed price of £3,000 per garage plus VAT.
20th April	Claimant enters site and commences work.
27th October	Work completed.
5th November	Claimant renders invoice for £180,000 (including VAT); payment due no later than 5th December.

2024

22nd January	Reminder sent.
12th February	Reminder warning of legal action in event of non-payment by 19th February.
22nd February	Claimant instructs solicitors.
1st March	Solicitors write letter before claim.

5th March	Claim form issued and served by 1st class post.
8th March	Defendant's solicitors acknowledge service and give Notice of Intention to Defend.
5th April	Claimant's solicitors issue Part 24 notice of application.

Claim Form

You may be able to issue your claim online which may save time and money. Go to www.moneyclaims.service.gov.uk/make-claim to find out more.

In the	High Court of Justice, King's Bench Division, Weyford District Registry
Fee Account no.	ABCD12345
Help with Fees - Ref no. (if applicable)	H W F - ☐☐☐ - ☐☐☐

For court use only

Claim no.	OM1527
Issue date	15 March 2024

Claimant(s) name(s) and address(es) including postcode

Richard Marks (trading as Marks Roofing) 17 Easthorpe Road, Westleigh, Blankshire BN1 2DP

Defendant(s) name and address(es) including postcode

Master Builder Homes Limited, Crown House, Jubilee Square, Easterham, Blankshire BE2 1RE

Brief details of claim

The claim is for £150,000 plus VAT (£180,000) for work done and materials supplied by the Claimant to the Defendant between 20 April 2023 and 27 October 2023

Value

The claim is for a specified sum of £180,000 plus interest of £5,425

Defendant's name and address for service including postcode

Master Builder Homes Ltd
Crown House
Jubilee Square
Easterham
Blankshire
BE2 1RE

	£
Amount claimed	185,425.00
Court fee	9,271.25
Legal representative's costs	100.00
Total amount	194,796.25

For further details of the courts www.gov.uk/find-court-tribunal.
When corresponding with the Court, please address forms or letters to the Manager and always quote the claim number.

N1 Claim form (CPR Part 7) (12.24) © Crown Copyright 2024

	Claim no.	OM1527

You must indicate your preferred County Court Hearing Centre for hearings here
(see notes for guidance)

Do you believe you, or a witness who will give evidence on your behalf, are vulnerable in any way which the court needs to consider?

☐ Yes. Please explain in what way you or the witness are vulnerable and what steps, support or adjustments you wish the court and the judge to consider.

☑ No

Does, or will, your claim include any issues under the Human Rights Act 1998?

☐ Yes
☑ No

	Claim no.	OM1527

Particulars of Claim

☐ attached

☐ to follow

The Claimant's claim is for £150,000 plus VAT at 20% being the sum due from the Defendant to the Claimant for work done and materials supplied by the Claimant to the Defendant at their request in connection with the construction of 50 garage roofs at the Defendant's Bishopwood Housing Development between 20 April 2023 and 27 October 2023 at the agreed price per roof of £3,000 plus VAT.

Particulars

5 December 2023

To account rendered 150,000
VAT at 20%   30,000
                  £180,000

1. The Claimant claims the sum of £180,000.
2. Interest pursuant to the Late Payment of Commercial Debts (Interest) Act 1998. For the purposes of the Act, both parties acted in the course of a business. The statutory interest began to run from and including 6 December 2023 at 8% over the base rate of 3% then in force, totalling 11% per annum. Interest due to the date of issue is £5,425 (6 December 2023 to 15 March 2024 inclusive being 100 days) and continuing until judgment or sooner payment at the daily rate of £54.25.
3. Compensation for late payment pursuant to the Late Payment of Commercial Debts (Interest) Act 1998 in the sum of £100.

Statement of truth

I understand that proceedings for contempt of court may be brought against a person who makes, or causes to be made, a false statement in a document verified by a statement of truth without an honest belief in its truth.

☑ **I believe** that the facts stated in this claim form and any attached sheets are true.

☐ **The claimant** believes that the facts stated in this claim form and any attached sheets are true. **I am authorised** by the claimant to sign this statement.

Signature

Richard Marks

☑ Claimant
☐ Litigation friend (where claimant is a child or protected party)
☐ Claimant's legal representative (as defined by CPR 2.3(1))

Date

Day	Month	Year
15	March	2024

Full name
Richard Marks

Name of claimant's legal representative's firm
ULaw LLP

If signing on behalf of firm or company give position or office held

Note: you are reminded that a copy of this claim form must be served on all other parties.

Claimant's or claimant's legal representative's address to which documents should be sent.

Building and street

2 Bunhill Row

Second line of address

Town or city

London

County (optional)

Postcode

| E | C | 1 | Y | 8 | H | Q |

If applicable

Phone number

DX number

Your Ref.

Email

Find out how HM Courts and Tribunals Service uses personal information you give them when you fill in a form:
https://www.gov.uk/government/organisations/hm-courts-and-tribunals-service/about/personal-information-charter

N244
Application notice

For help in completing this form please read the notes for guidance form N244Notes.

Find out how HM Courts and Tribunals Service uses personal information you give them when you fill in a form: https://www.gov.uk/government/organisations/hm-courts-and-tribunals-service/about/personal-information-charter

Name of court	Claim no.
HCoJ, King's Bench Division	OM1527

Fee account no. (if applicable)	Help with Fees – Ref. no. (if applicable)
	HWF- -

Warrant no. (if applicable)	N/A

Claimant's name (including ref.)
Richard Marks trading as Marks Roofing

Defendant's name (including ref.)
Master Builder Homes Ltd

Date	5 April 2024

1. What is your name or, if you are a legal representative, the name of your firm?
   ULaw LLP

2. Are you a ☐ Claimant ☐ Defendant ✓ Legal Representative
   ☐ Other (please specify)

   If you are a legal representative whom do you represent? The Claimant

3. What order are you asking the court to make and why?
   Summary judgment pursuant to CPR Part 24, rule 24.2(a)(ii) and (b) because the defendant has no real prospect of successfully defending the claim and there is no other compelling reason why the case should be disposed of at trial.

4. Have you attached a draft of the order you are applying for? ✓ Yes ☐ No

5. How do you want to have this application dealt with? ✓ at a hearing ☐ without a hearing
   ☐ at a remote hearing

6. How long do you think the hearing will last? ☐ Hours 20 Minutes
   Is this time estimate agreed by all parties? ✓ Yes ☐ No

7. Give details of any fixed trial date or period — N/A

8. What level of Judge does your hearing need? Judge

9. Who should be served with this application? The Defendant

9a. Please give the service address, (other than details of the claimant or defendant) of any party named in question 9.

N244 Application notice (06.22) © Crown copyright 2022

10. What information will you be relying on, in support of your application?

    ☑ the attached witness statement

    ☑ the statement of case

    ☐ the evidence set out in the box below

> If necessary, please continue on a separate sheet.

11. Do you believe you, or a witness who will give evidence on your behalf, are vulnerable in any way which the court needs to consider?

☐ Yes. Please explain in what way you or the witness are vulnerable and what steps, support or adjustments you wish the court and the judge to consider.

☑ No

Statement of Truth

I understand that proceedings for contempt of court may be brought against a person who makes, or causes to be made, a false statement in a document verified by a statement of truth without an honest belief in its truth.

[✓] **I believe** that the facts stated in section 10 (and any continuation sheets) are true.

[ ] **The applicant believes** that the facts stated in section 10 (and any continuation sheets) are true. **I am authorised** by the applicant to sign this statement.

Signature

Richard Marks

[ ] Applicant
[ ] Litigation friend (where applicant is a child or a Protected Party)
[ ] Applicant's legal representative (as defined by CPR 2.3(1))

Date

Day	Month	Year
5	April	2024

Full name

Richard Marks

Name of applicant's legal representative's firm

ULaw LLP

If signing on behalf of firm or company give position or office held

Applicant's address to which documents should be sent.

Building and street

| 2 Bunhill Road |

Second line of address

| |

Town or city

| London |

County (optional)

| |

Postcode

| E | C | 1 | Y | 8 | H | Q |

If applicable

Phone number

| |

Fax phone number

| |

DX number

| |

Your Ref.

| |

Email

| |

(4) CLAIMANT'S WITNESS STATEMENT

Claimant
1st
R Marks
5 April 2024

IN THE HIGH COURT OF JUSTICE Claim Nº OM1527
KING'S BENCH DIVISION
WEYFORD DISTRICT REGISTRY

BETWEEN RICHARD MARKS
(TRADING AS MARKS ROOFING) Claimant

and

MASTER BUILDER HOMES LIMITED Defendant

CLAIMANT'S WITNESS STATEMENT IN SUPPORT OF APPLICATION UNDER CPR PART 24

I, Richard Marks, of 17 Easthope Road, Westleigh, say as follows:-

1. The statements of fact in this statement are made from my own knowledge. I am the owner of the business Marks Roofing which specialises in providing flat roofing and I am the Claimant in this case. This statement has been prepared following discussions with my solicitor by telephone. The statements of fact in this statement are made from my own knowledge.

2. On 7 March 2023 the Defendant engaged me to provide and construct the roofs on 50 double garages for houses forming phase 1 of the Defendant's development at an estate at Bishopswood, Westerfield. I gave them a written quotation which Paul Walters, their managing director verbally agreed. I didn't keep a copy.

3. I agreed to build the garage roofs for £3,000 plus VAT per garage. I built all of the garages between 20 April 2023 and 27 October 2023. However, despite numerous written and telephone requests the Defendant has failed to pay for this work. The amount I am owed is set out in the Particulars of Claim in this action.

4. I believe that the Defendant has no real prospect of successfully defending my claim and there is no other compelling reason why this case should be disposed of at a trial.

I believe that the facts stated in this witness statement are true. I understand that proceedings for contempt of court may be brought against anyone who makes, or causes to be made, a false statement in a document verified by a statement of truth without an honest belief in its truth.

Signed: *Richard Marks*

Dated: 5 April 2024

(5) DEFENDANT'S WITNESS STATEMENT

on behalf of the Defendant
1st
P Walters
12 April 2024

IN THE HIGH COURT OF JUSTICE　　　　　　　　　　　　　　　　　Claim N° OM1527
KING'S BENCH DIVISION
WEYFORD DISTRICT REGISTRY

BETWEEN　　　　　　　　　　RICHARD MARKS
　　　　　　　　　　(TRADING AS MARKS ROOFING)　　　　　　　Claimant

and

MASTER BUILDER HOMES LIMITED　　　　　Defendant

**DEFENDANT'S WITNESS STATEMENT OPPOSING
CLAIMANT'S APPLICATION UNDER CPR PART 24**

I, Paul Walters, Managing Director of Master Builder Homes Limited, whose registered office is at Crown House, Jubilee Square, Easterham, say as follows:-

1. I am an employee and Director of the Defendant in this case and I am authorised by the Defendant to make this witness statement on its behalf. The statements of fact in this statement are made from my own knowledge. This statement has been prepared following discussions with my solicitor by telephone.

2. I have read a copy of the witness statement of Richard Marks made on 5 April 2024 on behalf of the Claimant and for the reasons set out below I deny that the Defendant is indebted to the Claimant as alleged or at all. The defendant has both a defence to the claim and its own counterclaim in this matter as I shall explain below.

3. The Defendant builds high quality executive housing and is presently developing an estate at Bishopswood, Westerfield. I agree that the Defendant engaged the Claimant to provide and construct the roofs on garages for the houses forming phase 1 of this development. They contracted to build 50 double garage roofs at an agreed price of £3,000 plus VAT per garage. The contract between us was purely oral. This is not unusual with contractors such as Richard Marks who we have used a lot in the past.

4. It was an implied term of the agreement between the parties that the Claimant would carry out the work in a proper and workmanlike manner and with all due care and skill and that any materials supplied would be of satisfactory quality and reasonably fit for their purpose.

5. In breach of these implied terms the roofs provided and constructed by the Claimant have the following defects:-

    Plots 3, 4, 8　　　　Garage roofs leak due to insufficient bitumen being applied. Damp has penetrated the timber joists, so roofs require stripping, joists replacing and roofs re-laying.

    Plots 10, 33, 42, 48　Garage roofs suffer from puddling and will require stripping off and completely re-laying.

    Plots 21, 22　　　　Bitumen has been applied carelessly so as to mark and deface the rendering on the adjacent houses.

    Plots 9, 14, 23, 28　Timber joists have twisted and warped so as to split the felting and leave gaps between the roof and supporting walls, so roofs require stripping, joists replacing and roofs re-laying.

I would estimate that the total cost of putting these defects right is in the region of £60,000 inclusive of VAT.

6. Quite apart from the cost of repairs referred to in paragraph 5 herein, the Defendant has suffered damage as it has been unable to offer these plots for sale and has been deprived of the profit therefrom. All the houses in phase 1 of the development are to be sold at £350,000 each. The budgeted net profit on each plot is £40,000. Furthermore, the poor condition of so many garages has given the whole development a bad reputation.

7. The Claimant has been well aware that these defects have existed since 11 February 2023 when I telephoned him in response to his letter of 10 February 2023 in which he threatened legal action. I informed him that he would get nothing until the defects were put right to which he replied that he did not know what I was talking about.

8. For the reasons set out above, I deny that the Defendant is indebted to the Claimant as alleged or at all, or alternatively the Defendant is entitled to claim damages by way of set-off that amount to a sum in excess of the sum claimed. Accordingly I would ask that the Claimant's application is dismissed as the defendant has a realistic prospect of its defence and associated counterclaim succeeding at trial.

I believe that the facts stated in this witness statement are true. I understand that proceedings for contempt of court may be brought against anyone who makes, or causes to be made, a false statement in a document verified by a statement of truth without an honest belief in its truth.

Signed: *Paul Walters*

Dated: 12 April 2024

(6) CLAIMANT'S SECOND WITNESS STATEMENT

Claimant
2nd
Richard Marks RM1
29 April 2024

IN THE HIGH COURT OF JUSTICE　　　　　　　　　　　　Claim N° OM1527
KING'S BENCH DIVISION
WEYFORD DISTRICT REGISTRY

BETWEEN

RICHARD MARKS
(TRADING AS MARKS ROOFING)　　　　Claimant

and

MASTER BUILDER HOMES LIMITED　　　　Defendant

CLAIMANT'S WITNESS STATEMENT IN REPLY

I, Richard Marks, of 17, Easthope Road, Westleigh, say as follows:-

1. The statements of fact in this witness statement are made from my own knowledge. This statement has been prepared following discussions with my solicitor by telephone.
2. I have read a copy of the witness statement of Paul Walters made on 12 April 2024 on behalf of the Defendant.
3. I dispute Paragraphs 5 and 6 since until 15 March 2024 I was wholly unaware that the Defendant was dissatisfied with any of the completed garages. I have never been given an opportunity to inspect the alleged defects and am therefore unable to comment either upon their existence or the alleged cost of effecting repairs.
4. I deny the contents of Paragraph 7. I have never spoken to Paul Walters on the telephone. I refer to a copy of a letter dated 14 March 2024 marked "RM1" which is the first intimation I have ever received about this particular problem.
5. I accordingly ask that this Honourable Court awards me summary judgment.

I believe that the facts stated in this witness statement are true. I understand that proceedings for contempt of court may be brought against anyone who makes, or causes to be made, a false statement in a document verified by a statement of truth without an honest belief in its truth.

Signed:　　*Richard Marks*

Dated:　　29 April 2024

IN THE HIGH COURT OF JUSTICE Claim N° OM 1527
KING'S BENCH DIVISION
WEYFORD DISTRICT REGISTRY

BETWEEN

RICHARD MARKS
(TRADING AS MARKS ROOFING) **Claimant**

and

MASTER BUILDER HOMES LIMITED **Defendant**

This is the exhibit marked "RM1" referred to in the witness statement of Richard Marks made this 29th day of April 2024.

Signed: *Richard Marks*

Dated: 29/4/2024

MASTER BUILDER HOMES LIMITED

**Crown House
Jubilee Square
Easterham
EH6 8DL**

Tel: 01409 255600
Fax: 01409 123321

Richard Marks 14 March 2024
Marks Roofing
17 Easthope Road
Westleigh
WT7 5AC

Dear Richard,

<u>Phase 1 - Bishopswood</u>

I have received court papers from your solicitors and frankly I am disappointed. We have always had an excellent working relationship and I am sad to see it threatened by legal action which, as we both know, benefits no-one but our lawyers.

We have had big problems with the roofs on plots 3, 4, 8, 9, 10, 14, 21-23, 28, 33, 42 and 48. I cannot really see how you can push for payment until these are rectified, the plots are unsaleable until then.

You also know just how tough things are in the industry at the moment. It is no secret that sales are at an all-time low and I cannot afford any delays in getting all the plots on the market. Bishopswood is getting a reputation with local surveyors and estate agents as a problem estate and you know how damaging that can be.

Please contact me as to when you can start on the roofs. Needless to say I expect you to do this free of charge since it is your responsibility to complete the job properly.

Yours sincerely

Paul Walters

CLAIMANT'S SUBMISSIONS

Judge, my name is Mr Holtam from ULaw LLP and I represent the Claimant Richard Marks, trading as Marks Roofing. Miss Gibson of Swallows and Co, acts for the Defendant, Master Builder Homes Ltd.

This is the Claimant's application for summary judgment.

Judge, do you have the bundle of documents?

[The judge replies that they have the bundle of documents.]

Judge, would a brief summary of the facts assist you?

[The judge replies that they are familiar with the facts and a brief summary is not required.]

Judge, the claim is a debt action concerning a contract in which the Claimant agreed to construct 50 Garage roofs at the Defendant's Bishopswood Housing Development.

The legal issue in this case is whether the defendant has a real prospect of successfully defending the claim at trial. The defendant is not suggesting there is any other compelling reason for a trial.

The purported defence is that 13 of the 50 garage roofs installed by the Claimant are defective. The defendant alleges that some of the roofs leak, some suffer from puddling, some have resulted in the rendering on adjoining houses being defaced and some have warped timber joists.

Judge, you will see from the particulars of claim that the garage roofs were constructed between April and October of last year at the agreed price per roof of £3,000 plus VAT. The total amount claimed is £180,000 plus interest.

Judge, I shall now take you to the first witness statement of Mr Marks.

Paragraphs 2 and 3 set out the contractual terms and in paragraph 3 you will see that despite numerous written and telephone requests for payment the amount is still outstanding.

In his witness statement on behalf of the Defendant, Mr Walters, at paragraph 3, agrees the terms of the contract and in paragraph 5 gives evidence of the alleged defects. The alleged defects are disputed and the defects alleged in relation to plots 21 and 22 are not defects to the garage roofs at all and can be easily remedied by cleaning. Mr Walters estimates that the total cost of putting these defects right is in the region of £60,000 inclusive of VAT and yet the total cost of installing the 11 allegedly defective flat roofs was only £39,600 inclusive of VAT. Even if what the Defendant says is true the figure for the repairs seems excessive. It is interesting to note that no detailed breakdown of how the figure of £60,000 is calculated is provided by Mr Walters.

In paragraph 6, Mr Walters states that he has been unable to offer these properties for sale and that he has been deprived of profit as a result. Judge, there is nothing stopping the Defendant offering these properties for sale. They can be shown to potential purchasers and the Defendant can assure potential purchasers that any defects will be remedied before they move into the houses. Also, as is well known, house prices have fallen since these houses were built and it is highly unlikely that these houses would now sell for £350,000. There is no independent evidence produced by Master Builder Homes of the current market value of these houses. It is unlikely that the Defendant will make a £40,000 profit on these houses in the present climate. The Defendant has not been deprived of the profit from the sale of these houses as a result of the alleged defects. Even if the defendant makes a profit, the profit has merely been delayed not extinguished. It is submitted that the Defendant is looking to the Claimant to compensate him for the depressed state of the current housing market.

In paragraph 6 Mr Walters states that the poor condition of so many garage roofs has given the estate a poor reputation. This is difficult to comprehend as the 11 houses with the alleged defects have not been offered for sale. The poor reputation of the development must therefore be due to the other houses that are being offered for sale; a matter which is outside the Claimant's control.

In paragraph 8 Mr Walters refers to a telephone conversation. It is the Claimant's case that no such telephone conversation took place.

Judge, you will see that Mr Marks has filed a second witness statement.

Moving to that, in paragraph 3 you will see that it was not until 15 March that Mr Marks knew Mr Walters was dissatisfied with his work. In paragraph 3 Mr Marks produces his exhibit, RM1: the letter he received from Mr Walters. Judge, in his letter Mr Marks refers to how tough things are in the industry at the moment. This reinforces the submission that I made earlier. The Defendant is looking to blame Mr Marks for matters which can be explained by the difficult market conditions in the property industry at the moment. Judge, you will see that no reference is made to the alleged telephone conversation between Mr Walters and Mr Marks that was referred to earlier. I submit that there is no reference to it because no such conversation took place.

Judge, you have the discretion under CPR 24.3(a) and (b) to enter summary judgment for the Claimant. The Defendant has no real prospect of succeeding on the defence and there is no other compelling reason why the case should be disposed of at trial.

I submit that the Claimant has discharged his burden of proof.

In conclusion, there is no realistic defence or counterclaim here. The Defendant alleges that some of the garage roofs are defective. The garage roofs were completed on 27 October 2023 yet he leaves it until a letter dated 14 March 2024 to bring the defects to the attention of the Claimant. Surely if there had been defects then this would have been brought to the attention of the Claimant when they were first discovered.

The Claimant has been denied the opportunity of inspecting the alleged defects. Again if there were such defects then you would expect the Defendant to be keen to show them to the Claimant. There is no independent expert evidence to support Mr Walters' contention that the garage roofs are defective.

Neither is there any supporting evidence for Mr Walters' contention that the garage roofs would cost some £60,000 to repair which is much more than the garage roofs cost to install in the first place. The Claimant contends that the Defendant is looking for someone to blame for the fact that this development has failed to sell. This is not the fault of the Claimant but a sign of the difficult market conditions in the property industry at the moment.

Unless I can assist you further Judge, I invite you to award summary judgment for the Claimant.

DEFENDANT'S SUBMISSIONS

Judge, I intend to refer to the same documents as Mr Holtam.

I agree with Mr Holtam that the legal issue for you to decide is whether the defendant has a real prospect of successfully defending the claim at trial. It is the Defendant's case that there is a defence with a real prospect of success at trial. The defence is that 13 of the garage roofs have problems. These include leaking roofs, puddling, the careless application of bitumen and warping. The garage roofs will need attention at significant cost.

Judge, from the particulars of claim you will see that there was one contract for the construction of 50 garage roofs.

The only dispute that the Defendant has with the evidence contained in Mr Marks' first witness statement is contained in paragraph 3 where he states that despite numerous written and telephone requests the Defendant has failed to pay for this work. Judge, there were only two written reminders and no telephone reminders for payment before ULaw LLP were instructed.

Judge, the Defendant's defence is contained in Mr Walters' witness statement.

Mr Walters in paragraph 3 gives evidence of the terms of the contract which are not in dispute. There was one contract for the Claimant to provide 50 garage roofs.

The contract contained the implied terms mentioned in paragraph 4 of Mr Walters' witness statement.

Paragraph 5 outlines the breaches of those implied terms.

The Defendant agrees with Mr Holtam's assertion that the roofs to Plots 21 and 22 are not defective. However, that does not absolve the Claimant from responsibility for careless application of bitumen to those Plots.

Mr Walters' estimate of the cost of putting these defects right is in excess of the original cost of the garage roofs. The cost is more because the existing roofs have to be stripped, joists replaced and the roofs re-laid; much more work than if the roofs had been properly installed by the Claimant. A detailed breakdown of how the £60,000 figure is calculated can be provided in due course.

The Defendant's decision not to offer these plots for sale is a simple one. No one would buy these houses with such obvious defects. Market conditions are such that any minor defect, let alone more serious ones such as these, will discourage potential purchasers from making offers.

Paragraph 7 refers to a telephone conversation that did take place between Mr Walters and Mr Marks on 11 February 2024.

Judge, I shall now address Mr Marks' second witness statement.

Paragraph 3 is disputed. It is the Defendant's case that Mr Marks did know of the defects as a result of the telephone conversation of 11 February.

Judge, I agree with Mr Holtam when he said earlier that under CPR 24.3(a) and (b) you have the discretionary power to award summary judgment if you conclude that the Defendant has no real prospect of succeeding on the defence.

Judge, this contract to provide garage roofs is a contract for the supply of goods and services. The Supply of Goods and Services Act 1982 contains implied terms that the garage roofs should be of satisfactory quality and reasonably fit for purpose and that the installation should be undertaken with reasonable care and skill. The Claimant has breached those implied terms under sections 4 and 13 of the Act.

I submit that the Defendant has a defence with a real prospect of success at trial. There was one contract to build 50 garage roofs. Only 37 were completed properly. Eleven of the garage roofs have defects and the construction of two others resulted in the careless application of bitumen to adjoining houses. Consequently the Defendant is entitled to withhold payment until the contract is successfully completed. The Defendant will also be counterclaiming for the loss of profit arising from the Defendant's inability to sell these houses. Such a counterclaim will exceed the amount that the Claimant is pursuing in this action.

The Defendant invites you not to exercise your discretion to award summary judgment in this case and to dismiss this application.

Unless I can assist you further Judge that concludes my submissions.

CLAIMANT'S SUBMISSIONS IN REPLY

Judge, you have the power to award summary judgement for the whole or part of the claim. The Defendant has not disputed that 39 of the 50 garage roofs were successfully completed. Therefore Judge, should you decide not to award summary judgment for the whole claim I invite you to award summary judgment for part of the claim. The total cost of installing 39 garage roofs amounted to £117,000 plus VAT making a total sum of £140,400.

Unless I can assist you further Judge, those are my submissions in reply.

13.11.3.4 Closing the case

The judge then gives a reasoned judgment and writes their order in note form on the court file. This indorsement forms the basis for the order subsequently drawn up.

If appropriate, the judge will give directions for the further conduct of the action. Be prepared to ask for any directions which you feel are necessary.

The party who has won usually asks for costs, and the loser is given the opportunity to reply. Be prepared to make submissions on the appropriate costs order.

13.11.3.5 Appeals

At the end of the hearing, the judge may ask the parties if they wish to appeal the decision. An application for permission to appeal may be made to the judge at the hearing. Permission to appeal may be given only where the court considers that the appeal would have a real prospect of success or there is some other compelling reason why the appeal should be heard.

13.11.3.6 Effective civil advocacy

Although the subject matter and nature of civil applications cover an enormous range, it is vitally important for the advocate to make their submissions as clearly and concisely as possible in order to help the court, especially since it hears so many applications during a working day.

13.12 CONCLUSION

Although this chapter could not deal in detail with the subject, it has provided an introduction to some of the salient features of the advocate's art. It should also have made clear the fact that many of the skills of the advocate can be acquired through study and observation. Remember that thorough preparation is the key: without that, no advocate can be fully effective, however fluent their oral skills may be.

Bibliography

Writing and drafting

Grammar and punctuation

J Butterfield, *Fowler's Concise Modern English Usage* (3rd edn, 2016)

RL Trask, *The Penguin Guide to Punctuation* (Penguin, 1997)

L Truss, *Eats, Shoots and Leaves* (Fourth Estate, 2009)

Plain English

M Adler, *Clarity for Lawyers* (3rd edn, 2017)

E Gowers, *The Complete Plain Words* (1987)

Inclusive language

Gov.uk, Guide to gender neutral drafting, 2019

The Law Society, A guide to race and ethnicity terminology and language, January 2025

Practical legal research

P Clinch, *Legal Research: A Practitioner's Handbook* (3rd edn, 2019)

J Knowles, *Effective Legal Research* (4th edn, 2016)

Oral communication skills

A Pease and B Pease, *The Definitive Book of Body Language* (2017)

Interviewing and advising

A Sherr, *Client Care for Lawyers* (2nd rev edn, 1999)

Law Society, *Client Care Practice Notes* at www.lawsociety.org.uk/topics/practice-notes

Negotiation

R Fisher and W Ury, *Getting Past No: Negotiating With Difficult People* (1992)

R Fisher and W Ury, *Getting to Yes* (rev edn, 2012)

D Kahneman, *Thinking, Fast and Slow* (2012)

D Stone, B Patton and S Heen, *Difficult Conversations* (2011)

Advocacy

K Evans, *Advocacy in Court* (2nd rev edn, 1995)

J Munkman, *The Technique of Advocacy* (1991)

SRA Code of Conduct for Solicitors 2023

Index

abbreviations database 73
ACAS (Advisory Conciliation and Arbitration Service) 178
active listening 122
addressee
  female 19
  letters 23
adverbs 12
advising techniques 128
advocacy 183–4
  addressing the court 187–8
    evidence 188
    objections 188
    opinions 188
    reference to opponent 188
  analysis 185, 186
  argument 184
  bail applications 198–9
  civil cases
    closing the case 196, 238
    ethical issues 197–8
    interim applications 214–18
    introducing real evidence 194
    opening the case 190–1
    witnesses 190
    witnesses not up to proof 193
  closing the case
    civil cases 196, 197
    criminal cases 196–7
    interim applications 238
    purpose of closing speech 196–7
  criminal cases
    bail applications 198–9
    closing the case 196–7
    defence advocate 197
    ethical issues 197–8
    example papers 200–6, 208–11
    introducing real evidence 193
    magistrates' court 190
    opening the case 190
    pleas in mitigation 207, 212–13
    prosecution advocate 197
    witnesses 190
    witnesses not up to proof 192
  cross-examination
    defining objectives 194–5
    discrediting evidence 195
    discrediting witnesses 195
    favourable matters 195
    leading questions 195
    no questions 195
    previous inconsistent statement 196
    tactics 194
    technique 195–6
  defence advocate 197
  effective 238
  ethical issues
    civil cases 197–8

advocacy – *continued*
  criminal cases 197
  examination-in-chief
    characteristics 191–2
    documents 193
    exchange of witness statements 193
    leading questions 191
    real evidence 193–4
    witnesses not up to proof 192–3
  fact gathering 185
  interim applications
    appeals 238
    applicant's case 215–16
    applicant's final word 216
    characteristics 214
    closing the case 238
    conduct of application 215–16
    example papers 217–37
    preparation 214–15
    respondent's case 216
  knowledge of law 185
  leading questions 191, 195
  magistrates' court 190
  modes of address
    court personnel 187–8
    opponent 188
  objections 188
  opening the case
    civil trials 190–1
    criminal trials 190
    magistrates' court 190
  oral skills 184
    argument 184
    presentation 184
    questioning witnesses 184
  organisational skills 185
    analysis 185, 186
    fact gathering 185
    knowledge of law 185
    paperwork 185–6
  paperwork 185–6
  pleas in mitigation 207, 212–13
  preparation 186
  presentation 184, 186–7
  prosecution advocate 197
  questioning witnesses 184
    know the answer 189
    objectives kept in view 189
    one question at time 189
    short questions 188–9
    when to stop 189
  re-examination 196
  witnesses
    civil cases 190
    court formalities 189–90
    criminal cases 190
    hostile 192

advocacy – *continued*
    leading questions 191
    not up to proof 192–3
    questioning *see* questioning witnesses
All England Law Reports 72, 73, 79
alternative dispute resolution (ADR)
    advantages 180
    arbitration 180–1
    commercial transactions 179, 181
    complaints and grievances procedures 178
    conciliation 178
    consideration 179–80
    disadvantages 180
    early neutral evaluation 178
    essential ingredients 177
    expert determination 178
    meaning 177–8
    mediation 177, 178–9
    negotiation *see* **negotiation**
    promotion by civil courts 178
    third parties 177, 178
ambiguity in drafting
    and/or 14
    discretion 15
    ejusdem generis rule 16
    expressions of time 15
    obligations 15
    pronouns 16
    shall/will 16
    similar words 15
    'undistributed middle' 15
    word order 14
AND 47
appeals
    interim applications 238
arbitration 180–1
    see also **alternative dispute resolution (ADR)**
archaic language 12
artificial intelligence (AI)
    internet research and 36, 49
asterisk 47
Atkin's Court Forms 107, 109–10
    online 109–10
    printed version 110
attendance notes 26
attestation 6

bail applications 198–9
BAILII
    case law search 71
bargaining 174–5
***Blackstone's EU Treaties and Legislation* 69, 99, 101**
blogs 52
body language 123, 128–9
Boolean operators 47
brainstorming 38
Brexit
    European law and 97–8
business information 52–4

***Cardiff Index to Legal Abbreviations* 70, 73**
case law
    All England Law Reports 72, 73, 79

case law – *continued*
    authorities
        citation 114–15
        selection 72–3
    BAILII 71
    Case Overview 75, 76–7
    citation 73–4
        conventions 73
        database of abbreviations 70, 73
        European cases 103
        incomplete information 74–5
        neutral 74
        OSCOLA 115
    Current Law Case Citator 67, 68, 70, 78
    Current Law Monthly Digest 67, 68, 70, 78
    Current Law Year Books 67, 70, 78
    European 103–5
        citation 103
        Common Market Law Reports 105
        EUR-Lex 104–5
        Europa website 103
        European Court Reports 103, 104, 105
        Lexis+ Legal Research 105
        sources 103–5
        Westlaw 105
    ex tempore judgment 72
    handing down judgment 71–2
    later decisions 78–9
    The Law Reports 72–3
    Lexis+ Legal Research 7, 67–8, 71, 73, 75, 76, 105
    newspaper reports 72
    printed resources 78–9
    publication of cases 71–2
    specialist law reports 80–1
    subject searches 79–81
    transcripts 71–2
    updating 75–9
    Weekly Law Reports 72, 73, 79
    Westlaw 67–8, 71, 73–80, 105
***Case Overview* 75, 76–7**
charging method 154–5
citation
    case law
        conventions 73
        database of abbreviations 70, 73
        European 103
        incomplete information 74–5
        neutral 74
        Weekly Law Reports 73
    legislation
        chapter numbers 83–4
        regnal years 84
        schedules 84
        sections 84
        statutory instruments 84
civil cases
    closing the case 196
    closing speech 197
    ethical issues 197–8
    interim applications
        advocacy 214–18
        appeals 238
        applicant's case 215–16

civil cases – *continued*
    applicant's final word 216
    characteristics 214
    closing the case 238
    conduct of application 215–16
    example papers 217–37
    preparation 214
    respondent's case 216
  introducing real evidence 194
  opening the case 190–1
  witnesses 190
  witnesses not up to proof 193
clauses
  categorical order 7
  chronological order 6–7
  Coode 8–9
  importance order 7
  numbering 7–8
  structuring 7–9
clients
  client care information sheet 142–3
  client care issues 136–7, 151–2
  money laundering 141
  proving identification 140–1
Common Market Law Reports **105**
communication skills
  addressing the court 187–8
  argument 184
  body language 123, 128–9
  with client 120–1
  with colleagues 121
  developing 121–2
  drafting *see* **drafting**
  importance 119–22
  listening 122
    acknowledgments 129
    active 122
    body language 128–9
    interviews 128–9
    invitations to continue 129
    passive 122
    reflecting feeling 129
    silence 128
  non-verbal communication 123, 128–9
  with other professionals 121
  presentation 184, 186–7
  questioning client
    closed questions 123, 130, 146
    cross-checking 133
    devil's advocate 133
    further clarification 132–3
    interviews 129–33
    leading questions 132, 195
    open questions 123, 129–30
    probing 132–3
    summarising 133
    T-funnel sequence 130–2, 148
  questioning witnesses 184
    know the answer 189
    objectives kept in view 189
    one question at time 189
    short questions 188–9
    when to stop 189

communication skills – *continued*
  writing *see* **writing**
complaints and grievances procedures 178
conciliation 178
conflict of interest 140
connectors 47
Coode, George 8–9
costs estimate 136–7, 154–5
criminal cases
  bail applications 198–9
  closing the case 196–7
  closing speech 196–7
  defence advocate 197
  ethical issues 197–8
  example papers 200–6, 208–11
  introducing real evidence 193
  magistrates' court 190
  opening the case 190
  pleas in mitigation 207, 212–13
  prosecution advocate 197
  witnesses 190
  witnesses not up to proof 192–3
cross-examination
  defining objectives 194–5
  discrediting evidence 195
  discrediting witnesses 195
  favourable matters 195
  leading questions 195
  no questions 195
  previous inconsistent statement 196
  tactics 194
  technique 195–6
Curia database **103**
Current Law Case Citator **78**
Current Law Legislation Citators **67, 68**
Current Law Monthly Digest **78**
Current Law Statutes **85–6**
  Service File 67, 68
Current Law Year Books **78**

databases
  see also **electronic databases**
  on-line 46–8
defence advocate
  duties 197
definitions
  in drafting 10–11
  positioning 11
  use 10–11
Directory of European Union Legislation **102**
discussion in negotiation 173–4
drafting
  ambiguity
    and/or 14
    discretion 15
    ejusdem generis rule 16
    expressions of time 15
    obligations 15
    pronouns 16
    shall/will 16
    similar words 15
    'undistributed middle' 15
    word order 14

drafting – *continued*
- amendment of other side's draft 18
- attestation 6
- basic structure 4–6
- checking the draft 18
- clauses
  - categorical order 7
  - chronological order 6–7
  - Coode 8–9
  - importance 7
  - numbering 7–8
  - structuring 7–9
- commencement 4
- copies 18
- date 4
- definitions
  - guidelines on use 11
  - positioning 11
  - use 10
- ethical considerations 18
- execution 6
- female addressees 19
- language
  - adjectives 12
  - adverbs 12
  - ambiguity 14–16
  - compound prepositions 12
  - gender neutral 19, 20–3
  - inclusive *see* **language**, inclusive
  - jargon 17
  - 'legalese' 17, 23
  - nouns derived from verbs 12
  - padding 11
  - paragraphs 12–13
  - sentences 12–13
  - tautology 11–12
  - verbs in passive 13–14, 22
  - word order 14
- layout 16
- negotiating a draft 18
- numbering systems 17
- operative part 5
- order of clauses 6–7
- paragraphs 12–13, 16
- parties 4, 10
- planning 4
- precedent use 9–10
- presentation 16
- process 3
- professional misconduct 18
- recitals 5
- researching law 4
- schedules 5–6
- sentences 12–13
- structure of document 4–6
- submission for approval 18
- tabulation 17
- taking instructions 4
- testimonium 5
- verbs 13–14

early neutral evaluation 178
ejusdem generis **rule 16**

electronic databases
- advantages 45–6
- *All England Law Reports* on Lexis+ Legal Research 79
- AND 47
- asterisk 47
- Boolean operators 47
- connectors 47
- *Curia* 103
- EUR-Lex 69, 98–102, 104–5
- exclamation marks 47
- field searching 47–8
- *Halsbury's Laws of England* on Lexis+ Legal Research 59–61
- legislation.gov.uk website 85, 88
- Lexis+ Legal Research *see* **Lexis+ Legal Research**
- NOT 47
- OR 47
- phrase searching 48
- refining search 48
- searching 46–8
- sort by relevance 79
- truncation 47
- updating 95–6
- *Westlaw see* **Westlaw**
- wildcard symbols 47

Emmerson, *Human Rights Practice* 70
***Encyclopaedia of Forms and Precedents* 107, 110–12**
- online 111–12
- printed version 112

English Reports
- Table of Cases 68

ethical issues
- advocacy
  - civil cases 198
  - criminal cases 197
- drafting 18
- negotiation 158

EUR-Lex
- case law 104–5
- cases 70
- legislation 69, 98–102

Europa website 98, 103
European Court of Human Rights
- cases and reports 70

European Court Reports 103, 104, 105
European Current Law 70
- monthly digests 69

European Current Law Year Books 69
European law
- *Blackstone's EU Treaties and Legislation* 99, 101
- Brexit and 97–8
- case law
  - citation 103
  - sources 103–5
- *Common Market Law Reports* 105
- *Curia* database 103
- EUR-Lex 69, 70, 98–102, 104–5
- *Europa* website 98, 103
- *European Court Reports* 104, 105
- legislation
  - in force 101–3
  - official texts 101
  - primary 99
  - secondary 100–3

European law – *continued*
   sources 99–103
   Lexis+ Legal Research 98, 105
   Official Journal of the European Union 98, 101, 103
   secondary legislation
     Decisions 100
     Directives 100
     Opinions 100
     Recommendations 100
     Regulations 100
     sources 100–1
   Westlaw 69, 98, 105
evidence
   discrediting 195
   previous inconsistent statement 196
   real 193–4
examination-in-chief
   characteristics 191–2
   documents 193
   exchange of witness statements 193
   leading questions 191
   real evidence 193–4
   witnesses not up to proof 192–3
exclamation mark 47
execution of document 6
expert determination 178

field searching 47–8
forms
   Atkin's Court Forms 107, 109–10
   Encyclopaedia of Forms and Precedents 107, 110–12
   research 107–12

Google 48, 50–1
   European law 98
grammar 26
   automated checks 18
grievances procedures 178

Halsbury's Laws of England 79
   Annual Abridgement volumes 67, 70
   consolidated index 58
   cumulative supplement 58
   electronic version 59–61
   footnotes 67, 69
   index 58
   main volume 58
   Monthly Review 70
   noter-up 58
   paper version 57–9
Halsbury's Laws of England on Lexis+ Legal Research
   scope 59
   searching 59–61
   using 59–61
Halsbury's Statutes 68, 69, 83, 86–7, 95, 96
   Consolidated Table of Cases 67
   cumulative supplement 69, 86, 87
   footnotes 68
   index 86
   main volumes 86
   noter-up 69, 86, 87
Halsbury's Statutes Citator 68, 96
Halsbury's Statutes of England see Halsbury's Statutes

Halsbury's Statutory Instruments 69, 83, 95
   EU Legislation implementator 69
Hansard 86
Hill and Redman's Law of Landlord and Tenant 67
Human Rights Practice (Emmerson) 70

Index to Legal Citations and Abbreviations (Raistrick) 70, 73
indexes
   Cardiff Index to Legal Abbreviations 70, 73
   Halsbury's Laws of England 58
   Halsbury's Statutes 86–7
   Raistrick Index to Legal Citations and Abbreviations 70, 73
   subject 40–1
   tables of primary sources 40–1
   Times Law Reports monthly cumulative indexes 68
interim applications
   advocacy 214–18
   appeals 238
   applicant's case 215–16
   applicant's final word 216
   characteristics 214
   closing the case 238
   conduct of application 215–16
   example papers 217–37
   preparation 214–15
   respondent's case 216
internet research 46
   see also on-line databases
   artificial intelligence (AI) and 36, 49
   authoritative material 48, 50–1
   blogs 52
   business information 52–4
   collections 54–5
   directories 51–2
   evaluation of material 55
   free sources 48–50
   Google 48, 50–1, 98
   legislation.gov.uk website 85, 88
   official websites 51
   portals 51–2
   professional conduct 49
   quality 48
   search engines 50–1
   social media 52
   Web 2.0 52
   Wikipedia 48
   wikis 52
interpreters 142, 144, 147
interview techniques
   advising 128, 148–51
     discussing options 149–50
     explaining legal position 148–9
     future plan of action 151
     helping to reach decision 150–1
   analysis 133–4
   background research 141
   charging, method 154–5
   checklists 141
   client care issues 136–7, 151–2
   closing stage 151–6
   conflict of interest 140
   contact names 153
   costs estimate 136–7, 154–5

interview techniques – *continued*
  costs of interview 145–6
  detail, filling in 128, 147–8
  environment 139
  explanation 134–6
  failings 127
  filling in details 128, 147–8
    note-taking 136
  follow-up tasks
    by client 153
    by solicitor 152–3
  funding 145
    charging method 154–5
    costs estimate 136–7, 154–5
  greeting 143–4
  identification of client 140–1
  importance 125–6
  interpreter 142, 144, 147
  interruptions 143
  Law Society guidance 126
  listening
    acknowledgments 129
    body language 128–9
    invitations to continue 129
    reflecting feeling 129
    silence 128
  model 143
  next contact 155–6
  note-taking 136, 147
  objectives of interview 126
  obtaining facts 146–7
  obtaining information 128
  parting 156
  post-interview actions 156
  practice 156
  preliminaries 144
  preparation 139–43
  questioning
    closed questions 130, 146
    cross-checking 133
    devil's advocate 133
    further clarification 132–3
    leading questions 132
    open questions 129–30
    probing 132–3
    summarising 133
    T-funnel sequence 130–2, 148
  relationship building 125–6
  reputation 125–6
  seating arrangements 139
  skills involved 127, 128–36
  structure 127–8, 137–8
  time available 144
  time frame for matter 153–4
  vulnerable clients 142
Is it in Force? **68, 87**

jargon 17, 23
judgment
  ex tempore 72
  handing down 71–2

Kelly's Legal Precedents **107**

language
  adjectives 12
  adverbs 12
  ambiguity 14–16
  archaic 12
  compound prepositions 12
  gender neutral 19, 20–3
  inclusive 18–23
    age 19
    characteristics 19–20
    disabilities, medical conditions and mental health 19
    forms of address 19
    gender neutral 19, 20–3
    pairing 21
    race and ethnicity 20
    sex, gender and sexuality 20
  jargon 17, 23
  'legalese' 17, 23
  nouns derived from verbs 12
  padding 11
  paragraphs 12–13
  sentences 12–13
  tautology 11–12
  verbs in passive 13–14, 22
  word order 14
law reports
  see also individual reports eg. ***Weekly Law Reports***
  specialist 80–1
The Law Reports **72–3**
  consolidated index 67
Law Society Gazette **68, 70, 72**
Law.com **54**
leading questions 191, 195
Legal Ombudsman
  complaints to 126
legal research *see* **research**
'legalese' 17, 23
legislation
  see also **statutory instruments**
  chapter numbers 83–4
  chronological 85
  citation 83–4
  commencement of statutes 87
  consolidated 85
  Current Law Statutes 68, 69, 85–6
  European *see* **legislation, European**
  in force 68, 87
  Halsbury's Statutes 69, 83, 86–7, 96
  Halsbury's Statutes Citator 96
  legislation.gov.uk website 85, 88
  official versions of Acts 85
  primary 83
  regnal years 84
  research, citation 83–4
  schedules 84
  secondary 83
  sections 84
  short title 83, 84
  updating 95–6
  Westlaw 68–9, 83, 85, 91–5, 95
legislation, European
  Blackstone's EU Treaties and Legislation 69, 99, 101
  in force 101–3

legislation, European – *continued*
   Official Journal of the European Union 98, 101, 103
   official texts 101
   primary 99
   secondary 100–3
   sources 99–103
Legislation Status Snapshots 68
legislation.gov.uk website 85, 88
letter writing
   addressees 23
   checking 24
   content 23–4
   editing 24
   ending 23
   form 23–4
   'ghosting' 23
   lay clients 23
   professional clients 23
   second thoughts 24
   starting 23
   structure 23
   style 23–4
Lexis+ Legal Research **49, 51**
   All England Law Reports 79
   case law 67–8, 71, 73, 75, 76–7, 105
   Case Overview 75, 76–7
   EU law 98, 105
   Halsbury's Laws of England 59–61
   Kelly's Legal Precedents 107
   legislation 68–9, 83, 85, 95
     scope 88
     searching 88–91
     statutory instruments 91
   precedents 107
Lexis+ Practical Guidance **63–5, 108–9**
listening skills 122
   acknowledgments 129
   active listening 122
   body language 123, 128–9
   interviews 128–9
   invitations to continue 129
   passive listening 122
   reflecting feeling 129
   silence 128

magistrates' court 190
mediation 177, 178–9
memoranda
   attendance notes 26
   internal 26
   writing 25–6
mitigation pleas 207, 212–13
money laundering 141

negotiation
   ADR *see* **alternative dispute resolution (ADR)**
   agreement 176
     reneging on 177
   bargaining 174–5
   closing negotiation 175–6
     agreement 176
     cost-benefit analysis 175
     tactics 176–7

negotiation – *continued*
   correspondence 169
   definition 157
   'dirty tricks' 176–7
   discussion 173–4
   environmental controls 177
   essentials 158
   ethical issues 158
   false deadlines 177
   feinting 176
   forum for 169–70
   'good person, bad person' 176
   last minute demands 177
   limited authority 177
   lying 177
   meetings 170–2
     adjournments 175
     agenda 171
     attendance 171
     bargaining 174–5
     clarification of purpose for 171
     closing negotiation 175–6
     'dirty tricks' 176–7
     discussion 173–4
     duration 170
     final preparation 171–2
     first bidder 171
     opening *see* opening negotiation
     readiness for 170
     resolving deadlocks 175
     seating arrangements 171, 177
     time 170
     venue 170
   negotiating styles
     accommodating 159, 160
     aggression 160
     avoiding 159, 160
     categories 158–9
     co-operating 159
     collaboration 159, 161–2
     competing 159, 160–1
     compromising 159, 160
   opening negotiation
     creating climate 172
     ground rules 172
     opening statement
       opponent's 173
       yours 172–3
     setting tone 172
   overview 172
   preparation
     BATNA 165
     closure 163
     control 162
     importance 162–3
     isolation of issues 165
     money 162
     objectives 162
     opening bids 166
     opening statement 169
     priority of issues 166
     resistance points 166–7, 174
     risk 162

negotiation – *continued*
    settlement zones 167–9
    standards 162–3
    strengths and weaknesses 164–5
    underlying interests 163–4
    unorthodox approaches 167
    variables 167
  reneging on agreement 177
  resistance points 166–7, 174
  resolving deadlocks 175
  settlement zones 167–9
  surprise attacks 176
  tactics
    'dirty tricks' 176–7
    environmental controls 177
    false deadlines 177
    feinting 176
    'good person, bad person' 176
    last minute demands 177
    limited authority 177
    lying 177
    reneging on agreement 177
    surprise attacks 176
  telephone 169–70
New Law Journal 68, 70, 72
non-verbal communication 123, 128–9
NOT 47
note-taking
  interview techniques 136, 147
  timing 136
numbering systems
  drafting 17

Official Journal of the European Union 98, 101, 103
official websites 51
ombudsman schemes 178
on-line databases 46–8
OR 47
organisational skills *see* **advocacy**
OSCOLA 115

Palmer's Company Law 67, 69
paragraphs 12–13, 16
Parker's Wills Precedents 107
passive listening 122
phrase searching 48
pleas in mitigation 207, 212–13
portals 51–2
Practical Law 61–3, 94
  Brexit 98
  precedents 107–8
practical legal research *see* **research**
practitioner books 65–6
practitioner databases 61–5
  Lexis+ Practical Guidance 63–5, 108–9
  Practical Law 61–3, 94, 98, 107–8
precedents
  Atkin's Court Forms 107, 109–10
  Encyclopaedia of Forms and Precedents 107, 110–12
  guidelines on use 10
  Kelly's Legal Precedents 107
  Lexis+ Practical Guidance 108–9
  Parker's Wills Precedents 107

precedents – *continued*
  Practical Law 107–8
  research 107–12
  use in drafting 9
presentation
  drafting 16
  reports 24–5
  research reports 39, 42
previous inconsistent statement 196
problem solving 36–9
  brainstorming 38
  problem analysis 37–9
  reporting 39
  solutions 38, 39
professional conduct
  internet research 49
professional misconduct
  drafting 18
pronouns 16
  gender neutral 21–2
prosecution advocate
  duties 197

questioning skills
  client
    closed questions 123, 130, 146
    cross-checking 133
    devil's advocate 133
    further clarification 132–3
    interviews 129–33
    leading questions 132, 195
    open questions 123, 129–30
    probing 132–3
    summarising 133
    T-funnel sequence 130–2
  closed questions 123
  leading questions 191, 195
  open questions 123
  witnesses 184
    know the answer 189
    one question at time 189
    short questions 188–9
    when to stop 189

Raistrick Index to Legal Citations and Abbreviations 70, 73
re-examination 196
recitals 5
regulators 178
report writing
  checks 25
  editing 25
  grammar 26
  layout 25
  planning 25
  presentation 25
  purpose 24
  research 24
  spelling 26
  style 25
research
  brainstorming 38
  case law
    All England Law Reports 72, 73, 79

research – *continued*
    BAILII 71
    Case Overview 75, 76–7
    citation 78
        conventions 73
        incomplete information 74–5
        neutral 74
    Current Law Year Books 78
    ex tempore judgment 72
    handing down judgment 71–2
    later decisions 78–9
    The Law Reports 72–3
    newspaper reports 72
    specialist law reports 80–1
    subject searches 79–81
    transcripts 71–2
    updating 75–9
    Weekly Law Reports 72, 73, 79
    Westlaw 67–8, 71, 73–80, 105
  citation of authorities 114–15
  drafting skills and 4
  electronic databases
    advantages 45–6
    AND 47
    asterisk 47
    Boolean operators 47
    connectors 47
    EUR-Lex 98–102, 104–5
    exclamation mark 47
    field searching 47–8
    Halsbury's Laws of England on Lexis+ Legal Research 59–61
    legislation.gov.uk website 85, 88
    Lexis+ Legal Research *see* **Lexis+ Legal Research**
    NOT 47
    on-line databases 46–8
    OR 47
    phrase search 48
    refining search 48
    updating 95
    Westlaw see **Westlaw**
    wildcard symbols 47
  European law *see* **research, European law**
  forms 107–12
  guidance 42–3
  Halsbury's Laws of England
    consolidated index 58
    cumulative supplement 58
    electronic version 59–61
    index 58
    main volume 58
    noter-up 58
    paper version 57–9
  Halsbury's Laws of England on Lexis+ Legal Research
    scope 59
    searching 59–61
  identification of sources 40
  indexes 40–1
    Halsbury's Laws of England 58
    Halsbury's Statutes 86–7
  internet 46
    see also on-line databases
  keywords 39–40
  legislation

research – *continued*
    see also **statutory instruments**
    citation 83–4
    commencement of statutes 87
    Current Law Statutes 68, 85–6
    in force 87
    Halsbury's Statutes 69, 83, 86–7, 96
    Halsbury's Statutes Citator 96
    legislation.gov.uk website 85, 88
    Lexis+ Legal Research 68–9, 83, 85, 88–91, 95
    official versions of Acts 85
    updating 95–6
    Westlaw 68–9, 83, 85, 91–5, 95
  model 37–9
  in office 35–6
  on-line databases 46–8
    see also electronic databases
  practitioner books 65–6
  precedents 107–12
  presentation format 42
  primary sources 66–70
  printed sources, advantages 46
  problem analysis 37–9
  problem solving approach 36–9
  publication of cases 71–2
  purpose 35–6
  record keeping 113–14
  recording trail 41
  reporting 39, 42, 114
  search terms 39–40
  searching 46–8
  solutions 38, 39
  source identification 40
  statutory instruments
    Halsbury's Statutory Instruments 69, 83, 95
    official versions 87–8
  suggested routes 67–70
  supporting fee earners 36
  updating information 41–2
    case law 75–9
    legislation 95–6
    noter-up
        Halsbury's Laws of England 58
        Halsbury's Statutes 86, 87
  writing reports 24
research, European law
  Blackstone's EU Treaties and Legislation 69, 99, 101
  case law
    citation 103
    EUR-Lex 104–5
  Common Market Law Reports 105
  Directory of European Union Legislation 102
  EUR-Lex 98–102, 104–5
  Europa website 98, 103
  European Court Reports 105
  legislation
    in force 101–3
    official texts 101
    primary 99
    secondary 100–3
  Lexis+ Legal Research 98, 105
  Official Journal of the European Union 98, 101, 103
  secondary legislation

research, European law – *continued*
    Decisions 100
    Directives 100
    Directory of European Union Legislation 102
    EUR-Lex 100–1
    Opinions 100
    Recommendations 100
    Regulations 100
    sources 100–1
  sources 103–5
  Westlaw 69, 98, 105
ResearchGate 54–5
resistance points 166–7, 174

schedules
  drafting 5–6
search engines 50–1
seating arrangements
  interviews 139
  negotiations 171, 177
secondary legislation
  European
    Decisions 100
    Directives 100
    Directory of European Union Legislation 102
    EUR-Lex 100–1
    Opinions 100
    Recommendations 100
    Regulations 100
    sources 100–1
  statutory instruments
    Halsbury's Statutory Instruments 69, 83, 95
    official versions 87–8
sentences 12–13
settlement zones 167–9
social media 52
specialist law reports 80–1
spelling 26
  automated checks 18
SSRN 55
statutory instruments
  articles 84
  citation 84
  Halsbury's Statutory Instruments 69, 83, 95
  legislation.gov.uk website 88
  Lexis+ Legal Research 91
  official versions 87–8
  Orders 84
  Regulations 84
  Rules 84

tabulation 17
telephone negotiation 169–70
testimonium 5

time
  drafting expressions of 15
***Times Law Reports* 72**
  monthly cumulative indexes 68
***Trusts and Estates Law and Tax Journal* 70**

verbs
  active voice 13
  passive voice 13–14, 22
vulnerable clients
  interviewing 142

Web 2.0 52
***Weekly Law Reports* 72, 73, 79**
Westlaw 49, 51
  case law 67–8, 71, 73–80, 105
    subject searches 79
  EU law 69, 98, 105
  legislation 68–9, 83, 85, 91–5, 95
Wikipedia 48
wikis 52
wildcard symbols 47
witness statements 193
witnesses
  civil cases 190
  court formalities 190
  criminal cases 190
  hostile 192
  leading questions 191
  not up to proof 192–3
  questioning 184
    know the answer 189
    one question at time 189
    short questions 188–9
    when to stop 189
writing
  attendance notes 26
  grammar 26
    automated checks 18
  memoranda
    attendance notes 26
    internal 26
    types 25
  reports
    checks 25
    editing 25
    layout 25
    planning 25
    presentation 25
    purpose 24
    research 24
    style 25
  spelling 26
    automated checks 18